EXAM CRAM

The CCENT Cram Sheet

This Cram Sheet contains key information as a final preparation tool for the ICND1 exam. Review this information as the last thing you do before you enter the testing center, paying special attention to those areas in which you think that you need the most review. Enjoy this additional study aid!

Networking Fundamentals

The OSI and TCP/IP Models

OSI—the layers are Application, Presentation, Session, Transport, Network, Data Link, Physical; TCP/IP[md]the layers are Application, Transport, Internet, Network Interface.

Protocols at Various Layers of the OSI Model

Layer	Examples
Application	FTP, HTTP, SMTP
Presentation	JPEG, MPEG
Session	NetBIOS, PPTP
Transport	TCP, UDP
Network	IP, ICMP
Data Link	PPP, ATM
Physical	Ethernet, USB

UDP is connectionless; UDP has very little overhead; UDP is often used for voice and video traffic forms; UDP can multiplex using port numbers to work with multiple applications.

TCP is connection-oriented; TCP has more overhead than UDP; TCP uses features like flow control, sequencing and acknowledgements to ensure reliable and ordered delivery of segments; TCP can multiplex using port numbers to work with multiple applications.

APPLICATIONS THAT USE TCP/UDP

TCP	UDP
HTTP	DHCP
FTP	RIP
Telnet	SNMP
SSH	TFTP
SMTP	*DNS

Well Known Port Numbers

Port Number	TCP or UDP?	Protocol
20	TCP	FTP Data
21	TCP	FTP Control
22	TCP	SSH
23	TCP	Telnet
25	TCP	
53	UDP	
67, 68	UDP	
69	UDP	
80	TCP	
110	TCP	
161	UDP	
443	TCP	
514	UDP	Syslog
520	UDP	RIP

The Verify MD5 Feature

```
R1# verify /md5 flash0:c2900-uni-
    versalk9-mz.SPA.154-3.M3.bin
    a79e325e6c498b70829d4db0afba2011
    ..............................
    ..............................
    ..................... .........
    ..............................
    ..............................
    ............
.....MD5 of flash0:c2900-universalk9-
    mz.SPA.154-3.M3.bin Done!
Verified (flash0:c2900-univer-
    salk9-mz.SPA.154-3.M3.bin)
    =a79e325e6c498b70829d4db0afba2011
```

ping Return Codes	
Character	Description
!	Reply success
.	Server timed out
U	Destination unreachable error received
Q	Source quench (destination too busy)
M	Could not fragment
?	Unknown packet type
&	Packet lifetime exceeded

Running an Extended ping

```
R1#ping
Protocol [ip]: ip
Target IP address: 4.4.4.4
Repeat count [5]: 8
Datagram size [100]: 1600
Timeout in seconds [2]: 4
Extended commands [n]: y
Source address or interface: 1.1.1.1
Type of service [0]: 1
Set DF bit in IP header? [no]: no
Validate reply data? [no]: no
Data pattern [0xABCD]: 0xAAAA
Loose, Strict, Record, Timestamp,
    Verbose[none]: none
Sweep range of sizes [n]: n
Type escape sequence to abort.
Sending 8, 1600-byte ICMP Echos to
    4.4.4.4, timeout is 4 seconds:
Packet sent with a source address
    of 1.1.1.1
Packet has data pattern 0xAAAA
!!!!!!!!
Success rate is 100 percent (8/8),
    round-trip min/avg/max =
    56/64/76 ms
R1#
```

An Extended traceroute

```
R1#traceroute
Protocol [ip]: ip
Target IP address: 4.4.4.4
Source address: 1.1.1.1
Numeric display [n]: y
Timeout in seconds [3]: 1
Probe count [3]: 5
Minimum Time to Live [1]: 1
Maximum Time to Live [30]: 10
Port Number [33434]: 33000
Loose, Strict, Record, Timestamp,
    Verbose[none]: none
Type escape sequence to abort.
Tracing the route to 4.4.4.4

  1 10.10.10.2 40 msec 16 msec 20
    msec 20 msec 16 msec
  2 10.20.20.3 24 msec 36 msec 36
    msec 72 msec 20 msec
  3 10.30.30.4 72 msec 60 msec 64
    msec 60 msec 64 msec
R1#
```

The **terminal monitor** command allows remote clients to view syslog messages.

Performing a Debug

```
R4#debug ip icmp
ICMP packet debugging is on
R4#
```

EXAM ✓ CRAM

CCENT
ICND1
100–105
Exam Cram

Anthony Sequeira, CCIE No. 15626

Pearson
800 East 96th Street
Indianapolis, Indiana 46240 USA

CCENT ICND1 100–105 Exam Cram

ISBN-13: 978-0-7897-5673-2

ISBN-10: 0-7897-5673-0

Library of Congress Control Number: 2016955445

Printed in the United States of America

3   18

Trademarks

All terms mentioned in this book that are known to be trademarks or service marks have been appropriately capitalized. Pearson IT Certification cannot attest to the accuracy of this information. Use of a term in this book should not be regarded as affecting the validity of any trademark or service mark.

Warning and Disclaimer

Every effort has been made to make this book as complete and as accurate as possible, but no warranty or fitness is implied. The information provided is on an "as is" basis. The author and the publisher shall have neither liability nor responsibility to any person or entity with respect to any loss or damages arising from the information contained in this book or from the use of the supplementary online content.

Special Sales

For information about buying this title in bulk quantities, or for special sales opportunities (which may include electronic versions; custom cover designs; and content particular to your business, training goals, marketing focus, or branding interests), please contact our corporate sales department at corpsales@pearsoned.com or (800) 382-3419.

For government sales inquiries, please contact governmentsales@pearsoned.com.

For questions about sales outside the U.S., please contact intlcs@pearson.com.

Editor-in-Chief
Mark Taub

Product Line Manager
Brett Bartow

Acquisitions Editor
Brett Bartow

Development Editor
Christopher A. Cleveland

Managing Editor
Sandra Schroeder

Project Editor
Mandie Frank

Copy Editor
Christopher Morris

Indexer
Cheryl Lenser

Proofreader
Deepa Ramesh

Technical Editor
Keith Barker

Publishing Coordinator
Vanessa Evans

Cover Designer
Chuti Prasertsith

Compositor
codeMantra

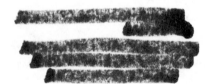

Contents at a Glance

Part VI: Command Reference, Practice Exams, and Glossary

To register this product and gain access to bonus content, go to www.pearsonitcertification.com/register to sign in and enter the ISBN. After you register the product, a link to the additional content will be listed on your Account page, under Registered Products.

Contents

Part II: LAN Switching Fundamentals

Part III: Routing Fundamentals

Preface

Why is this book so valuable? Why is it an excellent last resource prior to your exam? Let me outline that for you here:

▶ This book balances the two potential areas of expertise you need for each exam topic. You either need to focus on the theory of a technology, or you also need to be able to demonstrate mastery of configuration, verification, and troubleshooting. You can trust this text to guide you through the precise knowledge you need topic by topic.

▶ As alluded to above, this text remains tightly in scope with the exam. Although larger texts might provide background or peripheral information about a topic, this book is laser-focused on just those topics you need to master for success in the exam environment. We certainly encourage the reading and study of larger works for those that require it.

▶ Your author and technical reviewer have specialized in writing about and training candidates in all things CCNA since the inception of the certification in 1998.

▶ Your author and technical reviewer take the actual ICND1 as many times as Cisco permits us in a constant effort to be intimately familiar with the exam itself and Cisco's testing techniques.

▶ This book is filled with valuable resources to assist you immediately in your passing score—these resources include CramSavers, CramQuizzes, Review Questions, Final Exams, a Command Reference, and even Cram Sheets.

About the Author

Anthony Sequeira (CCIE No. 15626) began his IT career in 1994 with IBM in Tampa, Florida. He quickly formed his own computer consultancy, Computer Solutions, and then discovered his true passion—teaching and writing about Microsoft and Cisco technologies. Anthony has lectured to massive audiences around the world while working for Mastering Computers. Anthony has never been happier in his career than he is now as a full-time trainer for CBT Nuggets. He is an avid tennis player, a private pilot, a semi-professional poker player, and enjoys getting beaten up by women and children at the martial arts school he attends with his daughter.

Dedication

This book is dedicated to my remarkable wife Joette Sequeira.
Thank you for your understanding as I worked all those hours in
front of the Word Processor. You helped me improve the lives of readers
all over the world. I am sure they thank you as well.

Acknowledgments

I cannot thank Keith Barker enough! He helped me acquire this incredible opportunity, and he improved the book dramatically as its technical editor.

About the Technical Reviewer

Keith Barker began as a network technician for Electronic Data Systems (EDS) in 1985 and has had experience in IT and networking for more than 30 years. Keith creates training for CBT Nuggets, is a Cisco CCIE in Route/Switch and Security and has also earned certifications associated with VMware, Palo Alto, Check Point, ITIL, CCISP, and others. He can be reached through his Facebook page: Keith Barker Networking, on YouTube at Keith6783, or on Twitter @KeithBarkerCCIE.

We Want to Hear from You!

As the reader of this book, *you* are our most important critic and commentator. We value your opinion and want to know what we're doing right, what we could do better, what areas you'd like to see us publish in, and any other words of wisdom you're willing to pass our way.

We welcome your comments. You can email or write to let us know what you did or didn't like about this book—as well as what we can do to make our books better.

Please note that we cannot help you with technical problems related to the topic of this book.

When you write, please be sure to include this book's title and author as well as your name and email address. We will carefully review your comments and share them with the author and editors who worked on the book.

Email: feedback@pearsonitcertification.com
Mail: Pearson IT Certification
         ATTN: Reader Feedback
         800 East 96th Street
         Indianapolis, IN 46240 USA

Reader Services

Register your copy of CCENT ICND1 100–105 Exam Cram at www.pearsonitcertification.com for convenient access to downloads, updates, and corrections as they become available. To start the registration process, go to www.pearsonitcertification.com/register and log in or create an account*. Enter the product ISBN 9780789756732 and click **Submit**. When the process is complete, you will find any available bonus content under Registered Products.

*Be sure to check the box that you would like to hear from us to receive exclusive discounts on future editions of this product.

Introduction

Welcome to *CCENT Exam Cram*! This book covers the CCENT certification exam. Whether this is your first or your fifteenth *Exam Cram*, you'll find information here that will ensure your success as you pursue knowledge, experience, and certification. This introduction covers how the *Exam Cram* series can help you prepare for the CCENT exam.

This book is one of the *Exam Cram* series of books and will help by getting you on your way to becoming a CCENT.

This introduction discusses the basics of the CCENT exam. Included are sections covering preparation, how to take an exam, a description of this book's contents, how this book is organized, and, finally, author contact information.

Each chapter in this book contains practice questions. There are also two full-length practice exams at the end of the book. Practice exams in this book should provide an accurate assessment of the level of expertise you need to obtain to pass the test. Answers and explanations are included for all test questions. It is best to obtain a level of understanding equivalent to a consistent pass rate of at least 90 percent or more on the practice questions and exams in this book before you attempt the real exam.

Let's begin by looking at preparation for the exam.

How to Prepare for the Exam

This text follows the official exam objectives letter for letter. These official objective from Cisco Systems can be found here:

> https://learningnetwork.cisco.com/community/certifications/ccna/icnd1/exam-topics

Following the exam topics item by item and in their original order allows you to ensure you are ready for the real exam questions that will come your way on your actual test date.

Practice Tests

This book is filled with practice exam questions to get you ready! Enjoy the following:

▶ **CramSaver questions before each and every section**: These difficult, open-ended questions ensure you really know the material. Some readers use these questions in order to "test out" of a particular section.

▶ **CramQuizzes to end each section**: Another chance to demonstrate your knowledge after completing a section.

▶ **Review Questions to end each chapter**: Your final pass-through the material for that chapter.

▶ **Two full final exams**: These exams include explanations and tips for approaching each final exam question.

In addition, the book includes an additional two full practice tests in the Pearson Test Prep software that is available to you either online or as an offline Windows application. To access the practice exams that were developed with this book, please see the instructions in the card inserted in the sleeve in the back of the book. This card includes a unique access code that enables you to activate your exams in the Pearson Test Prep software.

If you are interested in more practice exams than are provided with this book, Pearson IT Certification publishes a Premium Edition eBook and Practice Test product. In addition to providing you with three eBook files (EPUB, PDF, and Kindle) this product provides you with two addition exams worth of questions. The Premium Edition version also offers you a link to the specific section in the book that presents an overview of the topic covered in the question, allowing you to easily refresh your knowledge. The insert card in the back of the book includes a special offer for a 70 percent discount off of this Premium Edition eBook and Practice Test product, which is an incredible deal.

Taking a Certification Exam

When you have prepared for the exam, you must register with Cisco Systems to take the exam. The CCENT (ICND1) exam is given at Pearson VUE testing centers. Check the Pearson VUE website at http://www.pearsonvue.com/ to get specific details.

You can register for an exam done online or by phone. After you register, you will receive a confirmation notice. Some locations may have limited test centers available which means you should schedule your exam in advance to make sure you can get the specific date and time you would like.

Arriving at the Exam Location

As with any examination, arrive at the testing center early. Be prepared! You will need to bring two forms of identification (one with a picture). The testing center staff requires proof that you are who you say you are and that someone else is not taking the test for you. Arrive early because if you are late, you will be barred from entry and will not receive a refund for the cost of the exam.

> **ExamAlert**
>
> You'll be spending a lot of time in the exam room. Plan on using the full two hours of time allotted for your exam and surveys. Policies differ from location to location regarding bathroom breaks—check with the testing center before beginning the exam.

In the Testing Center

You will not be allowed to take study materials or anything else into the examination room with you that could raise suspicion that you're cheating. This includes practice test material, books, exam prep guides, or other test aids. The Testing Center will provide you with scratch paper and a pen or pencil. These days, this often comes in the form of an erasable whiteboard.

After the Exam

Examination results are available after the exam. If you pass the exam, you will simply receive a passing grade—your exact score will not be provided. Candidates who do not pass will receive a complete breakdown on their score by domain. This allows those individuals to see what areas they are weak in.

About This Book

The ideal reader for an *Exam Cram* book is someone seeking certification. However, it should be noted that an *Exam Cram* book is a very easily readable, rapid presentation of facts. Therefore, an *Exam Cram* book is also extremely useful as a quick reference manual.

Most people seeking certification use multiple sources of information. Check out the links at the end of each chapter to get more information about subjects you're weak in.

This book includes other helpful elements in addition to the actual logical, step-by-step learning progression of the chapters themselves. *Exam Cram* books use elements such as examalerts, tips, notes, and practice questions to make information easier to read and absorb. This text also includes a very helpful Command Reference and Glossary to assist you.

Use the *Cram Sheet* to remember last-minute facts immediately before the exam. Use the practice questions to test your knowledge. You can always brush up on specific topics in detail by referring to the table of contents and the index. Even after you achieve certification, you can use this book as a rapid-access reference manual.

The Exam Blueprint

The table that follows outlines the CCENT exam domains and objectives and maps the objectives to the chapter(s) in the book that cover them in detail.

Exam Domain	Objective	Chapter in Book That Covers It
Network Fundamentals	Compare and contrast OSI and TCP/IP models	Chapter 1
Network Fundamentals	Compare and contrast TCP and UDP protocols	Chapter 1
Network Fundamentals	Describe the impact of infrastructure components in an enterprise network	Chapter 1
Network Fundamentals	Compare and contrast collapsed core and three-tier architectures	Chapter 1
Network Fundamentals	Compare and contrast network topologies	Chapter 1
Network Fundamentals	Select the appropriate cabling type based on implementation requirements	Chapter 1

Exam Domain	Objective	Chapter in Book That Covers It
Network Fundamentals	Apply troubleshooting methodologies to resolve problems	Chapter 1
Network Fundamentals	Configure, verify, and troubleshoot IPv4 addressing and subnetting	Chapter 2
Network Fundamentals	Compare and contrast IPv4 address types	Chapter 2
Network Fundamentals	Describe the need for private IPv4 addressing	Chapter 2
Network Fundamentals	Identify the appropriate IPv6 addressing scheme to satisfy addressing requirements in a LAN/WAN environment	Chapter 3
Network Fundamentals	Configure, verify, and troubleshoot IPv6 addressing	Chapter 3
Network Fundamentals	Configure and verify IPv6 Stateless Address Auto Configuration	Chapter 3
Network Fundamentals	Compare and contrast IPv6 address types	Chapter 3
LAN Switching Fundamentals	Describe and verify switching concepts	Chapter 4
LAN Switching Fundamentals	Interpret Ethernet frame format	Chapter 4
LAN Switching Fundamentals	Troubleshoot interface and cable issues (collisions, errors, duplex, speed)	Chapter 4
LAN Switching Fundamentals	Configure, verify, and troubleshoot VLANs (normal range) spanning multiple switches	Chapter 5
LAN Switching Fundamentals	Configure, verify, and troubleshoot interswitch connectivity	Chapter 5
LAN Switching Fundamentals	Configure, verify, and troubleshoot port security	Chapter 6
Routing Fundamentals	Describe the routing concepts	Chapter 7
Routing Fundamentals	Interpret the components of routing table	Chapter 7
Routing Fundamentals	Describe how a routing table is populated by different routing information sources	Chapter 7

Exam Domain	Objective	Chapter in Book That Covers It
Routing Fundamentals	Configure, verify, and troubleshoot inter-VLAN routing	Chapter 8
Routing Fundamentals	Compare and contrast static routing and dynamic routing	Chapter 9
Routing Fundamentals	Configure, verify, and troubleshoot IPv4 and IPv6 static routing	Chapter 9
Routing Fundamentals	Configure, verify, and troubleshoot RIPv2 for IPv4 (excluding authentication, filtering, manual summarization, redistribution)	Chapter 9
Infrastructure Services	Describe DNS lookup operation	Chapter 10
Infrastructure Services	Troubleshoot client connectivity issues involving DNS	Chapter 10
Infrastructure Services	Configure and verify DHCP on a router (excluding static reservations)	Chapter 10
Infrastructure Services	Troubleshoot client- and router-based DHCP connectivity issues	Chapter 10
Infrastructure Services	Configure and verify NTP operating in client/server mode	Chapter 10
Infrastructure Services	Configure, verify, and troubleshoot IPv4 standard numbered and named access list for routed interfaces	Chapter 11
Infrastructure Services	Configure, verify, and troubleshoot inside source NAT	Chapter 12
Infrastructure Maintenance	Configure and verify device-monitoring using syslog	Chapter 13
Infrastructure Maintenance	Configure and verify device management	Chapter 13
Infrastructure Maintenance	Configure and verify initial device configuration	Chapter 14
Infrastructure Maintenance	Configure, verify, and troubleshoot basic device hardening	Chapter 15
Infrastructure Maintenance	Perform device maintenance	Chapter 16
Infrastructure Maintenance	Use Cisco IOS tools to troubleshoot and resolve problems	Chapter 17

The Chapter Elements

Each *Exam Cram* book has chapters that follow a predefined structure. This structure makes *Exam Cram* books easy to read and provides a familiar format for all *Exam Cram* books. The following elements typically are used:

▶ Chapter topics

▶ Essential Terms and Components

▶ CramSavers

▶ CramQuizzes

▶ ExamAlerts

▶ Notes

▶ Exam preparation practice questions and answers

▶ An "Additional Resources" section at the end of each chapter

> **Note**
>
> Bulleted lists, numbered lists, tables, and graphics are also used where appropriate. A picture can paint a thousand words sometimes, and tables can help to associate different elements with each other visually.

Now let's look at each of the elements in detail.

▶ **Chapter topics**—Each chapter contains details of all subject matter listed in the table of contents for that particular chapter. The objective of an *Exam Cram* book is to cover all the important facts without giving too much detail; it is an exam cram. When examples are required, they are included.

▶ **Essential Terms and Components**—The start of every chapter contains a list of terms and concepts you should understand. These are all defined in the book's accompanying Glossary. They are also highlighted the first time they are encountered in a chapter.

▶ **CramSavers**—Each major section in the chapter kicks off with a brief short answer question quiz to help you assess your knowledge of the section topic. This chapter element is designed to help you determine if you need to read the whole section in detail or merely skim the material and skip ahead to the CramQuiz at the end of the section.

▶ **CramQuizzes**—Each major section in the chapter concludes with a multiple choice question quiz to help ensure that you have gained a familiarity with the section content.

▶ **ExamAlerts**—ExamAlerts address exam-specific, exam-related information. An ExamAlert addresses content that is particularly important, tricky, or likely to appear on the exam. An ExamAlert looks like this:

> **ExamAlert**
>
> Make sure you remember the different ways in which you can access a router remotely. Know which methods are secure, and which are not.

▶ **Notes**—Notes typically contain useful information that is not directly related to the current topic under consideration. To avoid breaking up the flow of the text, they are set off from the regular text.

> **Note**
>
> This is a note. You have already seen several notes.

▶ **Review Questions**—At the end of every chapter is a battery of exam practice questions similar to those in the actual exam. Each chapter contains a list of questions relevant to that chapter, including answers and explanations. Test your skills as you read.

▶ **Additional Resources section**—This section at the end of each chapter describes other relevant sources of information related to the chapter topics covered.

Other Book Elements

Most of this *Exam Cram* book on CCENT follows the consistent chapter structure already described. However, there are various, important elements that are not part of the standard chapter format. These elements apply to the entire book as a whole.

▶ **Practice exams**—In addition to exam-preparation questions at the end of each chapter, two full practice exams are included at the end of the book.

▶ **Answers and explanations for practice exams**—These follow each practice exam, providing answers and explanations to the questions in the exams.

▶ **Command Reference**—This valuable study guide appears at the end of the text.

▶ **Glossary**—The glossary contains a listing of important terms used in this book with explanations.

▶ **Cram Sheet**—The Cram Sheet is a quick-reference, tear-out cardboard sheet of important facts useful for last-minute preparation. Cram sheets often include a simple summary of facts that are most difficult to remember.

▶ **Companion Website**—The companion website for your book allows you to access several digital assets that come with your book, including:

▶ Pearson Test Prep software (both online and Windows desktop versions)

▶ Key Terms Flash Cards application

▶ A PDF version of the Command Reference

▶ A PDF version of the Cram Sheet

To access the book's companion website, simply follow these steps:

1. Register your book by going to: PearsonITCertification.com/register and entering the ISBN: 9780789756732.

2. Respond to the challenge questions.

3. Go to your account page and select the **Registered Products** tab.

4. Click on the **Access Bonus Content** link under the product listing.

Pearson Test Prep Practice Test Software

As noted previously, this book comes complete with the Pearson Test Prep practice test software containing four full exams (the two from the back of the book as well as two additional tests). These practice tests are available to you either online or as an offline Windows application. To access the practice exams that were developed with this book, please see the instructions in the card inserted in the sleeve in the back of the book. This card includes a unique access code that enables you to activate your exams in the Pearson Test Prep software. Note that this single access code can be used to activate both the online and offline versions of the software.

Accessing the Pearson Test Prep Software Online

The online version of this software can be used on any device with a browser and connectivity to the Internet, including desktop machines, tablets, and smartphones. To start using your practice exams online, simply follow these steps:

1. Go to: http://www.PearsonTestPrep.com.

2. Select **Pearson IT Certification** as your product group.

3. Enter your email/password for your account. If you don't have an account on PearsonITCertification.com or CiscoPress.com, you will need to establish one by going to PearsonITCertification.com/join.

4. In the **My Products** tab, click the **Activate New Product** button.

5. Enter the access code printed on the insert card in the back of your book to activate your product.

6. The product will now be listed in your My Products page. Click the **Exams** button to launch the exam settings screen and start your exam.

Accessing the Pearson Test Prep Software Offline

If you wish to study offline, you can download and install the Windows version of the Pearson Test Prep software. There is a download link for this software on the book's companion web site, or you can just enter this link in your browser:

http://www.pearsonitcertification.com/content/downloads/pcpt/engine.zip

To access the book's companion web site and the software, simply follow these steps:

1. Register your book by going to: PearsonITCertification.com/register and entering the ISBN: 9780789756732.

2. Respond to the challenge questions

3. Go to your account page and select the **Registered Products** tab.

4. Click on the **Access Bonus Content** link under the product listing.

5. Click the **Install Pearson Test Prep Desktop Version** link under the Practice Exams section of the page to download the software.

6. After the software finishes downloading, unzip all the files on your computer.

7. Double click the application file to start the installation, and follow the on-screen instructions to complete the registration.

8. When the installation is complete, launch the application and select **Activate Exam** button on the My Products tab.

9. Click the **Activate a Product** button in the Activate Product Wizard.

10. Enter the unique access code found on the card in the sleeve in the back of your book and click the **Activate** button.

11. Click **Next** and then the **Finish** button to download the exam data to your application.

12. You can now start using the practice exams by selecting the product and clicking the **Open Exam** button to open the exam settings screen.

Note that the offline and online versions will synch together, so saved exams and grade results recorded on one version will be available to you on the other as well.

Customizing Your Exams

Once you are in the exam settings screen, you can choose to take exams in one of three modes:

▶ Study Mode

▶ Practice Exam Mode

▶ Flash Card Mode

Study Mode allows you to fully customize your exams and review answers as you are taking the exam. This is typically the mode you would use first to assess your knowledge and identify information gaps. Practice Exam Mode locks certain customization options, as it is presenting a realistic exam experience. Use this mode when you are preparing to test your exam readiness.

Flash Card Mode strips out the answers and presents you with only the question stem. This mode is great for late stage preparation when you really want to challenge yourself to provide answers without the benefit of seeing multiple choice options. This mode will not provide the detailed score reports that the other two modes will, so it should not be used if you are trying to identify knowledge gaps.

In addition to these three modes, you will be able to select the source of your questions. You can choose to take exams that cover all of the chapters or you can narrow your selection to just a single chapter or the chapters that make up specific parts in the book. All chapters are selected by default. If you want to narrow your focus to individual chapters, simply deselect all the chapters then select only those on which you wish to focus in the Objectives area.

You can also select the exam banks on which to focus. Each exam bank comes complete with a full exam of questions that cover topics in every chapter. The two exams printed in the book are available to you as well as two additional exams of unique questions. You can have the test engine serve up exams from all four banks or just from one individual bank by selecting the desired banks in the exam bank area.

There are several other customizations you can make to your exam from the exam settings screen, such as the time of the exam, the number of questions served up, whether to randomize questions and answers, whether to show the number of correct answers for multiple answer questions, or whether to serve up only specific types of questions. You can also create custom test banks by selecting only questions that you have marked or questions on which you have added notes.

Updating Your Exams

If you are using the online version of the Pearson Test Prep software, you should always have access to the latest version of the software as well as the exam data. If you are using the Windows desktop version, every time you launch the software, it will check to see if there are any updates to your exam data and automatically download any changes that were made since the last time you used the software. This requires that you are connected to the Internet at the time you launch the software.

Sometimes, due to many factors, the exam data may not fully download when you activate your exam. If you find that figures or exhibits are missing, you may need to manually update your exams.

To update a particular exam you have already activated and downloaded, simply select the **Tools** tab and select the **Update Products** button. Again, this is only an issue with the desktop Windows application.

If you wish to check for updates to the Pearson Test Prep exam engine software, Windows desktop version, simply select the **Tools** tab and select the **Update Application** button. This will ensure you are running the latest version of the software engine.

Contacting the Author

Hopefully, this book provides you with the tools you need to pass the CCENT exam. Feedback is appreciated. You can contact the author at compsolv@me.com.

Thank you for selecting my book; I have worked to apply the same concepts in this book that I have used in the hundreds of training classes I have taught. Spend your study time wisely and you, too, can become a CCENT. Good luck on the exam, although if you carefully work through this text, you will certainly minimize the amount of luck required!

PART I

Network Fundamentals

This part of the text deals with one of five overall sections you must master for the ICND1 exam. There are three chapters total that make up Part 1. These three chapters, taken as a whole, represent 20 percent of the exam questions you face in your exam. This means that the Network Fundamentals area is the third-most important section of the five overall sections that you deal with on your testing day.

Here you master important models and designs, as well as key fundamentals of networking such as transport protocols and cabling. You also dig deep into the worlds of TCP/IP version 4 and TCP/IP version 6. Both of these protocol suites are already popular today. Version 4 should gradually fade away from usage (although perhaps never completely), whereas IPv6 installations should become more and more predominant.

Part 1 includes the following chapters:

CHAPTER 1   Network Fundamentals: Models and Designs

CHAPTER 2   Network Fundamentals: IPv4

CHAPTER 3   Network Fundamentals: IPv6

CHAPTER 1

Network Fundamentals: Models and Designs

This chapter covers the following official ICND1 100-105 exam topics:

▶ Compare and contrast OSI and TCP/IP models

▶ Compare and contrast TCP and UDP protocols

▶ Describe the impact of infrastructure components in an enterprise network

▶ Compare and contrast collapsed core and three-tier architectures

▶ Compare and contrast network topologies

▶ Select the appropriate cabling type based on implementation requirements

▶ Apply troubleshooting methodologies to resolve problems

This chapter ensures you are ready for the above topics from the Network Fundamentals section of the overall exam blueprint from Cisco Systems. Remember, this is just a portion of the Network Fundamentals area. Chapters Two and Three complete the Network Fundamentals grouping. Those chapters deal with IPv4 and IPv6 respectively.

Essential Terms and Components

▶ **Open Systems Interconnection (OSI) Model**

▶ **Transmission Control Protocol/Internet Protocol (TCP/IP) Model**

▶ **Transmission Control Protocol (TCP)**

▶ **User Datagram Protocol (UDP)**

▶ **Firewalls**

▶ **Access Points (APs)**

▶ **Wireless LAN Controllers (WLCs)**

▶ **Three-Tier Network Designs**

▶ **Collapsed Core Network Design**

▶ **Network Topologies**
▶ **Star Topologies**
▶ **Mesh Topologies**
▶ **Hybrid Topologies**
▶ **Network Cabling**
▶ **Troubleshooting Methodology**
▶ **Problem Isolation**
▶ **Escalation**
▶ **Resolution Monitoring**
▶ **Documentation**

Topic: Compare and contrast OSI and TCP/IP models

CramSaver

If you can correctly answer these CramSaver questions, save time by skimming the ExamAlerts in this chapter and then completing the CramQuiz at the end of each section and the Review Questions at the end of the chapter. If you are in doubt at all—read EVERYTHING in this chapter!

1. Name the missing levels of the OSI model from top to bottom.

   Application

   _____

   _____

   _____

   _____

   _____

   _____

2. Name the four layers of the TCP/IP model from top to bottom.

   _____

   _____

   _____

   _____

3. Name the PDUs of the bottom four layers of the OSI model from top to bottom.

   _____

   _____

   _____

   _____

4. Name the protocol that maps Layer 2 to Layer 3 addresses?

   _____

5. What two layers of the OSI model are associated with the network interface layer of the TCP/IP model?

_____

_____

Answers

1.

Application

Presentation

Session

Transport

Network

Data Link

Physical

2.

Application

Transport

Internet

Network Interface

3.

Segments

Packets

Frames

Bits

4.

ARP (Address Resolution Protocol)

5.

Data Link

Physical

Figure 1.1 shows the classic **Open Systems Interconnection (OSI) model** and **Transmission Control Protocol/Internet Protocol (TCP/IP) model** for networking. Notice how the layers between the two compare.

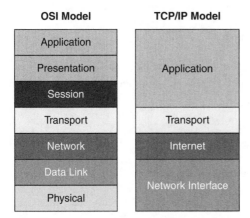

FIGURE 1.1 **The OSI and TCP/IP Models**

Here is a recap of the major functions of each of the layers of the OSI model:

▶ **Physical**: Defines the electrical and physical specifications.

▶ **Data Link**: Detects and, when possible, corrects errors found at the physical layer; defines the Layer 2 protocols to establish and terminate a connection between two physically connected devices.

▶ **Network**: Provides for logical network addressing; Address Resolution Protocol (ARP) is used to resolve Layer 3 network IP addresses to Layer 2 Ethernet addresses on LANs.

▶ **Transport**: This layer controls the reliability of communications through flow-control mechanisms; important examples of protocols used at this layer are **Transmission Control Protocol (TCP)** for reliable delivery or **User Datagram Protocol (UDP)** for unreliable delivery.

▶ **Session:** This layer controls the logical connections between two systems; it establishes, manages, and terminates the connections between the local and remote systems.

▶ **Presentation:** This layer is sometimes called the syntax layer because it ensures that network formats are converted in such a way that the application layer can understand them.

▶ **Application:** This layer provides services for end user applications so that communication with another application across the network is effective.

> **Note**
>
> As network engineers, we often deal with the bottom four layers intensely. As a result, you often hear them discussed as simply Layers 1 through 4. For example, you might say Layer 2 instead of the data link layer.

The data and header information (Protocol Data Units [PDUs]) that are built at each of the bottom four layers of the OSI model receive special names. Figure 1.2 shows the specific PDU names for each layer.

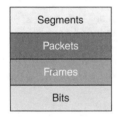

FIGURE 1.2   **The PDUs of the Bottom Four Layers**

> **ExamAlert**
>
> Be prepared to reference these PDU names for the bottom four layers of the OSI model. An easy way to remember them is the acronym—*Some People Fear Birthdays*. We refer to a Layer 2 switch as receiving and sending frames. A router works with packets. By the way, we tend to reference the information above Layer 4 as simply data.

Another important skill is identifying sample technologies we work with every day and at what layer of the OSI model they exist. Table 1.1 provides important sample information in this regard.

TABLE 1.1 **Protocols at Various Layers**

Layer	Examples
Application	FTP, HTTP, SMTP
Presentation	JPEG, MPEG
Session	NetBIOS, PPTP
Transport	TCP, UDP
Network	IP, ICMP
Data Link	PPP, ATM
Physical	Ethernet, USB

CramQuiz

1. What protocol is used for a host to discover the L2 address of the next device in the path towards a remote destination?

   ○ **A.** TCP

   ○ **B.** UDP

   ○ **C.** DNS

   ○ **D.** ARP

2. What layer of the OSI model coordinates with the Transport layer of the TCP/IP model?

   ○ **A.** Network

   ○ **B.** Transport

   ○ **C.** Session

   ○ **D.** Presentation

CramQuiz Answers

1. **D** is correct. This is the job of ARP.

2. **B** is correct. The Transport layer of the TCP/IP model coordinates directly with the Transport layer of the OSI model.

Topic: Compare and contrast TCP and UDP protocols

CramSaver

1. Name at least four key characteristics of UDP.

   _____

   _____

   _____

   _____

2. Name at least four key characteristics of TCP.

   _____

   _____

   _____

   _____

Answers

1.

   UDP is connectionless.

   UDP has very little overhead.

   UDP is often used for voice and video traffic forms.

   UDP can multiplex using port numbers to work with multiple applications.

2.

   TCP is connection-oriented.

   TCP has more overhead than UDP.

   TCP uses features like flow control, sequencing, and acknowledgements to ensure reliable and ordered delivery of segments.

   TCP can multiplex using port numbers to work with multiple applications.

Transmission Control Protocol (TCP) and User Datagram Protocol (UDP) are both protocols that operate at the transport layer (Layer 4). TCP is used for reliable, connection-oriented communications, whereas UDP is for connectionless transport. It might seem as if you would *never* want to send information in an unreliable manner using UDP, but keep in mind that TCP adds overhead and some inefficiencies to the process. This is the reason that UDP is often used for things like voice and video communications, where efficiency and non-delay of packets is key at the sacrifice of reliability mechanisms. In fact, sometimes applications use UDP and then use their own application layer mechanisms for reliability.

ExamAlert

Remember, not all traffic relies upon TCP or UDP at the Transport layer. A great clue for traffic forms that do not use them are those that have their own protocol identifier. Here is a list of examples of protocol identifiers from the IP header:

1 – ICMP

6 – TCP

17 – UDP

88 – EIGRP

89 – OSPF

What are some examples of applications that rely on TCP and UDP? Table 1.2 provides plenty of examples for you.

TABLE 1.2   **Applications That Rely on TCP versus UDP**

TCP	UDP
HTTP	DHCP
FTP	RIP
Telnet	SNMP
SSH	TFTP
SMTP	*DNS

* DNS also uses TCP in some instances, such as a DNS zone transfer, but is mainly considered a UDP example.

TCP and UDP can both multiplex using port numbers to work with multiple applications. For example, DHCP uses UDP ports 67 and 68, RIP uses UDP port 520, and HTTP uses TCP port 80. The overhead that TCP uses is a result of reliable delivery. For example, with TCP we have:

▶ Error recovery

▶ Flow control using windowing

▶ Connection establishment and termination

▶ Ordered data transfer

▶ Data segmentation

ExamAlert

You never know when Cisco might need you to prove that you know a TCP or UDP port number. This might even come in the clever form of you building a firewall statement (Access Control List) in the exam. I would encourage you to make flash cards to learn these well-known ports, shown below.

Port Number	TCP or UDP?	Protocol
20	TCP	FTP Data
21	TCP	FTP Control
22	TCP	SSH
23	TCP	Telnet
25	TCP	SMTP
53	UDP	DNS
67, 68	UDP	DHCP
69	UDP	TFTP
80	TCP	HTTP
110	TCP	POP3
161	UDP	SNMP
443	TCP	SSL/TLS
514	UDP	Syslog
520	UDP	RIP

CramQuiz

1. What Transport layer protocol does EIGRP rely upon in its operation?

   ○ **A.** TCP

   ○ **B.** UDP

   ○ **C.** ICMP

   ○ **D.** None of these answers are correct

2. What protocol and port does RIP use? (Choose two)

   ○ **A.** TCP

   ○ **B.** UDP

   ○ **C.** 514

   ○ **D.** 520

CramQuiz Answers

1. **D** is correct. EIGRP does not rely upon TCP or UDP in its operation. The protocol encapsulates inside of IP and provides its own reliable mechanisms for delivery from router to router. You should also note that ICMP is not a Transport layer protocol, but a Network layer protocol. Interestingly, ICMP does not rely upon TCP or UDP to function, but rather has its own protocol number.

2. **B** and **D** are correct. RIP relies on the connectionless UDP protocol and port number 520.

Topic: Describe the impact of infrastructure components in an enterprise network

CramSaver

1. Name a network device that is used to manage lightweight access points (APs).

   _____

2. Name a network device that protects certain networks from other networks in your infrastructure.

   _____

3. Name a network device that connects users to the network using multiple frequency bands.

   _____

Answers

1. Wireless Controllers—also known as Wireless LAN Controllers (WLC)
2. Firewalls
3. Access point

Networks today are growing in complexity. This means new devices appear and play critical roles in the network infrastructure and functionality. Although there are many specialized devices, the exam blueprint calls upon three that we must review:

▶ **Firewalls**: The firewall is implemented in a number of ways. It might be software running as an application on your operating system; it might be built into your operating system; or it might be a network appliance. No matter its form, the job is always the same, protect one portion of your network or computer system from another portion. The classic example (and most likely for your exam), is the network firewall. This device connects to "inside" protected networks and protects them from "outside" networks. Often, the main outside network is the Internet. The specific example of a network firewall appliance from Cisco Systems is the Adaptive Security Appliance or ASA. There is even a virtual version (ASAv) today that you can connect to a virtualized (VMware) network.

▶ **Access points (APs)**: It seems like you cannot go anywhere today without being in a wireless cell for Internet access. Some cities around the world (including my own) provide complimentary Internet access using WiFi. One of the key devices that make this a reality is the access point. These are often termed *dual band* because they support multiple frequency bands for various iterations of the 802.11 wireless standards. The role of the device is simple: connect users to the network as quickly and efficiently as possible with some level of security. This might be no security at all in the case of an open Guest network, or it might mean the highest levels of security available for a protected corporate network. For corporate environments, Cisco manufactures "lightweight" access points that rely on a wireless LAN controller for their instructions and management.

ExamAlert

Wireless networks often use an older method of allowing multiple devices to access the infrastructure "at the same time." They use carrier sense multiple access with collision avoidance (CSMA/CA). With CSMA/CA, carrier sensing is used, but nodes attempt to avoid collisions by transmitting only when the channel is sensed to be "idle." Contrast this to what happened in older hub–based local-area networks (LANs) with Ethernet cables. They used carrier sense multiple access with collision detection (CSMA/CD). This is a media access control method that uses a carrier sensing scheme in which a transmitting data station listens for other signals while transmitting a frame. If it detects that two devices are sending at the same time, the device stops transmitting that frame, transmits a jam signal, and then waits for a random time interval before trying to resend the frame.

▶ **Wireless LAN controllers (WLCs)**: In larger, more complex environments than the home, there might be many access points to fulfill the needs of the organization. A WLC is ideal in this situation to manage the many APs (access points) that exist. These devices often act as the brains of the operation and control aspects like security and frequency usage and antennae strength. As you might guess, Cisco is in the business of WLCs as well. Figure 1.3 shows the Cisco 8540 WLC.

Topic: Describe the impact of infrastructure components in an enterprise network

FIGURE 1.3 **The Cisco 8540 WLC**

ExamAlert

Probably the cleverest method of testing you on these devices is to describe what the device does, and then have you select that device from a multiple choice question. Keep in mind, you study routers and switches in preparation for the ICND1 exam, so expect those devices to be in the list of options as well.

CramQuiz

1. Ethernet LANs, when operating in half-duplex, rely on what technology in order to deal with collisions?

   ○ **A.** CSMA/CA

   ○ **B.** CSMA/CD

   ○ **C.** CSMA/CC

   ○ **D.** CSMA/CQ

2. What security device tends to be implemented in many different forms, including hardware and software?

   ○ **A.** WLC

   ○ **B.** Firewall

   ○ **C.** Access point

   ○ **D.** Router

CramQuiz Answers

1. **B** is correct. Half-duplex Ethernet LANs use carrier sense multiple access collision detection in order to guard against collisions.

2. **B** is correct. Firewalls protect some part of your system or network from another part of the system or network. They come in many different varieties. Some firewalls are hardware-based, whereas others are software-based.

Topic: Compare and contrast collapsed core and three-tier architectures

CramSaver

1. What are the three tiers of the classic hierarchical Cisco network design?

   _____

   _____

   _____

2. What layer of the classic hierarchical Cisco network design is typically eliminated in a collapsed design?

   _____

Answers

1.

   Core

   Distribution

   Access

2.

   Distribution

For years, Cisco has suggested that we break up our network into easy to understand and manage layers or tiers. The classic **three-tier network design** consists of the following:

▶ **Access layer**: This layer provides workgroup/user access to the network; as a result, this layer is sometimes called the workstation layer.

▶ **Distribution layer**: This layer provides policy-based connectivity and controls the boundary between the access and core layers.

▶ **Core layer**: This layer provides fast transport between distribution switches within the enterprise campus; this is sometimes called the backbone layer.

ExamAlert

You should be aware of particular functions that most often occur at different layers. Here are some examples:

The Access layer:

▶ Layer 2 switching

▶ Port security

▶ QoS classification and marking and trust boundaries

▶ Address Resolution Protocol (ARP) inspection

▶ Virtual access control lists (VACLs)

▶ Spanning tree

▶ Power over Ethernet (PoE) and auxiliary VLANs for VoIP

The Distribution layer:

▶ Aggregation of LAN or WAN links

▶ Policy-based security in the form of access control lists (ACLs) and filtering

▶ Routing services between LANs and VLANs and between routing domains

▶ Redundancy and load balancing

▶ A boundary for route aggregation and summarization configured on interfaces toward the core layer

▶ Broadcast domain control

The Core layer:

▶ Providing high-speed switching

▶ Providing reliability and fault tolerance

Now if you are in charge of a small, simple network right now, you might be thinking to yourself—really??? You expect me to buy all of this equipment to make all of that happen in layers? This is where the **collapsed core network design** might come in.

ExamAlert

The collapsed core design takes the functions of the distribution layer and moves them (or collapses them) into the core layer. So you dramatically simplify things with a Core and Access layer only. Keep in mind this also might be done in larger networks as well, especially when the Core/Distribution equipment is so sophisticated, it has no problem providing incredibly fast speeds at the same time it accomplishes the overhead of the Distribution layer functions.

CramQuiz

1. At what layer of the Cisco network model might you expect to find port security?

   - ○ **A.** Distribution
   - ○ **B.** Internet
   - ○ **C.** Access
   - ○ **D.** Core

2. At what layer of the Cisco network model is speed most important?

   - ○ **A.** Distribution
   - ○ **B.** Internet
   - ○ **C.** Access
   - ○ **D.** Core

CramQuiz Answers

1. **C** is correct. The access layer is where we find such mechanisms as port security, QoS classification, and Power over Ethernet, to name just a few.

2. **D** is correct. The core layer is where speed is of critical importance. In fact, speed is so important at this layer, it is why we often move functions like QoS and Security out of the core layer.

Topic: Compare and contrast network topologies

CramSaver

1. What topology is common today in the access layer that features a switch for network connectivity?

_____

2. What topology might be skipped due to cost concerns?

_____

Answers

1. The star topology
2. The full mesh topology

The exam blueprint calls out three **network topologies** that we should be mindful of:

▶ **Star**

▶ **Mesh**

▶ **Hybrid**

Let us actually elaborate on this list a bit more fully:

▶ **Star**

▶ **Full Mesh**

▶ **Partial Mesh**

▶ **Hybrid**

I presume the exam blueprint authors were thinking of the hybrid topology as a partial mesh, but let us stick with our elaboration for clarity.

The star refers to a network design where one central device connects to several others. If you locate the central device in the center of your drawing, the devices that connect look like shining beams of light from this star, thus the name. Figure 1.4 shows an example of a star topology.

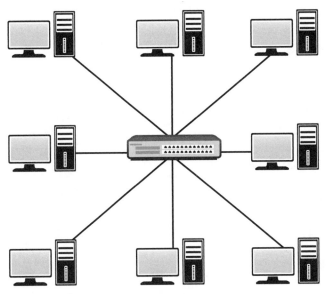

FIGURE 1.4   An Example of a Star Topology

ExamAlert

Note that this star topology shows an Ethernet switch from Cisco Systems connected to workstations. In reality, switched LANs are more of what we call an extended star topology, but this exam fails to enter that level of detail.

If your topology connects every single node to every other single node, it is a full mesh topology. There is a formula for calculating the number of connections you need in this type of topology. The formula is $n(n - 1)/2$ where n equals the number of nodes. So if you have 10 nodes, it is $10(10 - 1)/2$. That is 45 connections to fully mesh the 10 nodes! This is why full mesh environments typically have a high cost and/or an administrative overhead.

The partial mesh seeks to eliminate some of the connections in a full mesh. Perhaps we have a certain area where a key device connects to all other devices, but the remainder of these devices are not connected to every other device. Consider that the star is actually a form of a partial mesh topology. In Wide Area Networking (WAN) we term this a hub-and-spoke design, but it certainly looks just like the star topology.

Most networks today are quite complex and as such use a wide variety of topologies to make themselves up. If you were to have a star connected to a full mesh, technically you could say your network topology is a hybrid topology.

CramQuiz

1. What topology consists of an n(n - 1)/2 number of connections?
   - ○ **A.** Star
   - ○ **B.** Full mesh
   - ○ **C.** Partial mesh
   - ○ **D.** Hybrid

2. In a WAN environment, the hub-and-spoke design is most often termed what type of topology?
   - ○ **A.** Full mesh
   - ○ **B.** Hybrid
   - ○ **C.** Bus
   - ○ **D.** Partial mesh

CramQuiz Answers

1. **B** is correct. The full mesh might be skipped due to overhead and costs of the many connections that might be present. Notice the formula indicates an increasing number of connections as you add nodes.

2. **D** is correct. The hub-and-spoke topology is an excellent example of a partial mesh.

Topic: Select the appropriate cabling type based on implementation requirements

Ethernet is king today when it comes to **network cabling**.

Ethernet continues to evolve and get faster. Table 1.3 shows you some forms you should be aware of:

TABLE 1.3 **Examples of Ethernet Technologies**

Common Name	Speed	Standard	Cable Type, Max. Length
Ethernet	10 Mbps	10BASE-T	Copper, 100 m
Fast Ethernet	100 Mbps	100BASE-T	Copper, 100 m
Gigabit Ethernet	1000 Mbps	1000BASE-LX	Fiber, 5000 m
Gigabit Ethernet	1000 Mbps	1000BASE-T	Copper, 100 m
10 Gig Ethernet	10 Gbps	10GBASE-T	Copper, 100 m
40 Gig Ethernet	40 Gbps	40GBASE-LR4	Fiber, 10000 m

> **ExamAlert**
>
> For the longest time we had to worry about the way in which the copper cables inside a physical Ethernet cable were arranged. There was a straight-through pin out for connecting unlike devices (a router and a switch, for example). There was a crossover pin out for connecting like devices (a switch to switch, for example). Although these pin outs still exist, we care much less because a modern Cisco switch supports auto-mdix. This technology allows the switch to work correctly with whatever cable is connected between the switch and any other device.

The most popular forms of Ethernet use unshielded twisted pair (UTP) in their operations. There are many categories of this UTP abbreviated as follows: CAT1, CAT2, CAT3, CAT4, CAT5, CAT5e, CAT6, CAT6a and CAT 7. Each of the unshielded twisted pair cable categories is technically advanced compared to its predecessor. For example, Cat 5e is cable of 1 gigabit per second Ethernet, whereas Cat 6 is capable of 10 gigabit per second Ethernet.

What about serial connections? Of course we will still find them at use in data centers to make certain types of WAN connections. Unfortunately, things are more complex when selecting the correct serial cable. Here are just some of the questions you must answer:

▶ Is the router being connected to a data terminal equipment (DTE) or data communications equipment (DCE) device?

▶ Is a male or female connector required on the cable?

▶ What signaling standard does the device require?

Although it is not necessary for us to review the dozens of serial cables you might encounter in the data center, please pay attention to the next ExamAlert, of course.

> **ExamAlert**
>
> Although there are many types of serial cables that you can implement in your network, there is one critical command you use in order to check the type and the health of such a cable. The command is **show controllers**. Know this command and its sample output. Here is an example of its output:
>
> ```
> HD unit 0, idb = 0x29A82C, driver structure at 0x2A1DF0
> buffer size 1524 HD unit 0, V.35 DCE cable, clockrate 64000
> ```

CramQuiz

1. What technology eliminates the major concerns about crossover versus straight-through cables?

    ○ **A.** STP

    ○ **B.** RSTP

    ○ **C.** Auto-mdix

    ○ **D.** FabricPath

2. What is not an example of a question you might need to ask when provisioning your device with the correct serial cable?

    ○ **A.** Is the router being connected to a data terminal equipment (DTE) or data communications equipment (DCE) device?

    ○ **B.** Is the port part of the chassis or modular?

    ○ **C.** Is a male or female connector required on the cable?

    ○ **D.** What signaling standard does the device require?

CramQuiz Answers

1. **C** is correct. Auto-mdix permits the switch to adapt to the type of cable connected to the device.

2. **B** is correct. Whether the port you are connecting is part of a module or part of the chassis is not as critical a concern as the other questions listed here.

Topic: Apply troubleshooting methodologies to resolve problems

CramSaver

1. A technician examines the symptom reports from their junior tech in the field and decides to start troubleshooting at the network layer. This is an example of what troubleshooting approach?

   _____

2. What troubleshooting methodology allows others to learn from your troubleshooting experience?

   _____

Answers

1. This is an example of the divide-and-conquer approach.
2. Documentation allows others to easily benefit from your troubleshooting experience.

You will perform plenty of troubleshooting of specific technologies in this exam. As such, I guide you through these topics in many of the pages that follow. Here, I present the exam blueprint depiction of a very simple and brief **troubleshooting methodology**:

▶ Problem isolation: Determining at what layer of the OSI model and on what devices and links the problem may exist.

▶ Documentation: It is critical to document the processes you use and the information you find; it can not only help you in the current process, but can become critical for those that troubleshoot after you.

▶ **Resolve**: This is of course your ultimate goal; you find the root cause of the problem after your problem isolation process, you document what has happened, and then you fix the root cause of the problem; fixing the problem is what is meant by *resolving* the problem.

▶ **Escalate**: Should you not be able to fix the issue, there should be a written escalation process in your organization; this might involve even communicating to a third party that your company partners with in order to fix the issue.

▶ **Verify and monitor**: Many times it might take time to carefully verify and monitor your solution to ensure the issue(s) are truly resolved; this text provides very important guidance on exact verification and **resolution monitoring** procedures for various specific technologies.

ExamAlert

The OSI model is a critical tool when carrying out your troubleshooting. If a device is without power, you find it very quickly with a bottom up troubleshooting approach. This means starting at the physical layer and moving upward. A top-down approach starts at the application layer and works its way downward. Should you gather excellent and trustworthy problem evidence, you might even choose a divide and conquer approach. This permits you to begin at a very specific layer and then moving upwards or downward as required.

CramQuiz

1. What happens should you not be able to resolve a problem that one of your users is having regarding their e-mail?

   - ○ **A.** Further documentation
   - ○ **B.** Verification
   - ○ **C.** Monitoring
   - ○ **D.** Escalation

2. What are two steps of a troubleshooting methodology where Cisco **show** commands might prove most valuable? (Choose two)

   - ○ **A.** Escalation
   - ○ **B.** Monitoring
   - ○ **C.** Resolve
   - ○ **D.** Problem isolation

CramQuiz Answers

1. **D** is correct. We typically resolve the problem that an end user is having, or we must escalate the problem to another group or even a third party. Your enterprise should document the escalation procedure.

2. **B** and **D** are correct. Problem isolation, verification, monitoring, and documenting most often involve **show** commands.

Review Questions

1. What layers of the OSI model coordinate to the Application layer of the TCP/IP model? Choose all that apply.

   ○ **A.** Transport

   ○ **B.** Application

   ○ **C.** Presentation

   ○ **D.** Session

2. What layer of the OSI model exists just above the Network layer?

   ○ **A.** Session

   ○ **B.** Presentation

   ○ **C.** Application

   ○ **D.** Transport

3. What layer of the OSI model controls the logical connections between two systems (local and remote), establishing and maintaining, and terminating these connections as necessary?

   ○ **A.** Transport

   ○ **B.** Data Link

   ○ **C.** Session

   ○ **D.** Presentation

4. What are the terms for the four PDUs that exist at the bottom of the OSI model? Name these in order from bottom to top

   ○ **A.** Segments, Frames, Packets, Bits

   ○ **B.** Bits, Frames, Packets, Segments

   ○ **C.** Packets, Frames, Bits, Segments

   ○ **D.** Segments, Packets, Frames, Bits

5. Name two Transport layer protocols. (Choose two)

   ○ **A.** ICMP

   ○ **B.** TCP

   ○ **C.** UDP

   ○ **D.** FTP

6. What protocol uses windowing in order to implement flow control?

   ○ **A.** ICMP

   ○ **B.** TCP

   ○ **C.** UDP

   ○ **D.** RIP

7. What is the port number and protocol used by SSH? (Choose two)

   ○ **A.** TCP

   ○ **B.** UDP

   ○ **C.** 22

   ○ **D.** 23

8. What command allows you to see the type of serial cable connected to your device?

   ○ **A. show version**

   ○ **B. show controllers**

   ○ **C. show interface**

   ○ **D. show flash**

9. What topology do you find in a modern switched LAN?

   ○ **A.** Star

   ○ **B.** Mesh

   ○ **C.** Hybrid

   ○ **D.** Full mesh

10. What type of cable is used in order to connect a switch to another switch?

   ○ **A.** Straight-through

   ○ **B.** Crossover

   ○ **C.** Null

   ○ **D.** Dual band

Answers to Review Questions

1. **B, C,** and **D** are correct. The Application layer of the TCP/IP model coordinates to the Application, Presentation, and Session layers for the OSI model

2. **D** is correct. The Transport layer exists just above the Network layer in the OSI model.

3. **C** is correct. The Session layer controls the connections between two systems; it establishes, manages, and terminates the connections between the local and remote systems.

4. **B** is correct. From the bottom to the top, the PDUs are Bits, Frame, Packets, and Segments.

5. **B** and **C** are correct. The Transport layer features both TCP and UDP.

6. **B** is correct. Transmission Control Protocol uses several mechanisms in order to attempt to guarantee delivery of packets. Windowing is one of these.

7. **A** and **C** are correct. SSH uses TCP and port 22 in its operations.

8. **B** is correct. The **show controllers** command allows you to see what type of serial cable attaches to your interface.

9. **A** is correct. The modern switched LAN is an excellent example of a star topology.

10. **B** is correct. The crossover cable is used to connect like devices, such as two switches.

Additional Resources

Bring the OSI Model to Life—http://www.ajsnetworking.com/osi-life

OSI Reference Model—http://www.ajsnetworking.com/osi-anyone-guess-layer

CHAPTER 2

Network Fundamentals: IPv4

This chapter covers the following official ICND1 100-105 exam topics:

▶ Configure, verify, and troubleshoot IPv4 addressing and subnetting

▶ Compare and contrast IPv4 address types

▶ Describe the need for private IPv4 addressing

This chapter ensures you are ready for the above topics from the Network Fundamentals section of the overall exam blueprint from Cisco Systems. Remember, this is just a section of the Network Fundamentals area. Chapters One and Three also make up this grouping. Those chapters deal with networking models and IPv6 respectively.

Essential Terms and Components

▶ **IPv4 Addressing**

▶ **IPv4 Address Classes**

▶ **Subnet Masks**

▶ **IPv4 Subnetting**

▶ **IPv4 Address Configuration**

▶ **Broadcasts**

▶ **Unicasts**

▶ **Multicasts**

▶ **Private IPv4 Addressing**

▶ **Network Address Translation (NAT)**

Topic: Configure, verify, and troubleshoot IPv4 addressing and subnetting

CramSaver

If you can correctly answer these CramSaver questions, save time by skimming the ExamAlerts in this chapter and then completing the CramQuiz at the end of each section and the Review Questions at the end of the chapter. If you are in doubt at all—read EVERYTHING in this chapter!

1. What is 187 converted to binary?

   _____

2. What is 10010011 in decimal?

   _____

3. What class of address is 239.1.2.3?

   _____

4. You are using 5 mask bits in an octet. What is the decimal value in this octet of the subnet mask?

   _____

5. How many hosts can this network support: 10.0.0.0 255.255.255.128?

   _____

6. How many subnets can you create if you borrow 6 bits?

   _____

7. What is the broadcast address for the subnet 10.15.2.0 255.255.254.0?

   _____

8. What is the usable host range for 10.15.0.224/27?

   _____

Answers

1. 10111011
2. 147
3. Class D
4. 248
5. 126
6. 64
7. 10.15.3.255
8. 10.15.0.225–10.15.0.254

Remember, an IPv4 address is a 32-bit number that we like to represent in dotted decimal notation. Consider using a conversion chart for the 8 bits that exist in an octet to help you with the various subnetting exercises you might encounter in the exam. Figure 2.1 is the simple chart I build on scratch paper before starting the exam:

2^7	2^6	2^5	2^4	2^3	2^2	2^1	2^0
128	64	32	16	8	4	2	1

FIGURE 2.1 **A Conversion Chart for IPv4 Addressing and Subnetting Questions**

One task that is simple using this chart is converting a number from decimal to binary or vice versa. For example, to convert 186 to binary, we first note that you can successfully subtract 128 from this number, so the first bit is on (1). The remainder is 58 after this subtraction. Note we cannot subtract 64 from this number (without having a negative number), so we move to the next number after setting the 64 value to off (0). We then subtract 32 from 58. This places a 1 in the 32 column and leaves us with 26. We can subtract 16 from 26 so there is a 1 in that column. Continuing with this method, we easily calculate that 186 in binary is:

10111010

Converting from binary to decimal is even easier. Just examine what bit positions are on (1) and add those decimal values together. So for example, 11101111 equals:

239

Early on in the development of TCP/IP, the designers created address classes to attempt to accommodate networks of various sizes. Notice they did this by setting the initial bit values. Table 2.1 shows these classes.

TABLE 2.1 **The TCP/IP Version 4 Address Classes**

Address Class	High-Order Bit Setting	1st Octet Range in Decimal
A	0	1–127
B	10	128–191
C	110	192–223
D	1110	224–239

> **ExamAlert**
>
> It is an important skill to be able to recognize the class of address using the decimal value in the first octet. Note that addresses beginning with 127 are reserved for local loopback purposes. Also memorize that class D addresses are for multicasting. Multicast can be used to send a message to multiple devices across multiple networks and subnetworks.

Another critical memorization point here is the default subnet masks for these address classes. Remember, it is the job of the subnet mask to define what portion of the 32-bit address represents the network portion versus the host portion. Table 2.2 defines the default masks.

TABLE 2.2 **Default IPv4 Subnet Masks**

Address Class	Default Mask	Prefix Notation Mask Bits
A	255.0.0.0	/8
B	255.255.0.0	/16
C	255.255.255.0	/24

Note that subnet masks must use continuous on bits (1). This results in the only possible values in a subnet mask octet shown in Table 2.3.

TABLE 2.3 **The Possible Values in an IPv4 Subnet Mask Octet**

On Bits	Value
8	255
7	254
6	252
5	248
4	240
3	224
2	192
1	128
0	0

ExamAlert

Some students will write out this table on scratch paper, as well as other tables in this chapter before they begin their exam. I do not do so, as I find I can pretty quickly calculate these facts on an as-needed basis during the exam.

Remember, subnetting is the process of "stealing" or "borrowing" bits from the host portion of the IPv4 address in order to create additional subnets. Think of using the following IP address and subnet mask combination in your network:

10.0.0.0/8 or 10.0.0.0 255.0.0.0

This allows you to only create one giant network. Sure, this network can have many host systems (specifically $2^{24} - 2$), but they all must exist in the same network. With broadcast traffic and other potential issues, this would be terrible for efficient communications. Today, we like to divide networks into small sections (subnetworks) of about 100 computers or less.

ExamAlert

Notice that the formula for calculating the number of hosts a subnet can support is to take the number of bits remaining for host addressing (h), make this the exponent for the number 2, and then subtract 2 from this amount. Thus, the formula is $2^h - 2$. We subtract two in this formula because we cannot assign a host an IP address with all zeroes in the host bits or all ones in the host bits. These are reserved for the identification of the network itself (all zeroes), and the broadcast address (all ones) for that subnet.

In the preceding example, we might decide to borrow 4 bits for subnetting. Now the identifications look like this:

10.0.0.0 255.240.0.0 or 10.0.0.0/12

How many bits are left for host identification? The subnet mask now contains 12 bits, leaving 20 bits available for host identification. Note that our calculation (2^{20} – 2) requires a calculator. As a result, you would not see this question in your exam. The answer is an astounding 1,048,574 hosts per subnet.

ExamAlert

But how many subnets can we create? The answer is the formula 2^s where s is the number of subnet bits we are borrowing. So in this case, we have 2^4. Examining my scratch paper chart from Figure 2.1, I quickly see the answer is 16 subnets. Note that as we borrow more and more host bits, we can create more and more subnets, but each subnet supports fewer and fewer hosts.

Also important is to establish the exact subnets we create given a bit-borrowing scenario. The great news is: We once again rely on Figure 2.1 for assistance!

Using the preceding scenario, we have:

10.0.0.0 255.240.0.0 or 10.0.0.0/12

To determine the subnets—we determine our block size. The block size is the least significant bit (rightmost) decimal value that the mask extends in to. So, in our example here, we extend four bits into the second octet. The decimal value here from Figure 2.1 is 16. We start at 0 and then each new subnet increments by 16! So we have subnets numbered 0, 16, 32, 48, 64, 80, and so on. Plugging these values into our IP address, we have:

10.0.0.0/12

10.16.0.0/12

10.32.0.0/12

10.48.0.0/12

10.64.0.0/12

10.80.0.0/12

Etc.

What if we begin with 10.46.0.0/16 and we want to borrow 4 additional bits to create new subnets? No problem. We have:

10.46.0.0/20

10.46.16.0/20

10.46.32.0/20

10.46.48.0/20

10.46.64.0/20

10.46.80.0/20

Etc.

What if we begin with 192.168.1.0/24 and we need to create 6 subnets? Borrowing 3 bits does the job with some to spare ($2^3 = 8$). So we have subnets of:

192.168.1.0/27

192.168.1.32/27

192.168.1.64/27

192.168.1.96/27

192.168.1.128/27

192.168.1.160/27

There are two more subnets of course, but we do not care here because we only needed six.

> **Note**
>
> You can take unused subnets and further subnet them! This is known as *variable length subnet masking (VLSM)*.

What about usable addresses for hosts on a subnet? Look at 192.168.1.0/27 above. That is a reserved address—it is the subnet ID itself. Add 1 to this and you have the first usable host address on this subnet—so it would be 192.168.1.1/27. The last address before we get to the next subnet is 192.168.1.31/27. This is reserved as well. It is for the subnet broadcast. Remember from our earlier discussion these two reserved addresses are why we have the −2 in the hosts calculation formula. So the last usable address on the subnet is 192.168.1.30/27. The last usable address is always the next subnet ID minus two.

Here is one more example for you. If we have 10.10.0.0/16 and we want at least 15 new subnets, we create the scheme 10.10.0.0/20. Here are the usable host ranges for the first four subnets:

Subnet 10.10.0.0/20—First Usable 10.10.0.1—Last Usable 10.10.15.254

Subnet 10.10.16.0/20—First Usable 10.10.16.1—Last Usable 10.10.31.254

Subnet 10.10.32.0/20—First Usable 10.10.32.1—Last Usable 10.10.47.254

Subnet 10.10.48.0/20—First Usable 10.10.48.1—Last Usable 10.10.63.254

ExamAlert

Be ready to implement all of the above skills in the exam environment. Obviously there are a variety of ways in which questions can be asked of you, and this chapter provides plenty of examples through CramSavers, CramQuizzes, and Review Questions. Although initially these questions might seem like a lot of work, you eventually crave questions like this in the exam because they are just math. Math questions don't have the challenging gray areas other multiple-choice questions have.

CramQuiz

1. What is 203 converted to binary?
   - ○ **A.** 11001011
   - ○ **B.** 11101011
   - ○ **C.** 10101100
   - ○ **D.** 11001000

2. What is 01101111 in decimal?
   - ○ **A.** 112
   - ○ **B.** 111
   - ○ **C.** 120
   - ○ **D.** 110

3. What is the default subnet mask for a class B network?
   - ○ **A.** 255.255.255.0
   - ○ **B.** 255.0.0.0

    ◯ **C.** 255.255.0.0

    ◯ **D.** 255.255.255.255

4. If your mask uses three bits in an octet, what is the decimal value?

    ◯ **A.** 192

    ◯ **B.** 224

    ◯ **C.** 240

    ◯ **D.** 252

5. If you have a mask of 255.255.255.240—how many hosts can you support?

    ◯ **A.** 32

    ◯ **B.** 62

    ◯ **C.** 14

    ◯ **D.** 6

6. Your network needs to support 30 subnets. How many bits should you "borrow" in order to create the least waste in address space?

    ◯ **A.** 4

    ◯ **B.** 5

    ◯ **C.** 6

    ◯ **D.** 7

7. What is the last usable host on a subnet where your computer has been given the address of 172.16.7.1 255.255.254.0?

    ◯ **A.** 172.16.7.255

    ◯ **B.** 172.16.6.1

    ◯ **C.** 172.16.7.128

    ◯ **D.** 172.16.7.254

CramQuiz Answers

1. **A** is correct. Using the chart in Figure 2.1, you arrive at these decimal values 128 + 64 + 8 + 2 + 1 = 203.

2. **B** is correct. The bits we add here are 64 + 32 + 8 + 4 + 2 + 1 = 111.

3. **C** is correct. 255.255.0.0 or 16 bits is the default mask for a Class B address.

4. **B** is correct. Three bits would mean 128 + 64 + 32 = 224.

5. **C** is correct. With this mask, there are only 4 bits left for host addressing. Using the chart in Figure 2.1, we learn that 2 raised to the 4th power is 16. We subtract two from this number to arrive at 14 hosts.

6. **B** is correct. Borrowing 5 bits permits the creation of 32 subnets. You have the 30 you need, plus 2 additional subnets.

7. **D** is correct. The usable host range here is 172.16.6.1 through 172.16.7.254.

Topic: Compare and contrast IPv4 address types

Modern networking systems use three main forms of addressing in order to communicate in the network:

▶ Unicast

▶ Broadcast

▶ Multicast

Unicast transmission is most likely what you think of first. For example, you are in a home network with an IP address of 192.168.1.2, and you want to send data to print to a printer located at 192.168.1.10. You do not intend for any other system to receive this traffic. This is a classic example of unicast IPv4 traffic.

When you have a system that must send a frame to all members of the network, this is termed a *broadcast*. At Layer 2, the destination broadcast address is FF:FF:FF:FF:FF:FF. At Layer 3, an example of a broadcast IPv4 address is

255.255.255.255. Remember, there is another type of broadcast, however. This is when a packet is destined for all of the members of a subnet. You and I calculated the broadcast address for subnets in this chapter. So, for example, the broadcast address for Subnet 10.10.0.0/20 is 10.10.15.255.

> **Note**
>
> Because a directed broadcast to a remote subnet can introduce many potential security issues, most routers give you the opportunity to enable or disable directed broadcast capabilities.

What if you want your device to "tune into" traffic in much the same way we tune into a television station in order to enjoy a broadcast of some show? The network equivalent of this is multicasting. Remember, the multicast address range is 224–239 in the first octet. Computers can "subscribe" to or "join" the multicast group by participating in this address scheme (in addition to their unicast address). Multicast is a way of sending one message (or set of packets) to multiple hosts across multiple networks and subnetworks. Some routing protocols use multicast addressing. When you enable RIP on your router, it starts listening for traffic destined for its 224.0.0.9 address as this is the address used to send traffic to all RIPv2 routers.

CramQuiz

1. Your system is sending email to the local SMTP server. What type of IPv4 traffic is this most likely given that these two systems have communicated seconds ago?
   - ○ **A.** Broadcast
   - ○ **B.** Multicast
   - ○ **C.** Unicast
   - ○ **D.** Anycast

2. EIGRP uses 224.0.0.10 in its operation. What type of address is this?
   - ○ **A.** Unicast
   - ○ **B.** Broadcast
   - ○ **C.** Multicast
   - ○ **D.** Anycast

3. What does it mean when you see FF:FF:FF:FF:FF:FF as the destination address in an Ethernet frame?

○   **A.** It means the frame is a multicast.

○   **B.** It means the frame is a unicast.

○   **C.** It means the frame should be dropped.

○   **D.** It means the frame is a broadcast.

CramQuiz Answers

1. **C** is correct. Although an ARP broadcast may initially be needed, because these systems have already communicated, the traffic can be sent unicast.

2. **C** is correct. 224.0.0.10 is the all-EIGRP-routers multicast address.

3. **D** is correct. The destination address of FF:FF:FF:FF:FF:FF is a reserved MAC address to indicate a broadcast.

Topic: Describe the need for private IPv4 addressing

CramSaver

1. List the Class A private address space.

_____

2. List the Class B private address space.

_____

3. List the Class C private address space.

_____

Answers

1. 10.0.0.0 to 10.255.255.255
2. 172.16.0.0 to 172.31.255.255
3. 192.168.0.0 to 192.168.255.255

The designers of IPv4 created private address space to help alleviate the depletion of IPv4 addresses. This address space is not routable on the public Internet. This address space can be used as needed inside corporations. This address space would then be translated using Network Address Translation (NAT) to allow access to and through the public Internet. Of course, this is why you tend to see the same addresses used in homes today (typically in the 192.168.1.X range). Table 2.4 shows you the private address space.

TABLE 2.4 **The IPv4 Private Address Ranges**

Address Class	Range of Private Addresses
A	10.0.0.0 to 10.255.255.255
B	172.16.0.0 to 172.31.255.255
C	192.168.0.0 to 192.168.255.255

ExamAlert

Clearly a skill you must possess is to memorize these ranges. Although it is normally not important to memorize Request for Comment numbers, the RFC that defined these ranges is so famous you should know it. The above ranges are often termed RFC 1918 addresses.

CramQuiz

1. What technology permits many private addresses to communicate on the public Internet?

   ○ **A.** SMTP

   ○ **B.** POP3

   ○ **C.** SNMP

   ○ **D.** NAT

2. Which of the following is not a private address?

   ○ **A.** 10.10.10.1

   ○ **B.** 12.34.100.1

   ○ **C.** 172.16.1.10

   ○ **D.** 192.168.1.10

3. What famous RFC defined the private use only IP address space?

   ○ **A.** RFC 2020

   ○ **B.** RFC 2191

   ○ **C.** RFC 2001

   ○ **D.** RFC 1918

CramQuiz Answers

1. **D** is correct. Network Address Translation permits these private addresses to communicate.

2. **B** is correct. 12.X.X.X is part of the public IP address space.

3. **D** is correct. RFC 1918 defined the private address space.

Review Questions

1. What is two raised to the seventh power?

    ○ **A.** 64

    ○ **B.** 128

    ○ **C.** 32

    ○ **D.** 16

2. What is the meaning of this IP address—127.0.0.1?

    ○ **A.** This is a multicast address

    ○ **B.** This is a Class A unicast address

    ○ **C.** This is a loopback address

    ○ **D.** This is an invalid IP address

3. What is the subnet mask if you began with the default Class A mask and then "borrowed" four bits for subnetting?

    ○ **A.** 255.255.128.0

    ○ **B.** 255.255.240.0

    ○ **C.** 255.240.0.0

    ○ **D.** 255.255.255.240

4. If you need to create six subnets, and want to waste as little IP address space as possible, how many bits should you "borrow"?

    ○ **A.** 2

    ○ **B.** 3

    ○ **C.** 4

    ○ **D.** 5

5. Examine the following diagram. What is the most likely reason HostA is unable to ping HostB?

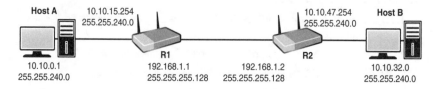

- ○ **A.** The subnet masks are incorrect for the link between R1 and R2.
- ○ **B.** HostA has an invalid IP address.
- ○ **C.** HostB is attempting to use the subnet ID as an IP address.
- ○ **D.** The R2 interface to R1 is attempting to use a subnet broadcast IP address.

6. What is the Layer 3 broadcast address?

- ○ **A.** 127.255.255.255
- ○ **B.** 0.0.0.0
- ○ **C.** 1.1.1.1
- ○ **D.** 255.255.255.255

7. What is the range of Class B private addresses?

- ○ **A.** 172.16.0.0 to 172.16.255.255
- ○ **B.** 172.0.0.0 to 172.255.255.255
- ○ **C.** 172.16.0.0 to 172.31.255.255
- ○ **D.** 172.32.0.0 to 172.36.255.255

Answers to Review Questions

1. **B** is correct. Two raised to the seventh power is on our quick reference sheet shown in Figure 2.1. The value is 128.

2. **C** is correct. 127.0.0.1 is a loopback address.

3. **C** is correct. The default Class A subnet mask is 255.0.0.0. Borrowing four bits from the next octet creates a new mask of 255.240.0.0.

4. **B** is correct. Borrowing three bits permits the creation of eight subnets.

5. **C** is correct. The HostB IP address is the subnet identifier for that subnet and is reserved.

6. **D** is correct. The Layer 3 broadcast address is simply 255.255.255.255.

7. **C** is correct. The RFC 1918 range is 172.16.0.0 to 172.31.255.255 for Class B.

Additional Resources

Reverse Engineering an IPv4 Host Address—
http://www.ajsnetworking.com/reverse-ipv4

Online IP Subnet Calculator—http://www.subnet-calculator.com

CHAPTER 3

Network Fundamentals: IPv6

This chapter covers the following official ICND1 100-105 exam topics:

▶ Identify the appropriate IPv6 addressing scheme to satisfy addressing requirements in a LAN/WAN environment

▶ Configure, verify, and troubleshoot IPv6 addressing

▶ Configure and verify IPv6 Stateless Address Auto Configuration

▶ Compare and contrast IPv6 address types

This chapter ensures you are ready for the above topics from the Network Fundamentals section of the overall exam blueprint from Cisco Systems. Remember, this is just a portion of the Network Fundamentals area. Chapters One and Two also exist in this grouping. These other chapters deal with networking models and IPv4 respectively.

Essential Terms and Components

▶ **IPv6 Addressing**

▶ **IPv6 Stateless Address Auto Configuration**

▶ **Global unicast**

▶ **Unique local**

▶ **Link local**

▶ **IPv6 Multicast**

▶ **Modified EUI 64**

▶ **IPv6 Autoconfiguration**

▶ **IPv6 Anycast**

Topic: Identify the appropriate IPv6 addressing scheme to satisfy addressing requirements in a LAN/WAN environment

CramSaver

If you can correctly answer these CramSaver questions, save time by skimming the ExamAlerts in this chapter and then completing the CramQuiz at the end of each section and the Review Questions at the end of the chapter. If you are in doubt at all—read EVERYTHING in this chapter!

1. How many bits are in an IPv6 IP address?

   _____

2. Rewrite this IPv6 address as short as possible: 2001:0000:0011:0001:0000: 0000:0001:1AB1

   _____

3. What is the "standard" host portion for an IPv6 address?

   _____

Answers

1. 128 bits
2. 2001:0:11:1::1:1AB1
3. 64 bits

IPv6 attacks the address exhaustion issues with IPv4 head-on. The 32-bit address space of IPv4 expands to 128 bits with IPv6. Because this is such an incredibly long address, hexadecimal is used to represent the address.

The header IPv6 uses in packets is larger than IPv4's. Figure 3.1 shows this new header.

Version	Class	Flow Label	
Payload Length		Next Header	Hop Limit
Source Address (16 Bytes)			
Destination Address (16 Bytes)			

FIGURE 3.1 **The IPv6 Header**

The IPv6 address format is eight sets of four hex digits. A colon separates each set of four digits. For example:

2001:1111:A231:0001:2341:9AB3:1001:19C3

Remember, there are two rules for shortening these IPv6 address:

▶ Once in the address, you can represent consecutive sections of 0000's with a double colon (::).

▶ As many times as you can in the address, you can eliminate leading 0's; you can even take a section of all zeroes (0000) and represent it as simply 0.

Here is an example of the application of these rules to make an address more convenient to read and type:

2001:0000:0011:0001:0000:0000:0001:1AB1

2001:0:11:1::1:1AB1

You present the subnet mask in prefix notation only. For example, an IPv6 address that uses the first 64 bits to represent the network could be shown as:

2001:0:11:1::1:1AB1/64

This section of your exam blueprint focuses on the global unicast address space for IPv6. These function like the public IPv4 addresses that we are accustomed to. Other types of IPv6 addresses are elaborated upon later in this chapter.

The management of the IPv6 address space is done by the Internet Assigned Numbers Authority (IANA). IANA assigns blocks of address spaces to regional registries, who then allocate address space to network service providers. Your organization requests address space from a service provider. For example, a company may be assigned the address space similar to 2001:DB8:6783::/48 From that network address space, they can create and use subnets.

> **Note**
>
> With the massive address space, you immediately have more subnet and host capabilities than you should ever need.

To simplify subnetting in IPv6, companies often use a /64 mask. Remember, this means a 64-bit network portion and a 64-bit host portion.

> **ExamAlert**
>
> Although the section sounds like it might be a "real world only" bit of information, please understand that these facts are frequently tested in the ICND1 exam.

CramQuiz

1. What is the size of the source address field in an IPv6 header?

   - ○ **A.** 6 bytes
   - ○ **B.** 8 bytes
   - ○ **C.** 12 bytes
   - ○ **D.** 16 bytes

2. What are the two rules you can use to shorten an IPv6 address? (Choose two.)

   - ○ **A.** You can trim all trailing zeroes in all sections.
   - ○ **B.** You can trim all leading zeroes in all sections.
   - ○ **C.** You can use :: twice in an address.
   - ○ **D.** You can use :: once in an address.

3. What is the typical network portion of an IPv6 global unicast address?

- ○ **A.** 32 bits
- ○ **B.** 48 bits
- ○ **C.** 64 bits
- ○ **D.** 128 bits

CramQuiz Answers

1. **D** is correct. The source and destination address fields are 16 bytes in length to accommodate the IPv6 addresses.

2. **B** and **D** are correct. You can trim all leading zeroes in all sections. Once in an address, you can use :: in order to represent a successive section of all zeroes.

3. **C** is correct. The network portion is typically 64 bits and the host portion is 64 bits as well.

Topic: Configure, verify, and troubleshoot IPv6 addressing

CramSaver

1. What is the term for running IPv4 and IPv6 on the same network interface?

   _____

2. What command would you use to configure the IPv6 address of 2001:aaaa:bbbb::1 on an interface with a 64-bit mask?

   _____

3. Which method uses the interface hardware address as part of the IPv6 Layer 3 host address?

   _____

4. What is the equivalent command for IPv6 for the IPv4 command **show ip interface brief**?

   _____

Answers

1. Dual stack
2. **ipv6 address 2001:aaaa:bbbb::1/64**
3. Modified EUI-64
4. **show ipv6 interface brief**

IPv6 address configuration is pleasantly simple. Examine the configuration shown in Example 3.1. Note how this interface is now dual stack. It runs IPv4 and IPv6 simultaneously. This is a quite common configuration since IPv4 may be around for the rest of our lifetimes and beyond. Keep in mind, of course, that IPv4 is not required for the configuration of IPv6.

EXAMPLE 3.1 **A Sample IPv6 Address Configuration**

```
R1(config)#interface fastethernet0/0
R1(config-if)#ip address 10.10.10.1 255.255.255.0
R1(config-if)#ipv6 address 2001:aaaa:bbbb::1/64
R1(config-if)#no shutdown
```

> **Note**
>
> A global configuration command you will often use is **ipv6 unicast-routing**.
> This permits your router to run IPv6-related routing protocols such as EIGRP for IPv6
> or OSPF version 3. This command is not shown in Example 3.1 because it is not
> required for the configuration of IPv6 addresses.

What about verification? No problem—Example 3.2 provides two different approaches:

EXAMPLE 3.2 **Two Sample IPv6 Address Verifications**

```
R1#show ipv6 interface brief
FastEthernet0/0            [up/up]
    FE80::C801:6FF:FE65:0
    2001:AAAA:BBBB::1
R1#show ipv6 interface fa0/0
FastEthernet0/0 is up, line protocol is up
  IPv6 is enabled, link-local address is FE80::C801:6FF:FE65:0
  No Virtual link-local address(es):
  Global unicast address(es):
    2001:AAAA:BBBB::1, subnet is 2001:AAAA:BBBB::/64
  Joined group address(es):
    FF02::1
    FF02::1:FF00:1
    FF02::1:FF65:0
  MTU is 1500 bytes
  ICMP error messages limited to one every 100 milliseconds
  ICMP redirects are enabled
  ICMP unreachables are sent
  ND DAD is enabled, number of DAD attempts: 1
  ND reachable time is 30000 milliseconds (using 30000)
R1#
```

Many engineers will not want the extra work of manually assigning host addresses to their systems, however. IPv6 offers an excellent feature termed modified EUI-64. This process takes the MAC address from the device and uses it to automatically generate a host portion! Example 3.3 show the configuration and verification of an IPv6 address using this very groovy approach.

EXAMPLE 3.3 **Modified EUI-64 Host Portion Assignment and Verification**

```
R1(config)#interface fastEthernet 0/0
R1(config-if)#ipv6 address 2001:AAAA:BBBB::/64 eui-64
R1(config-if)#no shutdown
R1(config-if)#end
R1#
%SYS-5-CONFIG_I: Configured from console by console
R1#show ipv6 interface brief
FastEthernet0/0            [up/up]
    FE80::C801:6FF:FE65:0
    2001:AAAA:BBBB:0:C801:6FF:FE65:0
R1#show ipv6 interface fa 0/0
FastEthernet0/0 is up, line protocol is up
  IPv6 is enabled, link-local address is FE80::C801:6FF:FE65:0
  No Virtual link-local address(es):
  Global unicast address(es):
    2001:AAAA:BBBB:0:C801:6FF:FE65:0, subnet is 2001:AAAA:BBBB::/64
  [EUI]
  Joined group address(es):
    FF02::1
    FF02::1:FF65:0
  MTU is 1500 bytes
  ICMP error messages limited to one every 100 milliseconds
  ICMP redirects are enabled
  ICMP unreachables are sent
  ND DAD is enabled, number of DAD attempts: 1
  ND reachable time is 30000 milliseconds (using 30000)
R1#
```

CramQuiz

1. What command do you need in order to enable IPv6 routing capabilities on a
   Cisco router?

   ○ **A.** ipv6 unicast-routing

   ○ **B.** ipv6 routing

   ○ **C.** ipv6 routing enable

   ○ **D.** ipv6 unicast-enable

2. What command configures IPv6 on your interface and eliminates your requirement
   of manually configuring a host address?

   ○ **A.** ipv6 address 2001:aaaa:bbbb::/64 auto

   ○ **B.** ipv6 address 2001:aaaa:bbbb::/64

   ○ **C.** ipv6 address 2001:aaaa:bbbb::/64 eui-64

   ○ **D.** ipv6 address 2001:aaaa:bbbb::/64 slaac

3. What two commands could you use to verify your IPv6 interface address?
(Choose two.)

   ○ **A. show ipv6 interface brief**

   ○ **B. show interface ipv6 details**

   ○ **C. show ipv6 interface**

   ○ **D. show interface ipv6 info**

CramQuiz Answers

1. **A** is correct. The command required to enable IPv6 routing capabilities on a Cisco router is **ipv6 unicast-routing**.

2. **C** is correct. Use the **eui-64** keyword with the IPv6 address command in order to automatically have the device generate its host portion.

3. **A** and **C** are correct. The **show ipv6 interface brief** and **show ipv6 interface** commands are the equivalents of **show ip interface brief** and **show ip interface** commands.

Topic: Configure and verify IPv6 Stateless Address Auto Configuration

CramSaver

1. Describe the difference between stateful and stateless address assignment.

   _____

2. What is the command on a Cisco router to assign an IPv6 address using SLAAC?

   _____

Answers

1. Stateful address assignment refers to a device "tracking" the automatic assignment of addressing information. A typical example is DHCP for IPv4. Stateless assignment refers to a lack of tracking information.

2. **ipv6 address autoconfig**

If you think the ability to have the IPv6 network device configure its own host address (modified EUI) is pretty awesome, what is even more exciting is having one network device assist another in the assignment of the entire address. This is stateless address auto-configuration (SLAAC). _Stateless_ simply means that a device is not keeping track of the address information. For example, in IPv4 and IPv6 you can use a DHCP server in a "stateful" manner. A DHCP device provides the address information that devices need, and tracks this information in a database. Obviously, there is a fair amount of overhead involved in this process for the DHCP server. Fortunately, in IPv6 you can use SLAAC and stateless DHCP to provide a host with all of the information it might need. This of course includes things like the IPv6 address, the prefix length, the default gateway address, and the DNS server(s) address.

With SLAAC, the IPv6 device learns its prefix information automatically over the local link from another device (such as the router), then can randomly assign its own host portion of the address, or use the modified EUI method discussed earlier in this chapter.

Remember, because SLAAC cannot provide additional information such as DNS server addresses, we often combine SLAAC with the use of stateless DHCP in IPv6.

ExamAlert

How does the SLAAC host communicate with its neighbor if it does not yet possess the IPv6 address information it needs? Remember, this is the job of the link-local address in IPv6. We review this information in the next topic.

What does the configuration look like on a Cisco router for having an interface acquire its IPv6 address using SLAAC? Example 3.4 shows how remarkably simple it is.

EXAMPLE 3.4 **Using SLAAC for Address Assignment on a Cisco Router**

```
R1(config)#interface fa0/0
R1(config-if)#ipv6 address autoconfig
```

ExamAlert

Remember, Cisco routers that support IPv6 are ready for any of the IPv6 interface addressing methods with no special configuration. However, if the router needs to run IPv6 routing protocols (such as OSPF or EIGRP), you must use the **ipv6 unicast-routing** command, as discussed earlier in this chapter.

CramQuiz

1. Why might a stateless DHCP server be used in addition to SLAAC?

   - ○ **A.** In order to conserve address space
   - ○ **B.** In order to assign the prefix information needed by the host
   - ○ **C.** In order to track address assignments
   - ○ **D.** In order to provide DNS address information

2. How might a device create its host portion of the address once acquiring its prefix via SLAAC?

   - ○ **A.** Using stateless DHCP
   - ○ **B.** Using Modified EUI
   - ○ **C.** Using NAT
   - ○ **D.** Using a DNS server

3. How can a SLAAC host communicate with its neighbor that is providing network prefix information?

- ○ **A.** The Link Local address
- ○ **B.** CDP
- ○ **C.** NAT
- ○ **D.** The Anycast address

CramQuiz Answers

1. **D** is correct. SLAAC provides information such as prefix and prefix length, but cannot assign additional information such as DNS servers.

2. **B** is correct. SLAAC works perfectly with Modified EUI. SLAAC provides the prefix and length, allowing the host to use Modified EUI in order to assign its own host portion.

3. **A** is correct. SLAAC is able to function thanks to Link Local addressing used in IPv6.

Topic: Compare and contrast IPv6 address types

CramSaver

1. What type of IPv6 address is similar to an RFC 1918 address in IPv6?

   _____

2. What type of IPv6 address allows a variety of IPv6 services to function between two devices on the same network?

   _____

3. What type of IPv6 address has you configure identical addresses on different devices?

   _____

Answers

1. A Unique Local address
2. A Link Local address
3. An Anycast address

ExamAlert

For success in the exam regarding IPv6, it is critical that you master the following IPv6 address types. Notice we have reviewed many of these already, but they are covered again here in order to stay consistent with the exam blueprint.

Global Unicast—This is the unique IPv6 address that may be used on the public Internet.

Unique Local—This is similar to the concept of private use only addresses (RFC 1918) in IPv4. These addresses are not routable on the Internet. In IPv6, these addresses begin with FD. For example, fde4:8dba:82e1::1/64 is an example of a unique local address.

Link Local—As the name makes clear, these addresses only function on the local link. IPv6 devices automatically generate them in order to perform many automated functions between devices. The Link Local address uses the prefix FE80::/10.

Multicast—Just like in an IPv4 environment, multicast traffic is beneficial in IPv6. Remember, multicasting means a packet is sent to a group of devices interested in receiving the information. In IPv6, multicasting actually replaces completely the IPv4 approach of broadcasting. In IPv6, if your device wants to reach all devices, it sends traffic to the IPv6 multicast address of FF02::1.

Modified EUI 64—This is the approach a device uses to assign itself its host portion of the IPv6 address.

IPv6 Autoconfiguration—This refers to an IPv6 address achieved through the stateless address auto-configuration (SLAAC) process.

IPv6 Anycast—This feature allows you to configure *identical* IPv6 addresses on your devices. Now, when clients attempt to reach this address, IPv6 routers can send the traffic to the nearest anycast device. The configuration is simple for this addressing feature involving the keyword **anycast** following the address.

ExamAlert

A confusing command for many students is the interface command **ipv6 enable**. This command is not required to enable IPv6 on an interface, but what it does do is configure a Link Local address and prepare the interface for processing IPv6 information.

CramQuiz

1. What does a Link Local address begin with?

   ○ **A.** FD80::/10

   ○ **B.** FE80::/10

   ○ **C.** FF80::/10

   ○ **D.** FC80::/10

2. What address does IPv6 use in order to multicast traffic to all devices?

   ○ **A.** FF02::1

   ○ **B.** FF02::2

   ○ **C.** FF02::5

   ○ **D.** FF02::6

3. When troubleshooting an IPv6 network, you notice that two devices have identical IPv6 addresses. If the network is actually configured correctly, why might this occur?

   ○ **A.** The devices are using broadcasts for routing protocol traffic.

   ○ **B.** The devices are using Anycast.

   ○ **C.** The devices are using matching Link Local addresses for the purpose of SLAAC.

   ○ **D.** The devices are using Unique Local addresses.

CramQuiz Answers

1. **B** is correct. The FE80::/10 space is reserved for Link Local addressing.

2. **A** is correct. This is the all nodes IPv6 multicast address. The other multicast addresses listed in this question are valid—but for other purposes. For example, FF02::2 is for all routers.

3. **B** is correct. If the devices are properly configured and have matching configured addresses, they must be using Anycast addresses.

Review Questions

1. How many more bits are used in an IPv6 address compared to an IPv4 address?

   ○ **A.** 96

   ○ **B.** 128

   ○ **C.** 48

   ○ **D.** 64

2. What is the significance of :: in the following IPv6 address—2001:0:11:1:: 1:1AB1/64?

   ○ **A.** It is used to represent a single section of 0000.

   ○ **B.** It is used to represent one or more continuous sections of 0000.

   ○ **C.** It is used to represent a single section of 1111.

   ○ **D.** It is used to represent one or more continuous sections of 1111.

3. What command causes your router interface to configure its own host portion of the address?

   ○ **A. ipv6 address 2001:aaaa:bbbb::1/64 auto**

   ○ **B. ipv6 address 2001:aaaa:bbbb::1/64 eui-64**

   ○ **C. ipv6 address 2001:aaaa:bbbb::/64 eui-64**

   ○ **D. ipv6 address 2001:aaaa:bbbb::/64 auto**

4. What command allows you to see the multicast addresses that an interface has joined in IPv6?

   ○ **A. show ipv6 interface brief**

   ○ **B. show ipv6 interface**

   ○ **C. show ipv6 interface multicast**

   ○ **D. show multicast ipv6**

5. If you are using DHCP in IPv6 combined with the SLAAC feature, you are most likely using what version of DHCP?

   ○ **A.** Stateful

   ○ **B.** Stateless

   ○ **C.** Headless

   ○ **D.** Auto

6. If you use the **ipv6 enable** command on an interface, what address do you have on that interface?

○ **A.** Global Unicast

○ **B.** Autoconfiguration

○ **C.** Unique Local

○ **D.** Link Local

Answers to Review Questions

1. **A** is correct. An IPv4 address is 32 bits, while an IPv6 is 128 bits.

2. **B** is correct. The :: may be used once in an address in order to represent one or more continuous sections of 0000.

3. **C** is correct. The modified EUI method is in the correct syntax in this example.

4. **B** is correct. The **show ipv6 interface** command provides this level of detail. It shows the multicast and link local addressing joined.

5. **B** is correct. The stateless DHCP feature often combines with SLAAC.

6. **D** is correct. The **ipv6 enable** command ensures a Link Local address exists.

Additional Resources

IPv6 EUI-64 Calculation on an IOS Router—
http://www.ajsnetworking.com/eui-64

Stateless DHCP with IPv6—http://www.ajsnetworking.com/
stateless-dhcp-ipv6

PART II

LAN Switching Fundamentals

This part of the text deals with one of five overall sections you must master for the ICND1 exam. There are three chapters total that make up Part 2. These three chapters taken as a whole represent 26 percent of the exam questions you face in your exam. This means that the LAN Switching Fundamentals area is the most important section of the five overall sections that you deal with on your testing day!

Here you begin with a high-level overview of the world of switches, but then quickly move into details of their configuration and even security best practices. Part 2 includes the following chapters:

CHAPTER 4

LAN Switching Fundamentals: Switching Concepts

This chapter covers the following official ICND1 100-105 exam topics:

▶ Describe and verify switching concepts

▶ Interpret Ethernet frame format

▶ Troubleshoot interface and cable issues (collisions, errors, duplex, speed)

This chapter ensures you are ready for the above topics from the LAN Switching Fundamentals section of the overall exam blueprint from Cisco Systems. Remember, this chapter is just a portion of the LAN Switching Fundamentals area. Chapters Five and Six also exist in this grouping. These other chapters deal with VLANs and trunking configurations and an important feature called Port Security.

Essential Terms and Components

▶ **Ethernet Switching**

▶ **MAC Learning**

▶ **MAC Aging**

▶ **Frame Switching**

▶ **Frame Flooding**

▶ **MAC Address Table**

▶ **Ethernet Frame Format**

▶ **Collisions**

▶ **Errors**

▶ **Speed and Duplex Mismatches**

Topic: Describe and verify switching concepts

CramSaver

If you can correctly answer these CramSaver questions, save time by skimming the ExamAlerts in this chapter and then completing the CramQuiz at the end of each section and the Review Questions at the end of the chapter. If you are in doubt at all—read EVERYTHING in this chapter!

1. What specific field of an Ethernet frame does a switch "learn" from and then record in a database?

   _____

2. What is the process called when a MAC address that is no longer communicating on the network is removed from the switch database?

   _____

3. What happens when a frame enters the switch and the destination MAC address is known by the switch?

   _____

4. What happens when a frame enters the switch and the destination MAC address is not known by the switch?

   _____

5. What command can you use to view the MAC address table on a Cisco switch?

   _____

Answers

1. The switch "learns" and records the source MAC address.

2. This process of removing stale MAC addresses is termed *aging*.

3. When the destination MAC address is known by the switch, the switch can intelligently forward the information out the correct port, filtering the traffic from all other ports.

4. Frame flooding occurs when the destination MAC address is unknown; this is the process where the frame is sent out all ports (for the same VLAN) except the port on which the frame entered.

5. The command **show mac address-table** allows you to view the MAC address table.

Figure 4.1 and the list that follows provide the context for the discussion of several fundamental **Ethernet switching** concepts that you must review.

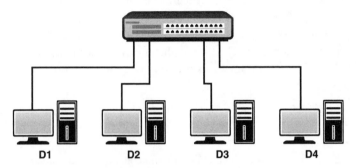

FIGURE 4.1   **A Simple Switch Layout**

▶ **MAC learning and MAC aging**: What is one of the responsibilities of the switch? It is to learn MAC addresses. The switch transparently observes incoming frames. It records the source MAC address of these frames in its MAC address table. It also records the specific port for the source MAC address. Based on this information, it can make intelligent frame forwarding (switching) decisions. Notice that a network machine could be turned off or moved at any point. As a result, the switch must also age MAC addresses and remove them from the table after they have not been seen for some duration.

▶ In Figure 4.1, it will not take long before all four systems send some traffic. Keep in mind that many protocols broadcast information periodically. When these frames enter the switch, it records the source MAC address and port information in its MAC address table.

ExamAlert

You can manipulate the aging of MAC addresses on your Cisco switch. Depending on the model of switch, the range of time you can set is from 0 to 1,000,000 seconds. The default is 300 seconds. You can even disable MAC address aging on some switches.

▶ **Frame switching**: Along with building a MAC address table (learning MAC address to port mappings), the switch also forwards (switches) frames intelligently from port to port. Think about this as the opposite of how a Layer 1 hub works. The device hub takes in a frame and always forwards this frame out all other ports. In a hub-based network, every port is part of the same collision domain. The switch is too smart for that. If its MAC address table is fully populated for all ports, then it "filters" the frame from being forwarded out ports unnecessarily. It forwards the frame to the correct port based on the destination MAC address. Using Figure 4.1 as an example, if D1 sends a unicast frame destined for D4, the switch examines the MAC address table, finds the destination MAC address in this table, and forwards the frame out only the port connecting to D4.

ExamAlert

Remember, the switch learns based on source MAC information, but then switches frames from port to port based on the destination MAC information.

▶ **Frame flooding**: What happens when a frame has a destination address that is not in the MAC address table? The frame is flooded out all ports (other than the port on which the frame was received). This also happens when the destination MAC address in the frame is the broadcast address.

▶ **MAC address table**: Obviously the MAC address table is a critical component in the modern switch. It really is the brains of the operation. It contains the MAC-address–to–port mappings so the switch can work its network magic. Example 4.1 shows how easy it is to examine the MAC address table of a Cisco switch.

EXAMPLE 4.1 **Examining a Real MAC Address Table**

```
Switch#show mac address-table
          Mac Address Table
-------------------------------------------

Vlan    Mac Address      Type       Ports
----    -----------      --------   -----
   1    e213.5864.ab8f   DYNAMIC    Gi0/0
   1    fa16.3ee3.7d71   DYNAMIC    Gi1/0
```

ExamAlert

Note that the switch dynamically learns MAC address entries by default. You can also program the switch with static MAC address entries.

CramQuiz

1. What is the default aging time for MAC address entries on a typical Cisco switch?
   - ○ **A.** 60 seconds
   - ○ **B.** 120 seconds
   - ○ **C.** 300 seconds
   - ○ **D.** 1200 seconds

2. If a MAC address of fa16.3ee3.7d71 exists in the MAC address table of a switch and is associated with the port gi0/1, which statement is true?
   - ○ **A.** Traffic with a source MAC address of fa16.3ee3.7d71 entering the switch is forwarded out port gi0/1.
   - ○ **B.** Traffic with a source MAC address of fa16.3ee3.7d71 entering the switch resets the aging timer.
   - ○ **C.** Traffic with a destination MAC address of fa16.3ee3.7d72 entering the switch is forwarded out port gi0/1.
   - ○ **D.** Traffic with a destination MAC address of fa16.3ee3.7d71 entering the switch is flooded.

3. What happens to a frame with a destination MAC address of ffff.ffff.ffff?
   - ○ **A.** The frame is dropped.
   - ○ **B.** The frame is forwarded out the gi0/0 port only.
   - ○ **C.** The frame is buffered.
   - ○ **D.** The frame is flooded out all ports except for the port the frame entered the switch on.

4. Which statement about a transparent Ethernet switch is true?
   - ○ **A.** The switch must use dynamic learning only.
   - ○ **B.** The switch records the destination MAC address from received frames.
   - ○ **C.** The switch drops broadcast frames by default.
   - ○ **D.** The switch aging process can be disabled.

CramQuiz Answers

1. **C** is correct. The default aging time on most Cisco switches is 300 seconds.
2. **B** is correct. The aging timer is reset when traffic enters the switch with a known source MAC address.
3. **D** is correct. Notice the MAC address shown is the broadcast MAC address. This triggers switch flooding behavior.
4. **D** is correct. The switch aging process can be disabled. This is done by setting the aging time to 0.

Topic: Interpret Ethernet frame format

CramSaver

1. What is the first field of a common Ethernet frame format today?

   _____

2. What is the last field of a common Ethernet frame format today?

   _____

3. What is the job of the SFD in an Ethernet frame?

   _____

Answers

1. The Preamble.
2. The Frame Check Sequence (FCS).
3. The SFD is the Start Frame Delimiter. This is one byte in length. It also has a simple job. It marks the end of the Preamble and indicates the beginning of the Ethernet frame.

Figure 4.2 shows the most common **Ethernet frame format**.

Preamble	SFD	Dest. MAC	Source MAC	Type	Data and Pad	FCS

FIGURE 4.2   **The Ethernet Frame Format**

Here is information you should know regarding this format:

▶ The fields before the **Data and Pad** are collectively termed the **header**.

▶ The field after the **Data and Pad** is known as the **trailer**.

▶ The **Preamble** is seven bytes in length. It is simply a pattern of alternating 1 and 0 bits, allowing devices on the network to easily synchronize their receiver clocks.

▶ The **SFD** is the **Start Frame Delimiter**. This is one byte in length. It also has a simple job. It marks the end of the **Preamble** and indicates the beginning of the Ethernet frame.

▶ The **Destination MAC** address field is six bytes in length to store the appropriate destination MAC address for the frame.

▶ The **Source MAC** address field is also six bytes in length. It stores the appropriate source MAC.

▶ The **Type** field is two bytes in length and identifies the protocol in the frame. For example, this field might indicate IPv4 or IPv6 in a network today.

▶ The **Data and Pad** section ranges from 46 to 1500 bytes. The padding might exist so that the section can meet the minimum length require-ment for this field of 46 bytes. Of course, the data portion represents the actual data being sent from a higher layer of the OSI model. Some Cisco switches have the capability to support larger than default frames. These frame sizes include baby giants (up to 1600 bytes), and jumbo frames (up to 9216 bytes), depending on the switch model.

▶ The **FCS** field is the **Frame Check Sequence**. It is four bytes in length. The purpose of this field is to determine whether the frame experienced transmission errors in its journey through the network.

CramQuiz

1. What field of the Ethernet frame ensures the frame was not damaged in transit?

  ○ **A.** SFD

  ○ **B.** Type

  ○ **C.** FCS

  ○ **D.** Preamble

2. What field of the Ethernet frame indicates whether IPv4 or IPv6 is the protocol?

  ○ **A.** SFD

  ○ **B.** Type

  ○ **C.** FCS

  ○ **D.** Preamble

3. What is the default MTU of the Data and Pad section of the Ethernet frame?

  ○ **A.** 1200

  ○ **B.** 900

  ○ **C.** 1500

  ○ **D.** 1600

CramQuiz Answers

1. **C** is correct. The Frame Check Sequence field determines whether there was an error in the transmission of the frame.

2. **B** is correct. The Type field indicates the protocol being carried.

3. **C** is correct. The MTU for Ethernet is 1500 bytes in size. See the next section for much more information on this question.

Topic: Troubleshoot interface and cable issues (collisions, errors, duplex, speed)

CramSaver

1. What command allows you to quickly see the various errors that might have occurred on Gi0/1 on a Cisco switch?

   _____

2. What is the typical size of a Giant frame in a Gigabit Ethernet data center?

   _____

3. What is the typical size of a Baby Giant frame in a modern network?

   _____

4. Runts are frames that are beneath what size?

   _____

5. Name the two types of duplex options?

   _____

Answers

1. **show interface gi0/1**
2. Approximately 9216 bytes
3. 1600 bytes
4. 64 bytes
5. Full duplex and half duplex

There are many things that can go wrong when you are dealing with a technology as complex as local area networking! Here are many issues you should be aware of. Note that many of these were not explicitly listed in the Cisco exam blueprint, but are very likely to be tested.

▶ The **show interface** command on a switch displays a ton of potential errors and problems that might happen due to interface and cable issues. Notice these is the last section of the output shown in Example 4.2.

EXAMPLE 4.2 **The show interface Output on a Cisco Switch**

```
Switch#show interface gi0/1
GigabitEthernet0/1 is up, line protocol is up (connected)
  Hardware is iGbE, address is fa16.3eb4.b62b (bia fa16.3eb4.b62b)
  MTU 1500 bytes, BW 1000000 Kbit/sec, DLY 10 usec,
      reliability 255/255, txload 1/255, rxload 1/255
  Encapsulation ARPA, loopback not set
  Keepalive set (10 sec)
  Unknown, Unknown, link type is auto, media type is unknown media type
  output flow-control is unsupported, input flow-control is
  unsupported
  Auto-duplex, Auto-speed, link type is auto, media type is unknown
  input flow-control is off, output flow-control is unsupported
  ARP type: ARPA, ARP Timeout 04:00:00
  Last input never, output 00:00:00, output hang never
  Last clearing of "show interface" counters never
  Input queue: 0/75/0/0 (size/max/drops/flushes); Total output drops:
  32562
  Queueing strategy: fifo
  Output queue: 0/0 (size/max)
  5 minute input rate 0 bits/sec, 0 packets/sec
  5 minute output rate 0 bits/sec, 0 packets/sec
      6783 packets input, 0 bytes, 0 no buffer
      Received 14 broadcasts (0 multicasts)
      0 runts, 0 giants, 0 throttles
      0 input errors, 0 CRC, 0 frame, 0 overrun, 0 ignored
      0 watchdog, 0 multicast, 0 pause input
      108456 packets output, 7107939 bytes, 0 underruns
      0 output errors, 0 collisions, 2 interface resets
      0 unknown protocol drops
      0 babbles, 0 late collision, 0 deferred
      0 lost carrier, 0 no carrier, 0 pause output
      0 output buffer failures, 0 output buffers swapped out
Switch#
```

▶ **Collisions** should not occur in your properly designed switched network. Today, we have the ability to design full duplex networks using
switches that intelligently filter frames from being sent out all interfaces.
This leads to what is termed microsegmentation. This is the construction of your network so that all hosts exist as the only device in a collision
domain. Each port on a switch is a separate collision domain.

▶ **Errors** might occur in your network for a wide a variety of reasons. For example, there could be electrical interference somewhere or a bad Network Interface Card that is not able to frame things correctly for the network. Remember, the Frame Check Sequence often is the source for catching these errors. Each time a router forwards a packet on an Ethernet network, it replaces and rewrites the Layer 2 Ethernet header information, along with a new FCS.

▶ **Duplex** used to be a big concern in Ethernet LANs. Because you might be using half-duplex due to having hubs in your network, you needed to ensure that **duplex mismatches** did not occur between full-duplex (switched) areas and half-duplex areas. Today, autonegotiation to full-duplex between devices is common. For the exam, just understand that if an older device is hard-coded to half-duplex and you code the LAN device connected to full duplex, a duplex mismatch can still result. These can be difficult to track down because some packets typically make it through the connection fine, whereas others are dropped. In networks that operate in half duplex, the technology of Carrier Sense Multiple Access with Collision Detection (CSMA/CD) is used to allow devices to operate on a half-duplex network.

▶ **Speed** is another area where conflict can occur, but this is also becoming a less common problem as technologies advance. For example, 1 Gigabit per second interfaces are quite common now and operate with each other seamlessly at 1 Gbps. The issue again becomes older equipment that might default to a slower speed causing a **speed mismatch**.

▶ **Runts** are Ethernet frames that are less than 64 bytes and may be caused by excessive collisions. Of course, these frames have become more rare as networks have become nearly collision-free.

▶ **Jumbo Frames (Giants)**: Today many technologies are enhancing networks by adding information to Ethernet frames. This results in **Jumbo Frames (Giants)**. This often indicates frames of 9216 bytes for Gigabit Ethernet, but technically can refer to anything over the standard IP MTU (Maximum Transmission Unit) of 1500 bytes.

▶ **Baby Giant Frames**: What if your Ethernet frame is just a little larger than the standard MTU of 1500 bytes? Specifically, what if your frame is 1600 bytes in size? You have what networkers term a **Baby Giant**.

ExamAlert

Although the indicators in the preceding list are by far the most likely to appear in your exam, here is a list of other conditions often included in **show interface** outputs:

▶ **Output Hang**: The number of hours, minutes, and seconds since the interface was last reset because of a transmission that took too long.

▶ **Input Drops**: The number of frames dropped on the input interface. Typically, this is a result of congestion on the interface.

▶ **Output Drops**: The number of frames dropped on the output interface.

▶ **No Buffer**: The number of input packets dropped because of no available buffers.

▶ **Broadcasts**: The number of broadcasts received on the interface.

▶ **Throttles**: The number of times the local interface requested another local interface within the switch to slow down.

▶ **Input Errors**: The total of no buffer, runts, giants, CRCs, frame, overrun, ignored, and abort errors.

▶ **CRC**: The Cyclic Redundancy Check failed on an input packet. This is made possible to detect thanks to the Frame Check Sequence on frame formats.

▶ **Frame**: The number of frames received that did not end on an eight-bit byte boundary.

▶ **Overrun**: The number of times the receiver hardware was unable to transfer received data to a hardware buffer because the input rate exceeded the receiver's ability to process the data.

▶ **Ignored**: The frames dropped because the interface hardware buffers ran low on internal buffers.

▶ **Abort**: An illegal sequence of 1 bits was detected in a frame received.

▶ **Dribble Condition Detected**: A Dribble bit error indicates that a frame is slightly too long. The frame is still accepted in this case.

▶ **Underruns**: The number of times the sender has been running faster than the switch can handle.

▶ **Interface Resets**: The number of times the interface had a reset. This is normally the result of missed keepalives from a neighboring device.

▶ **Babbles**: The number of frames transmitted greater than 1518 bytes in size.

▶ **Late Collision**: A collision that occurs after the interface has started transmitting the frame.

▶ **Deferred**: The number of frames that were transmitted successfully after waiting because the media was busy.

▶ **Lost Carrier**: The number of times the carrier was lost during transmission.

▶ **No Carrier**: The number of times the carrier was not present during the transmission.

▶ **Output Buffer Failures**: The number of times a frame was not output from the output hold queue because of a shortage of shared memory.

▶ **Output Buffers Swapped Out**: The number of frames stored in main memory when the output queue is full.

CramQuiz

1. Which of the following is not a valid error typically seen in a **show interface** output?

   ○ **A.** Babble
   ○ **B.** Late Collision
   ○ **C.** Ignored
   ○ **D.** Trickle

2. What counter increments if the number of frames transmitted is greater than 1518 bytes in size?

   ○ **A.** Babble
   ○ **B.** Late Collision
   ○ **C.** Runt
   ○ **D.** Ignored

3. What process on a Cisco device attempts to dynamically resolve speed and duplex between two devices?

   ○ **A.** Negotiation
   ○ **B.** Autonegotiation
   ○ **C.** CDP
   ○ **D.** LLDP

CramQuiz Answers

1. **D** is correct. There is no Trickle reported in the output as this is not a valid counter.

2. **A** is correct. A Babble increments when the number of frames over 1518 bytes increases.

3. **B** is correct. Autonegotiation attempts to resolve a common duplex and speed between two Cisco devices.

Review Questions

1. When a frame enters a Cisco switch, what field does the switch "learn" from?

   ○ **A.** Preamble

   ○ **B.** FCS

   ○ **C.** Source MAC

   ○ **D.** Destination MAC

2. What is the name of the database that stores address information in a Cisco switch?

   ○ **A.** The MAC address table

   ○ **B.** The routing table

   ○ **C.** The interface table

   ○ **D.** The buffer table

3. What command allows you to view the addresses learned by a Cisco switch?

   ○ **A. show mac-address-table**

   ○ **B. show mac address-table**

   ○ **C. show addresses**

   ○ **D. show mac addresses**

4. Why might padding be used in an Ethernet frame?

   ○ **A.** To bring the entire length of the frame to 1500 bytes

   ○ **B.** To bring the length of the data field to 46 bytes

   ○ **C.** To bring the length of the FCS field to 64 bytes

   ○ **D.** To bring the length of the SFD field to 1 byte

5. If a switch has five workstations attached, how many collision domains are created?

   ○ **A.** 1

   ○ **B.** 0

   ○ **C.** 5

   ○ **D.** 6

Answers to Review Questions

1. **C** is correct. The switch examines and learns the source MAC addresses of incoming frames.

2. **A** is correct. The database is termed the MAC address table.

3. **B** is correct. The command is **show mac address-table**.

4. **B** is correct. Padding might be used in the Data and Pad field in order to bring it to the required minimum length of 46 bytes.

5. **C** is correct. Five workstations connected to a switch are each in their own collision domain.

Additional Resources

Using Layer 2 Virtual Switches Inside of GNS3—
http://www.ajsnetworking.com/l2-gns3

Bridging and Switching Basics—http://bit.ly/2cBGaGu

CHAPTER 5

LAN Switching Fundamentals: VLANs and Interswitch Connectivity

> **This chapter covers the following official ICND1 100-105 exam topics:**
>
> ▶ Configure, verify, and troubleshoot VLANs (normal range) spanning multiple switches
>
> ▶ Configure, verify, and troubleshoot interswitch connectivity
>
> ▶ Configure and verify Layer 2 protocols

This chapter ensures you are ready for the above topics from the LAN Switching Fundamentals section of the overall exam blueprint from Cisco Systems. Remember, this chapter is just a portion of the LAN Switching Fundamentals area. Chapters Four and Six also exist in this grouping. These other chapters deal with switching fundamentals and Port Security for switches.

Essential Terms and Components

- ▶ **Virtual Local Area Networks (VLANs)**
- ▶ **Data Access Ports**
- ▶ **Voice Access Ports**
- ▶ **The Default VLAN**
- ▶ **Interswitch Links**
- ▶ **Trunk ports**
- ▶ **802.1Q**
- ▶ **The Native VLAN**
- ▶ **Layer 2 Protocol**
- ▶ **Cisco Discovery Protocol**
- ▶ **Link Layer Discovery Protocol (LLDP)**

Topic: Configure, verify, and troubleshoot VLANs (normal range) spanning multiple switches

CramSaver

If you can correctly answer these CramSaver questions, save time by skimming the ExamAlerts in this chapter and then completing the CramQuiz at the end of each section and the Review Questions at the end of the chapter. If you are in doubt at all—read EVERYTHING in this chapter!

1. From an IP perspective, what does a VLAN equate to?

   _____

2. What is the default VTP mode on a Cisco switch?

   _____

3. What VTP mode effectively disables VTP?

   _____

4. What command creates VLAN 30?

   _____

5. What is the default VLAN on a Cisco switch?

   _____

6. What protocol allows a Cisco IP phone to function properly with the Voice VLAN and the Cisco switch?

   _____

Answers

1. A VLAN equates to an IP subnet.
2. The default VTP mode is Server.
3. VTP Transparent mode effectively disables VTP. Some switches also support the mode of Off in addition to Server, Client, and Transparent.
4. **vlan 30**; the creation of the VLAN occurs when exiting VLAN configuration mode.
5. VLAN 1.
6. Cisco Discovery Protocol (CDP).

Remember, a **Virtual Local Area Network (VLAN)** is a broadcast domain you create on a switch. This domain also coordinates to a TCP/IP subnet. Figure 5.1 shows an example of VLANs created on a Cisco switch.

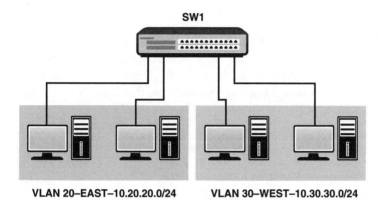

SW1

VLAN 20–EAST–10.20.20.0/24   **VLAN 30–WEST–10.30.30.0/24**

FIGURE 5.1   **VLANs on a Cisco Switch**

Cisco provides *VLAN Trunking Protocol (VTP)* in order to assist you with VLAN creation across many switches. In fact, this is why the word Trunking appears in the name. In order for VLAN creation to automatically span switches, the switches must be connected with special interswitch links called **trunks**. The next section of this chapter focuses on these trunks.

Example 5.1 shows the default VTP status of a Cisco switch.

EXAMPLE 5.1   **The VTP Status of a Default Configuration for a Cisco Switch**

```
Switch#show vtp status
VTP Version capable             : 1 to 3
VTP version running             : 1
VTP Domain Name                 :
VTP Pruning Mode                : Disabled
VTP Traps Generation            : Disabled
Device ID                       : fa16.3ebb.cb23
Configuration last modified by 0.0.0.0 at 0-0-00 00:00:00
Local updater ID is 0.0.0.0 (no valid interface found)

Feature VLAN:
--------------
VTP Operating Mode              : Server
Maximum VLANs supported locally : 1005
Number of existing VLANs        : 5
Configuration Revision          : 0
```

```
MD5 digest                       : 0x57 0xCD 0x40 0x65 0x63 0x59
                                   0x47 0xBD
                                   0x56 0x9D 0x4A 0x3E 0xA5 0x69
                                   0x35 0xBC
Switch#
```

Note the VTP Operating Mode is set to **Server** by default. This permits you to create and modify VLANs on this local device. Another mode termed **Transparent** basically disables VTP, whereas a mode termed **Client** allows switches to inherit the VLAN information from a server(s). Note that you cannot create VLANs locally on a VTP Client device.

Example 5.2 shows the creation of a VLAN on a Cisco switch.

EXAMPLE 5.2 **Creating a VLAN on a Cisco Switch**

```
Switch(config)#vlan 20
Switch(config-vlan)#name EAST
Switch(config-vlan)#end
Switch#
%SYS-5-CONFIG_I: Configured from console by console
Switch#
```

ExamAlert

Example 5.3 demonstrates several critical exam points. Notice that one powerful command for verifying your VLANs is **show vlan brief**. Also notice that the new VLAN of WEST does not appear in the output because you have not exited from (config-vlan) mode. Also, if you want to configure a hostname for the switch itself, use the hostname command from global configuration mode. The limits for the hostname are 63 characters, letters, numbers, or hyphens and no spaces. The name also must begin and end with a letter or number.

EXAMPLE 5.3 **Configuring and Verifying a VLAN**

```
Switch#configure terminal
Enter configuration commands, one per line.  End with CNTL/Z.
Switch(config)#vlan 30
Switch(config-vlan)#name WEST
Switch(config-vlan)#do show vlan brief

VLAN Name                             Status    Ports
---- -------------------------------- --------- --------------------
1    default                          active    Gi0/0, Gi0/1, Gi0/2,
                                                Gi0/3
                                                Gi1/0
```

```
20   EAST                              active
1002 fddi-default                     act/unsup
1003 token-ring-default               act/unsup
1004 fddinet-default                  act/unsup
1005 trnet-default                    act/unsup
Switch(config-vlan)#
```

> **ExamAlert**
>
> Notice that there is a VLAN 1 by default on a Cisco switch and that all non-trunk
> ports are listed as participants of this VLAN. This is termed the **default VLAN**. It is a
> best practice to remove all ports from this default VLAN. Typically, engineers create a
> special unused VLAN for any ports they are not using on the switch. By default, two
> hosts connected to the same switch will be in separate collision domains (one per
> port), but will both be part of the same Layer 2 broadcast domain and VLAN.

But what good is a VLAN if interfaces (ports) are not participating in it?
Example 5.4 demonstrates configuring an interface for participation in a data
VLAN as well as the simple verification.

EXAMPLE 5.4 **Configuring and Verifying an Interface for a VLAN**

```
Switch#configure terminal
Enter configuration commands, one per line.   End with CNTL/Z.
Switch(config)#interface gi0/1
Switch(config-if)#switchport mode access
Switch(config-if)#switchport access vlan 20
Switch(config-if)#end
Switch#
%SYS-5-CONFIG_I: Configured from console by console
Switch#show vlan brief

VLAN Name                             Status    Ports
---- -------------------------------- --------- --------------------
1    default                          active    Gi0/0, Gi0/2, Gi0/3,
                                                 Gi1/0
20   EAST                             active    Gi0/1
30   WEST                             active
40   TEST                             active
1002 fddi-default                     act/unsup
1003 token-ring-default               act/unsup
1004 fddinet-default                  act/unsup
1005 trnet-default                    act/unsup
Switch#
```

> **ExamAlert**
>
> Another big concern for your ICND1 exam is the configuration of a Voice VLAN for
> IP phones to send their data in. Example 5.5 demonstrates the Voice VLAN
> configuration and verification. Note the **Cisco Discovery Protocol (CDP)** is required
> for Cisco IP phones to function properly with this configuration. Because this is a
> default on the switch, no configuration for CDP is shown here.

EXAMPLE 5.5 **The Configuration and Verification of the Voice VLAN**

```
Switch#configure terminal
Enter configuration commands, one per line.  End with CNTL/Z.
Switch(config)#vlan 50
Switch(config-vlan)#name VOICE
Switch(config-vlan)#exit
Switch(config)#interface gi0/2
Switch(config-if)#switchport mode access
Switch(config-if)#switchport access vlan 30
Switch(config-if)#switchport voice vlan 50
Switch(config-if)#end
Switch#
%SYS-5-CONFIG_I: Configured from console by console
Switch#show vlan brief

VLAN Name                             Status    Ports
---- -------------------------------- --------- ----------------------
1    default                          active    Gi0/0, Gi0/3, Gi1/0
20   EAST                             active    Gi0/1
30   WEST                             active    Gi0/2
40   TEST                             active
50   VOICE                            active    Gi0/2
1002 fddi-default                     act/unsup
1003 token-ring-default               act/unsup
1004 fddinet-default                  act/unsup
1005 trnet-default                    act/unsup
Switch#show interface gi0/2 switchport
Name: Gi0/2
Switchport: Enabled
Administrative Mode: static access
Operational Mode: static access
Administrative Trunking Encapsulation: negotiate
Operational Trunking Encapsulation: native
Negotiation of Trunking: Off
Access Mode VLAN: 30 (WEST)
Trunking Native Mode VLAN: 1 (default)
Administrative Native VLAN tagging: enabled
```

```
Voice VLAN: 50 (VOICE)
Administrative private-vlan host-association: none
Administrative private-vlan mapping: none
Administrative private-vlan trunk native VLAN: none
Administrative private-vlan trunk Native VLAN tagging: enabled
Administrative private-vlan trunk encapsulation: dot1q
Administrative private-vlan trunk normal VLANs: none
Administrative private-vlan trunk associations: none
Administrative private-vlan trunk mappings: none
Operational private-vlan: none
Trunking VLANs Enabled: ALL
Pruning VLANs Enabled: 2-1001
Capture Mode Disabled
Capture VLANs Allowed: ALL

Protected: false
Appliance trust: none
Switch#
```

> **ExamAlert**
>
> Notice in the output in Example 5.5, the **show interface switchport** command is
> used for verifying the Voice VLAN functionality.

CramQuiz

1. Your Cisco switch has been configured with five different VLANs. How many
   broadcast domains exist on the switch?

   ○ **A.** 0

   ○ **B.** 1

   ○ **C.** 5

   ○ **D.** 10

2. What command allows you to easily verify your VTP mode?

   ○ **A.** show vtp mode

   ○ **B.** show vtp status

   ○ **C.** show vtp server

   ○ **D.** show vtp brief

3. What VTP mode would prevent you from creating a VLAN on the local switch?

   ○ **A.** Client
   ○ **B.** Server
   ○ **C.** Transparent
   ○ **D.** Off

4. What command allows you to view the VLANs and interface assignments on your switch?

   ○ **A. show vlan brief**
   ○ **B. show vlan status**
   ○ **C. show vlan information**
   ○ **D. show vlan database**

5. What command assigns an access port to VLAN 20?

   ○ **A. switchport vlan 20**
   ○ **B. switchport mode vlan 20**
   ○ **C. switchport assign vlan 20**
   ○ **D. switchport access vlan 20**

6. What command assigns an access port to Voice VLAN 10?

   ○ **A. switchport voice vlan 10**
   ○ **B. switchport access vlan 10 voice**
   ○ **C. switchport vlan 10 voice**
   ○ **D. switchport access vlan 10**

7. What command allows you to verify the Voice VLAN configuration?

   ○ **A. show interface gi0/1 voice**
   ○ **B. show interface gi0/1 switchport**
   ○ **C. show interface gi0/1 vlan**
   ○ **D. show interface gi0/1 vlan assign**

CramQuiz Answers

1. **C** is correct. Each VLAN is a broadcast domain. If there are five defined on the switch, then you have five broadcast domains.

2. **B** is correct. The **show vtp status** command allows you to verify many basic VTP parameters.

3. **A** is correct. Client mode prevents local VLAN creation.

4. **A** is correct. The **show vlan brief** command allows you to easily verify the VLANs and the interface assignments.

5. **D** is correct. The command is **switchport access vlan 20**.

6. **A** is correct. The command is **switchport voice vlan 10**.

7. **B** is correct. The command **show interface gi0/1 switchport** is very powerful and displays verbose information regarding the interface configuration, including the Voice VLAN.

Topic: Configure, verify, and troubleshoot interswitch connectivity

CramSaver

1. What is the most common Ethernet trunking protocol in use today?

   _____

2. What is the name of the VLAN that is not tagged on an Ethernet trunk?

   _____

3. What is the default Native VLAN in Cisco networking?

   _____

4. Why are administrators typically concerned about the Native VLAN?

   _____

Answers

1. 802.1Q is the most common Ethernet trunking protocol in use today.
2. The Native VLAN is not tagged.
3. The default Native VLAN is VLAN 1.
4. There are security concerns brought about by the Native VLAN.

How does a switch move the traffic of different VLANs from switch to switch? It is a trunk link. Specifically, an **802.1Q** trunk link.

Cisco originally created their own method of marking traffic with a VLAN ID for transport over an **interswitch link**. It was called Inter Switch Link (ISL), and it took an interesting approach. It fully re-encapsulated the frame in order to add a VLAN marking. 802.1Q takes a different approach. It injects in a tag value in the existing frame. Figure 5.2 shows the 802.1Q approach, which is inserted between the Source MAC address and Type fields of the frame. 802.1Q allows multiple VLANs to be supported over a single trunk interface.

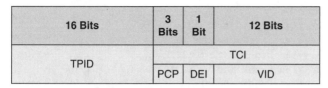

FIGURE 5.2   **The 802.1Q Tag**

Here is the breakdown of these values:

▶ **Tag protocol identifier (TPID)**: A 16-bit field set to a value of 0x8100 in order to identify the frame as an IEEE 802.1Q-tagged frame.

▶ **Tag control information (TCI)**: This section consists of the following:

  ▶ **Priority code point (PCP)**: A three-bit field that refers to the IEEE 802.1p class of service and maps to the frame priority level.

  ▶ **Drop eligible indicator (DEI)**: A one-bit field that may be used separately or in conjunction with PCP to indicate frames eligible to be dropped in the presence of congestion.

  ▶ **VLAN identifier (VID)**: A 12-bit field specifying the VLAN to which the frame belongs.

Example 5.6 demonstrates the configuration and verification of 802.1Q trunking on a Cisco switch.

EXAMPLE 5.6   **The Configuration and Verification of Trunking**

```
Switch#configure terminal
Enter configuration commands, one per line.  End with CNTL/Z.
Switch(config)#interface gi1/0
Switch(config-if)#switchport trunk encapsulation dot1q
Switch(config-if)#switchport mode trunk
Switch(config-if)#end
Switch#
%SYS-5-CONFIG_I: Configured from console by console
Switch#show interface gi1/0 switchport
Name: Gi1/0
Switchport: Enabled
Administrative Mode: trunk
Operational Mode: trunk
Administrative Trunking Encapsulation: dot1q
Operational Trunking Encapsulation: dot1q
Negotiation of Trunking: On
Access Mode VLAN: 1 (default)
Trunking Native Mode VLAN: 1 (default)
Administrative Native VLAN tagging: enabled
```

```
Voice VLAN: none
Administrative private-vlan host-association: none
Administrative private-vlan mapping: none
Administrative private-vlan trunk native VLAN: none
Administrative private-vlan trunk Native VLAN tagging: enabled
Administrative private-vlan trunk encapsulation: dot1q
Administrative private-vlan trunk normal VLANs: none
Administrative private-vlan trunk associations: none
Administrative private-vlan trunk mappings: none
Operational private-vlan: none
Trunking VLANs Enabled: ALL
Pruning VLANs Enabled: 2-1001
Capture Mode Disabled
Capture VLANs Allowed: ALL
Protected: false
Appliance trust: none
Switch#show interface trunk

Port        Mode           Encapsulation  Status       Native vlan
Gi1/0       on             802.1q         trunking     1

Port        Vlans allowed on trunk
Gi1/0       1-4094

Port        Vlans allowed and active in management domain
Gi1/0       1,20,30,40,50

Port        Vlans in spanning tree forwarding state and not pruned
Gi1/0       1,20,30,40,50
Switch#
```

There is a very special VLAN in your infrastructure by default. It is the termed the **Native VLAN**. This VLAN is not tagged. It is the only untagged VLAN in the infrastructure. By default, the Native VLAN is VLAN 1—the default VLAN. Why would Cisco introduce a Native VLAN feature? The idea was to use this for management traffic and this critical traffic can still flow between devices even if a link loses its trunking status. CDP messages are sent over the Native VLAN by default.

CramQuiz

1. Where is an 802.1Q tag inserted in a frame?

   O **A.** Between the Preamble and the SFD

   O **B.** Between the Source and Destination MAC addresses

    ○ **C.** Between the Source MAC and Type fields

    ○ **D.** Between the Source MAC and FCS fields

2. What command configures an interface to trunk?

    ○ **A. switchport trunk**

    ○ **B. switchport trunk dot1q**

    ○ **C. switchport mode trunk**

    ○ **D. switchport trunk enable**

3. What command allows you to quickly view all of the trunks on your switch?

    ○ **A. show vlans trunk**

    ○ **B. show interface trunk**

    ○ **C. show trunk interface**

    ○ **D. show trunk all**

4. What was the intent of the Native VLAN feature?

    ○ **A.** Security traffic

    ○ **B.** Monitoring traffic

    ○ **C.** Voice VLAN traffic

    ○ **D.** Management traffic

5. What are two methods that a network engineer might use in order to stop security issues with the Native VLAN? (Choose two.)

    ○ **A.** Eliminate VLAN 1

    ○ **B.** Disable VLAN 1

    ○ **C.** Tag the Native VLAN

    ○ **D.** Use an unused VLAN for the Native VLAN

CramQuiz Answers

1. **C** is correct. The tag is inserted between the Source MAC and Type fields.

2. **C** is correct. The command is **switchport mode trunk**.

3. **B** is correct. The command is **show interface trunk**.

4. **D** is correct. The intent of the Native VLAN was to carry management traffic in the event the 802.1Q trunking function failed.

5. **C** and **D** are correct. Today, engineers will tag the Native VLAN or use an unused VLAN for the Native VLAN. This reduces some vulnerabilities.

Topic: Configure and verify Layer 2 protocols

CramSaver

1. What is the Cisco Layer 2 protocol for discovering neighbors?

   _____

2. What is the open standard protocol for discovering neighboring devices?

   _____

3. What is the default status of for Cisco's Layer 2 protocol for discovering neighbors?

   _____

Answers

1. Cisco Discovery Protocol (CDP).
2. Link Layer Discovery Protocol (LLDP).
3. CDP is enabled by default.

Cisco Discovery Protocol is a **Layer 2 protocol** that allows Cisco devices to communicate information about each other to their directly connected neighbors. This can prove useful when you are unsure of the topology. Cisco IP phones also use it to communicate their capabilities and VLAN information to their local switch. CDP messages from a Cisco router are not forwarded by a directly connected Cisco switch. Two routers connected to the same switch would not see each other's CDP messages.

CDP is enabled by default on Cisco routers and switches, on all interfaces. To ensure it has not been disabled globally on the device, or to ensure it has not been "trimmed" off an interface, you can use the commands shown in Example 5.7.

EXAMPLE 5.7 **Ensuring CDP is Running on the Device and an Interface**

```
Switch#configure terminal
Enter configuration commands, one per line.  End with CNTL/Z.
Switch(config)#cdp run
Switch(config)#interface gi1/0
```

```
Switch(config-if)#cdp enable
Switch(config-if)#end
Switch#
%SYS-5-CONFIG_I: Configured from console by console
Switch#
```

Why might an administrator disable CDP globally or on certain interfaces? The answer is clear—they are concerned about their device sharing information with an unauthorized neighbor. This concern is legitimate and often leads to disabling CDP from specific public facing interfaces.

ExamAlert

Remember, CDP is its own Layer 2 protocol. It does not rely on other protocols. To quote Cisco themselves: "Cisco Discovery Protocol is a Layer 2, media-independent, and network-independent protocol that networking applications use to learn about nearby, directly connected devices."

CDP is obviously a Cisco-specific solution. The open standard approach is **Link Layer Discovery Protocol (LLDP)**. Note that CDP and LLDP basically serve the same purpose, they provide a method for network devices to communicate information about themselves.

Unlike CDP, LLDP is not enabled globally by default. Example 5.8 shows the commands that may be used to configure LLDP.

EXAMPLE 5.8 **Ensuring LLDP is Running Globally and on an Interface**

```
Switch#configure terminal
Enter configuration commands, one per line.  End with CNTL/Z.
Switch(config)#lldp run
Switch(config)#interface gi1/0
Switch(config-if)#lldp transmit
Switch(config-if)#lldp receive
Switch(config-if)#end
Switch#
%SYS-5-CONFIG_I: Configured from console by console
Switch#
```

CramQuiz

1. What technology does CDP rely upon in its operation?

   ○ **A.** TCP

   ○ **B.** UDP

   ○ **C.** ICMP

   ○ **D.** Layer 2

2. What Cisco technology heavily relies upon CDP?

   ○ **A.** VoIP

   ○ **B.** Video on Demand

   ○ **C.** STP

   ○ **D.** NTP

3. What command disables CDP globally on a device?

   ○ **A. no cdp run**

   ○ **B. no cdp enable**

   ○ **C. cdp disable**

   ○ **D. cdp stop**

CramQuiz Answers

1. **D** is correct. CDP operates at Layer 2, and does not use TCP, UDP, or ICMP.

2. **A** is correct. VoIP relies upon CDP for neighbor discovery and capabilities exchange.

3. **A** is correct. The **no cdp run** command is how you globally disable CDP on a device.

Review Questions

1. What protocol exists to assist you in creating VLANs across different devices with ease?

   ○ **A.** VTP

   ○ **B.** STP

   ○ **C.** SPAN

   ○ **D.** CDP

2. What must you do in order to place VLAN 20 in the VLAN database on your local device?

   ○ **A.** Exit from config-vlan mode

   ○ **B.** Restart the device

   ○ **C.** Place the device in Client mode

   ○ **D.** Save the running configuration

3. What is the default VLAN in Cisco networking?

   ○ **A.** VLAN 10

   ○ **B.** VLAN 0

   ○ **C.** VLAN 4092

   ○ **D.** VLAN 1

4. Which statement about CDP is correct?

   ○ **A.** CDP relies upon TCP.

   ○ **B.** CDP is disabled by default.

   ○ **C.** CDP is disabled on all serial interfaces by default.

   ○ **D.** CDP is a Layer 2 protocol.

Answers to Review Questions

1. **A** is correct. VTP allows you to configure or modify VLANs on a central device and then have these configurations synchronize across multiple switches.

2. **A** is correct. In order to complete a VLAN configuration, you must exit from config-vlan mode.

3. **D** is correct. VLAN 1 is the default VLAN in Cisco.

4. **D** is correct. CDP is a media and protocol independent Layer 2 protocol.

Additional Resources

What is a VLAN—http://www.ajsnetworking.com/what-is-a-vlan

VLANs—What, Why, and How?—http://www.ajsnetworking.com/vlans-what-why-and-how

CHAPTER 6

LAN Switching Fundamentals: Port Security

This chapter covers the following official ICND1 100-105 exam topics:

▶ Configure, verify, and troubleshoot port security

This chapter ensures you are ready for the above topic from the LAN Switching Fundamentals section of the overall exam blueprint from Cisco Systems. Remember, this chapter is just a portion of the LAN Switching Fundamentals area. Chapters Four and Five also exist in this grouping. These other chapters deal with switching fundamentals, VLANs, and trunks.

Essential Terms and Components

▶ **Port Security**

▶ **Dynamic Port Security**

▶ **Port Security Violation Actions**

▶ **Static Port Security**

▶ **Sticky Learning**

▶ **Maximum MAC Addresses**

▶ **errdisable recovery**

Topic: Configure, verify, and troubleshoot port security

CramSaver

If you can correctly answer these CramSaver questions, save time by skimming the ExamAlerts in this chapter and then completing the CramQuiz at the end of each section and the Review Questions at the end of the chapter. If you are in doubt at all—read EVERYTHING in this chapter!

1. If you issue the single **switchport port-security** command in interface configuration mode, name the resulting Port Security mode, violation action, and maximum number of MAC addresses permitted.

   _____

2. What form of Port Security combines aspects of dynamic learning with static?

   _____

3. What command allows you to verify the Port Security settings of the Gi0/1 interface?

   _____

Answers

1. The mode is Dynamic Port Security, the violation action is Shutdown, and the maximum MAC addresses is 1.

2. Sticky Learning

3. **show port-security interface gi0/1**

Port Security can control which source MAC addresses, and the quantity of source MAC source addresses that the switch will allow to be associated with the switch port.

Let us enable Port Security on a switch port and observe the results. Example 6.1 shows this.

EXAMPLE 6.1 **Configuring and Verifying Port Security**

```
Switch#configure terminal
Enter configuration commands, one per line.  End with CNTL/Z.
Switch(config)#interface gi0/1
```

```
Switch(config-if)#switchport mode access
Switch(config-if)#switchport port-security
Switch(config-if)#end
Switch#
%SYS-5-CONFIG_I: Configured from console by console
Switch#show port-security interface gi0/1
Port Security              : Enabled
Port Status                : Secure-up
Violation Mode             : Shutdown
Aging Time                 : 0 mins
Aging Type                 : Absolute
SecureStatic Address Aging : Disabled
Maximum MAC Addresses      : 1
Total MAC Addresses        : 0
Configured MAC Addresses   : 0
Sticky MAC Addresses       : 0
Last Source Address:Vlan   : 0000.0000.0000:0
Security Violation Count   : 0
Switch#
```

Notice how simple a basic configuration is! Notice the port must *not* be a negotiated access or trunk port. The port must be configured as a static access or static trunk port. It is most common to use port security on access ports. The interface configuration command **switchport mode access** causes the switch to be statically configured as an access port. If the port is dynamically negotiated, the **switchport port-security** command cannot be entered. Notice also that a basic configuration involves the one simple command. This configures a basic and default **Dynamic Port Security** configuration.

Let us examine some important sections of the **show port-security interface** output:

▶ Notice first that Port Security is indeed enabled for the interface we are examining.

▶ The status indicates Secure-up, meaning that Port Security is functioning and the port is not disabled due to a security violation.

▶ The **Port Security Violation Mode (Action)** is the default of Shutdown. There are three options here we may configure. You remember them using the order of the alphabet. There is Protect, Restrict, and Shutdown. Shutdown is the most severe and Protect is the least. With Protect, offending MAC addresses are blocked from speaking on the port but the administrator is never notified. Restrict blocks offending MAC addresses and generates a log message. Shutdown is very severe indeed. An offending MAC address causes the entire interface to disable. As an administrator, you must manually re-enable the port after correcting the security problem, or you may use the **errdisable recovery** command to cause the port to emerge from the error condition automatically after some time passes.

▶ Notice the default **Maximum MAC Addresses** permitted on the interface is 1. So, in this very basic configuration, only 1 MAC address is dynamically learned on the interface, and no other MAC addresses are permitted.

ExamAlert

Know these defaults of the basic Port Security configuration for the exam and know them well!

Example 6.2 provides a very different configuration. This time we engage in **Static Port Security**.

EXAMPLE 6.2 **Configuring Static Port Security**

```
Switch#configure terminal
Enter configuration commands, one per line.  End with CNTL/Z.
Switch(config)#interface gi1/0
Switch(config-if)#switchport mode access
Switch(config-if)#switchport port-security maximum 2
Switch(config-if)#switchport port-security mac-address fa16.3e20.58f1
Switch(config-if)#switchport port-security mac-address fa16.3e20.aabb
Switch(config-if)#switchport port-security
Switch(config-if)#end
%SYS-5-CONFIG_I: Configured from console by console
Switch#show port-security interface gi1/0
Port Security               : Enabled
Port Status                 : Secure-up
Violation Mode              : Shutdown
Aging Time                  : 0 mins
Aging Type                  : Absolute
SecureStatic Address Aging  : Disabled
Maximum MAC Addresses       : 2
Total MAC Addresses         : 2
Configured MAC Addresses    : 2
Sticky MAC Addresses        : 0
Last Source Address:Vlan    : fa16.3e20.58f1:1
Security Violation Count    : 0
Switch#
```

Notice this configuration begins exactly the same as a dynamic configuration. We set the port to access mode. This time, we then indicate that two MAC addresses are permitted. Then things get really secure! We provide the exact MAC addresses expected. This is what makes the configuration static.

ExamAlert

Notice something interesting about this configuration. First, we set all of the Port Security parameters. Then we actually enable Port Security. It is very easy to forget this last and critical step! This is one reason verification is always mandatory following your configurations, both in the exam and in the real world.

I am betting you are not a huge fan of running around your network recording MAC addresses for your devices. I am not either. Thankfully, there is a nice combination approach to dynamic and static Port Security. It has the one of the most colorful names in all of Cisco networking—it is **Sticky Learning**.

The idea here is: You physically inspect that the correct systems are connected to your switches. You then enable Port Security with the sticky learning feature. The learned MAC addresses are dynamically inserted in the running configuration for you! All you need to do as the administrator is save the running-configuration to the startup-configuration. Example 6.3 demonstrates this configuration.

EXAMPLE 6.3 **Configuring Sticky MAC Address Learning**

```
Switch#configure terminal
Enter configuration commands, one per line.  End with CNTL/Z.
Switch(config)#interface gi0/2
Switch(config-if)#switchport mode access
Switch(config-if)#switchport port-security maximum 2
Switch(config-if)#switchport port-security mac-address sticky
Switch(config-if)#switchport port-security
Switch(config-if)#end
Switch#
%SYS-5-CONFIG_I: Configured from console by console
Switch#show port-security interface gi0/2
Port Security              : Enabled
Port Status                : Secure-up
Violation Mode             : Shutdown
Aging Time                 : 0 mins
Aging Type                 : Absolute
SecureStatic Address Aging : Disabled
Maximum MAC Addresses      : 2
Total MAC Addresses        : 2
Configured MAC Addresses   : 2
```

```
Sticky MAC Addresses      : 2
Last Source Address:Vlan  : 0000.0000.0000:0
Security Violation Count  : 0
Switch#copy running-config startup-config
Switch#
```

CramQuiz

1. What command proceeds the **switchport port-security** command typically?

   ○ **A. switchport port-security enable**

   ○ **B. switchport mode access**

   ○ **C. switchport mode secure**

   ○ **D. switchport data enable**

2. Which violation mode does prevents the MAC address on a port but does not generate a log message?

   ○ **A.** Restrict

   ○ **B.** Shutdown

   ○ **C.** Error

   ○ **D.** Protect

3. What are two options for recovering from an error-disabled port due to Port Security? (Choose two.)

   ○ **A.** Port Security Auto Recovery

   ○ **B.** errdisable recovery

   ○ **C.** Manual recovery

   ○ **D.** Port Security Disable

CramQuiz Answers

1. **B** is correct. The **switchport mode access** command typically proceeds the **switchport port-security** command as the port must be configured as an access or trunk mode. The command **switchport mode access** configures the port as a static access port.

2. **D** is correct. Cisco does not recommend this mode because it does not alert the administrator of any violation.

3. **B** and **C** are correct. You can have automatic recovery with **errdisable recovery** or you can manually (using the command-line interface) recover from the errdisable state.

Review Questions

1. What is the Port Status when there is no issue with the port, but it is secure?

   ○ **A.** Enabled-up

   ○ **B.** Shutdown-up

   ○ **C.** Secure-up

   ○ **D.** Locked-safe

2. What command sets the maximum MAC addresses permitted to four?

   ○ **A. set port-security max mac-address 4**

   ○ **B. switchport port-security maximum 4**

   ○ **C. switchport port-security maximum mac-address 4**

   ○ **D. switchport port-security 4**

3. What command creates a static entry for aaaa.bbbb.cccc?

   ○ **A. set port-security mac-address aaaa.bbbb.cccc**

   ○ **B. switchport port-security mac-address aaaa.bbbb.cccc**

   ○ **C. switchport port-security address aaaa.bbbb.cccc**

   ○ **D. switchport port-security aaaa.bbbb.cccc**

Answers to Review Questions

1. **C** is correct. The state is Secure-up.

2. **B** is correct. The command is **switchport port-security maximum 4**.

3. **B** is correct. The command is **switchport port-security mac-address aaaa.bbbb.cccc**.

Additional Resources

CAM Table Overflow Attack—http://www.ajsnetworking.com/
cam-table-overflow-attack

Port Security Basics—http://www.ajsnetworking.com/port-security-basics

PART III

Routing Fundamentals

This part of the text deals with one of five overall sections you must master for the ICND1 exam. There are three chapters total that make up Part 3. These three chapters, taken as a whole, represent 25 percent of the exam questions you face in your exam. This means that the Routing Fundamentals area is the second most important section of the five overall sections that you deal with on your testing day!

Here you begin with a high-level overview of routing concepts, but then quickly move into details of router configurations, including inter-VLAN routing, static routing, and RIP for dynamic routing. Part 3 includes the following chapters:

CHAPTER 7

Routing Fundamentals: Routing Concepts

This chapter covers the following official ICND1 100-105 exam topics:

▶ Describe the routing concepts

▶ Interpret the components of routing table

▶ Describe how a routing table is populated by different routing information sources

This chapter ensures you are ready for the above topic from the Routing Fundamentals section of the overall exam blueprint from Cisco Systems. Remember, this is just a section of the Routing Fundamentals area. Chapters Eight and Nine also exist in this grouping.

Essential Terms and Components

▶ **Packet Handling**

▶ **Route Lookups**

▶ **Frame Rewrite**

▶ **Routing Table**

▶ **Prefix**

▶ **Network Mask**

▶ **Next Hop**

▶ **Routing Protocol Code**

▶ **Administrative Distance**

▶ **Metric**

▶ **Gateway of Last Resort**

▶ **Administrative Distance**

Topic: Describe the routing concepts

CramSaver

If you can correctly answer these CramSaver questions, save time by skimming the ExamAlerts in this chapter and then completing the CramQuiz at the end of each section and the Review Questions at the end of the chapter. If you are in doubt at all—read EVERYTHING in this chapter!

1. What criteria is used for the best match in a routing table lookup?

   _____

2. What does a router rewrite in a packet when forwarding data on Ethernet networks?

   _____

Answers

1. The best match is the longest match prefix in the routing table.

2. The router rewrites the Layer 2 header, including the source and destination MAC addresses, along with a new frame check sequence (FCS) as part of the trailer in a newly encapsulated frame.

We begin with a discussion of how routing really works. We know a packet enters the router and a routing lookup is done, but what does this really mean? What are the details of the **packet handling** process?

When a IPv4 packet arrives on a router interface, the router de-encapsulates the Layer 2 frame and examines the Layer 3 IPv4 header. The router identifies the destination IPv4 address and proceeds through the **route lookup** process. The router scans the routing table to find a best match for the destination IPv4 address. The best match is the longest match in the table. For example, if the destination IPv4 address is 172.16.0.10 and the entries in the routing table are for 172.16.0.0/12, 172.16.0.0/18, and 172.16.0.0/26, the longest match and the entry used for the packet is 172.16.0.0/26. Remember, for any of these routes to be considered a possible match, there must be at least the number of matching bits indicated by the subnet mask of the routing table prefix.

Another critical aspect for us to understand is the **frame rewrite** procedure by the router. For the router to do its job, it encapsulates the IP packet with the same source and destination IP address that was sent from the original sending device into a new Layer 2 frame. It changes the source MAC address to the forwarding interface of the local router. The router changes the destination MAC address to the receiving interface of the next hop device. An FCS as part of the trailer is also added. This process continues from hop to hop on Ethernet networks until the packet reaches the destination host.

CramQuiz

1. Given the following routing table entries, what is the next router (or hop) to be used for a packet destined for 172.16.1.23/24?

172.16.0.0/16 via 10.10.10.1

0.0.0.0/0 via 192.168.1.1

172.16.1.0/24 via 10.20.20.2

172.16.2.0/24 via 10.30.30.3

   ○ **A.** 10.30.30.3

   ○ **B.** 192.168.1.1

   ○ **C.** 10.10.10.1

   ○ **D.** 10.20.20.2

2. When performing a Layer 2 rewrite, what does the router use for the source MAC address?

   ○ **A.** The next hop interface MAC address

   ○ **B.** The sending interface MAC address on the local router

   ○ **C.** The previous hop sending interface MAC address

   ○ **D.** The receiving interface MAC address of the local router

CramQuiz Answers

1. **D** is correct. Here the longest match entry is 172.16.1.0/24 via 10.20.20.2 for the destination IP address of 172.16.1.23/24.

2. **B** is correct. During this rewrite process, the router changes the source MAC to its own sending interface MAC address.

Topic: Interpret the components of routing table

CramSaver

1. In a routing table, the word "via" indicates what?

   _____

2. What does the routing protocol code of EX stand for?

   _____

3. What do the two numbers of [120/1] mean when seen in a routing table entry?

   _____

4. What is the metric value used by RIP?

   _____

5. What is the Gateway of Last Resort?

   _____

Answers

1. **Via** indicates the next hop IP address. This is the IP address of the next router for forwarding packets to the final destination.
2. EIGRP External
3. 120 is the administrative distance, and 1 is the metric.
4. The metric used by RIP is Hop Count.
5. This is the default gateway for any unknown prefixes; the prefix match is 0.0.0.0/0.

It is time to examine in great detail the vast amount of information communicated in a key network component—the IP **routing table** of a Cisco router. Example 7.1 shows a sample table.

EXAMPLE 7.1 **The IP Routing Table on a Cisco Router**

```
R1#show ip route
Codes: L—local, C—connected, S—static, R—RIP, M—mobile, B—BGP
       D—EIGRP, EX—EIGRP external, O—OSPF, IA—OSPF inter area
       N1—OSPF NSSA external type 1, N2—OSPF NSSA external type 2
       E1—OSPF external type 1, E2—OSPF external type 2
       i—IS-IS, su—IS-IS summary, L1—IS-IS level-1, L2—IS-IS level-2
       ia—IS-IS inter area, *—candidate default, U—per-user static route
       o—ODR, P—periodic downloaded static route, +—replicated route

Gateway of last resort is not set

      10.0.0.0/8 is variably subnetted, 2 subnets, 2 masks
C        10.10.10.0/24 is directly connected, FastEthernet0/0
L        10.10.10.1/32 is directly connected, FastEthernet0/0
      172.16.0.0/24 is subnetted, 3 subnets
R        172.16.1.0 [120/1] via 10.10.10.3, 00:00:19, FastEthernet0/0
R        172.16.2.0 [120/1] via 10.10.10.3, 00:00:19, FastEthernet0/0
R        172.16.3.0 [120/1] via 10.10.10.3, 00:00:19, FastEthernet0/0
      192.168.1.0/32 is subnetted, 1 subnets
O        192.168.1.2 [110/2] via 10.10.10.2, 00:00:37, FastEthernet0/0
      192.168.2.0/32 is subnetted, 1 subnets
O        192.168.2.2 [110/2] via 10.10.10.2, 00:00:37, FastEthernet0/0
R1#
```

Specifically, in this output, we must master the meaning and location of the following components:

▶ **Prefix**: Notice that the routing table lists the parent and children prefixes reachable in the table. For example, in the table above, the entry **172.16.0.0/24 is subnetted, 3 subnets** listing the parent prefix, and the specific child prefixes below of **172.16.1.0**, **172.16.2.0**, and **172.16.3.0**.

▶ **Network Mask**: Notice the parent prefix lists the network mask in prefix notation. So for the 172.16.0.0 example above, the network mask is **/24**. Remember, in non-prefix notation, this is 255.255.255.0.

▶ **Next Hop**: The next hop IP address follows the **via** word for a child prefix entry. Note that it is **10.10.10.3** for our 172.16.0.0/24 entries. The **next hop** refers to the IP address of the next router in the path when forwarding packets to a remote destination.

▶ **Routing Protocol Code**: Located at the very beginning of a routing table entry is the routing protocol code. Cisco is kind to us and even provides a legend at the beginning of the show output to explain what each value means. Here are those values for your ease of reference:

   ▶ L—local

   ▶ C—connected

   ▶ S—static

   ▶ R—RIP

   ▶ M—mobile

   ▶ B—BGP

   ▶ D—EIGRP

   ▶ EX—EIGRP external

   ▶ O—OSPF

   ▶ IA—OSPF inter area

   ▶ N1—OSPF NSSA external type 1

   ▶ N2—OSPF NSSA external type 2

   ▶ E1—OSPF external type 1

   ▶ E2—OSPF external type 2

   ▶ i—IS-IS

   ▶ su—IS-IS summary

   ▶ L1—IS-IS level-1

   ▶ L2—IS-IS level-2

   ▶ ia—IS-IS inter area

   ▶ *—candidate default

   ▶ U—per-user static route

   ▶ o—ODR

   ▶ P—periodic downloaded static route

   ▶ +—replicated route

▶ **Administrative Distance**: The **administrative distance** (AD) for the prefix. This text details AD in the last section of this chapter. Note the AD associated with the 172.16.0.0/24 prefixes is **120**. This is because these routes were learned via RIP, and 120 is the default administrative distance for RIP.

▶ **Metric**: The metric varies for the dynamic routing protocol involved. It is a measure of the "distance" to reach the prefix. In our 172 prefixes, it is a hop count. This is the simple metric used by RIP. It indicates how many routers you must cross to reach the destination prefix in question.

▶ **Gateway of Last Resort**: Notice our routing table example above indicates there is no Gateway of Last Resort set. This indicates there is no default route 0.0.0.0/0 setup that allows the router to send traffic somewhere if it does not have a specific prefix entry for the destination IP address. The Gateway of Last Resort can be dynamically learned, or it can be set using three different commands: **ip default-gateway**, **ip default-network**, and **ip route 0.0.0.0 0.0.0.0**.

ExamAlert

Yes, you must memorize small details like the routing protocol codes. As I indicate later in this chapter, flash cards can really help with these matters. Especially for non-obvious codes like D for EIGRP.

CramQuiz

1. What is the decimal network mask for a prefix notation of /22?

   ○ **A.** 255.255.252.0

   ○ **B.** 255.255.254.0

   ○ **C.** 255.255.248.0

   ○ **D.** 255.255.240.0

2. What is the routing protocol code for a connected prefix?

   ○ **A.** S

   ○ **B.** L

   ○ **C.** C

   ○ **D.** i

3. What aspect of the routing table is impacted by the command **ip route 0.0.0.0 0.0.0.0**?

   ○ **A.** Network mask

   ○ **B.** Metric

   ○ **C.** Administrative distance

   ○ **D.** Gateway of Last Resort

CramQuiz Answers

1. **A** is correct. 255.255.252.0 equates to /22.

2. **C** is correct. C is used for Connected prefixes.

3. **D** is correct. **ip route 0.0.0.0 0.0.0.0** is one way to set the default route and Gateway of Last Resort.

Topic: Describe how a routing table is populated by different routing information sources

CramSaver

1. What is the meaning of an administrative distance value?

   _____

2. What is preferred, a lower or a higher administrative distance number?

   _____

3. What is the default administrative distance value for a static route?

   _____

4. What is the default administrative distance value for Internal BGP?

   _____

Answers

1. Administrative distance is a measure of the trustworthiness of the routing information source—note that a directly connected prefix is by far the most believable to the router.
2. The router prefers administrative distances that have a lower numeric value.
3. 1
4. 200

What happens when multiple different routing sources indicate they know how to reach a network/prefix? The router needs to be able to break this "tie" between routing information sources. As a result, the router uses **Administrative Distance**. This can be a bit of a misleading term since the value has nothing to do with actual distance of any kind. Some administrators like to call it administrative trustworthiness. Cisco ranks the trustworthiness of the various routing information sources. A lower score is better, just like in golf. Is it any surprise that Cisco rated their own inventions of IGRP and EIGRP so trustworthy?

Table 7.1 shows the default administrative distance values.

TABLE 7.1   **Default Administrative Distance Values**

Routing Information Source	Default Administrative Distance
Connected interface	0
Static route	1
Enhanced IGRP summary route	5
External BGP	20
Internal Enhanced IGRP	90
IGRP	100
OSPF	110
IS-IS	115
RIP	120
EGP	140
External Enhanced IGRP	170
Internal BGP	200
Unknown	255

> **Note**
>
> On Cisco gear, the maximum configurable administrative distance for a route is 255. This makes the route unusable. If the administrative distance is 255, the router does not believe the source of that route and does not install the route in the routing table.

> **ExamAlert**
>
> You should have the above values memorized for success in the exam. Without a ton of experience at the command line, this can be tough. I recommend you make some flash cards to help you in memorizing information like this. Notice also that logic comes into play. For example, RIP scores relatively poorly because it is so prone to problems.

> **Note**
>
> Remember, the administrative distance is shown in the prefix entries in the routing table with the **show ip route** command.

CramQuiz

1. What is the default administrative distance value for RIP?

   ○ **A.** 100
   ○ **B.** 60
   ○ **C.** 200
   ○ **D.** 120

2. What is the default administrative distance value for External BGP?

   ○ **A.** 60
   ○ **B.** 20
   ○ **C.** 110
   ○ **D.** 200

3. What is the default administrative distance value for OSPF?

   ○ **A.** 100
   ○ **B.** 110
   ○ **C.** 120
   ○ **D.** 140

4. What is the default administrative distance value for a connected interface?

   ○ **A.** 5
   ○ **B.** 1
   ○ **C.** 0
   ○ **D.** 20

CramQuiz Answers

1. **D** is correct. RIP features a default admin distance of 120.
2. **B** is correct. External BGP features an excellent admin distance of 20.
3. **B** is correct. OPSF features an AD of 110.
4. **C** is correct. A directly connected interface has the best possible AD of 0.

Review Questions

1. If a router cannot find a best match, what might the router use to route the traffic?
   - ○ **A.** 255.255.255.255/0
   - ○ **B.** 127.0.0.1/32
   - ○ **C.** 0.0.0.0/32
   - ○ **D.** 0.0.0.0/0

2. When a router forwards packets on Ethernet, what is rewritten?
   - ○ **A.** The source and destination IP addresses
   - ○ **B.** Only the source IP address
   - ○ **C.** Only the source MAC address
   - ○ **D.** The source and destination MAC addresses

3. What does the routing protocol code B indicate in the routing table?
   - ○ **A.** EIGRP
   - ○ **B.** IGRP
   - ○ **C.** RIP
   - ○ **D.** OSPF
   - ○ **E.** BGP

4. What is the administrative distance of Internal EIGRP?
   - ○ **A.** 5
   - ○ **B.** 20
   - ○ **C.** 90
   - ○ **D.** 100

5. What is the unreachable AD?
   - ○ **A.** 0
   - ○ **B.** 100
   - ○ **C.** 200
   - ○ **D.** 255

Answers to Review Questions

1. **D** is correct. Routers use the default route to send packets that have no other better match in the routing table.

2. **D** is correct. The router must rewrite the source and destination MAC addresses.

3. **E** is correct. B indicates BGP.

4. **C** is correct. Internal Enhanced IGP receives an AD of 90.

5. **D** is correct. An AD of 255 indicates the prefix is unreachable.

Additional Resources

What is VIRL?—http://www.ajsnetworking.com/what-is-virl

What is Administrative Distance—http://bit.ly/1OkgevM

CHAPTER 8

Routing Fundamentals: Inter-VLAN Routing

> **This chapter covers the following official ICND1 100-105 exam topics:**
>
> ▶ Configure, verify, and troubleshoot inter-VLAN routing

This chapter ensures you are ready for the above topic from the Routing Fundamentals section of the overall exam blueprint from Cisco Systems. Remember, this is just a section of the Routing Fundamentals area. Chapters Seven and Nine also exist in this grouping. These other chapters deal with basic routing concepts and static and dynamic routing protocol.

Essential Terms and Components

▶ **Inter-VLAN Routing**

▶ **Router on a Stick**

▶ **Subinterfaces**

Topic: Configure, verify, and troubleshoot inter-VLAN routing

CramSaver

If you can correctly answer these CramSaver questions, save time by skimming the ExamAlerts in this chapter and then completing the CramQuiz at the end of each section and the Review Questions at the end of the chapter. If you are in doubt at all—read EVERYTHING in this chapter!

1. What is required in order to move traffic from VLAN to VLAN?

2. What type of interface(s) allows a physical router interface to carry the traffic of multiple VLANs?

3. What command sets the encapsulation to 802.1Q for VLAN 10 on a virtual interface?

4. What two methods allow for the traffic of a Native VLAN in a router on a stick (ROAS) configuration?

Answers

1. A routing engine (RE), also known as a device that can do IPv4 layer 3 routing

2. Subinterfaces

3. **encapsulation dot1q 10**

4. Setting the appropriate IP address under the physical interface, or using a subinterface with the **native** keyword on the **encapsulation** statement

Inter-VLAN routing is an interesting topic in the scope of ICND1. The specific variation of this technology we must master is called **router on a stick (ROAS).** You very rarely encounter this in production any longer because of the popularity of multilayer switches. A multilayer switch possesses a routing engine (RE) in its components. This RE allows the device to very efficiently route between the various VLANs the device participates in.

The router on a stick configuration provides us with the ability to perform inter-VLAN routing.

Figure 8.1 and Examples 8.1 and 8.2 show the topology and configuration of this feature. I walk you through these configurations in the text that follows.

FIGURE 8.1   The ROAS Topology

EXAMPLE 8.1   **The ROAS Configuration of R1**

```
R1#
R1#configure terminal
Enter configuration commands, one per line.  End with CNTL/Z.
R1(config)#interface gi0/1
R1(config-if)#no shutdown
R1(config-if)#
%LINK-3-UPDOWN: Interface GigabitEthernet0/1, changed state to up
%LINEPROTO-5-UPDOWN: Line protocol on Interface GigabitEthernet0/1,
  changed state to up
R1(config-if)#! Notice no IP address is configured on the physical
  interface
R1(config-if)#interface gi0/1.10
R1(config-subif)#encapsulation dot1q 10
R1(config-subif)#ip address 10.1.10.1 255.255.255.0
R1(config-subif)#exit
R1(config)#interface gi0/1.20
R1(config-subif)#encapsulation dot1q 20
R1(config-subif)#ip address 10.1.20.1 255.255.255.0
R1(config-subif)#end
%SYS-5-CONFIG_I: Configured from console by console
R1#
```

EXAMPLE 8.2   **The ROAS Configuration of SW1**

```
SW1#
SW1#configure terminal
Enter configuration commands, one per line.  End with CNTL/Z.
SW1(config)#interface gi0/1
SW1(config-if)#switchport trunk encapsulation dot1q
```

```
SW1(config-if)#switchport mode trunk
SW1(config-if)#end
SW1#
```

> **Note**
>
> Example 8.2 above does not include the configuration you need of the VLANs and their interface assignments. Chapter 5, "LAN Switching Fundamentals: VLANs and Interswitch Connectivity," covers this configuration in detail.

Notice that router R1 has an issue. It has only one physical interface that connects to SW1. This is an issue because this device needs to route between two VLANs (VLAN 10 and VLAN 20). This is where subinterfaces come to the rescue in the ROAS configuration. Subinterfaces gi0/1.10 and gi0/1.20 solve the issue. This allows the router to use one single physical interface and multiple subinterfaces to properly encapsulate and route traffic for multiple VLANs.

> **ExamAlert**
>
> In the example, I used an IP network address that had as part of it the same VLAN ID number. I also chose the subinterface ID number to match the VLAN ID. This is not required. I do it in practice to help my configuration to be easier to read and troubleshoot. In the exam, do not expect the exam authors to be "nice" to you like this. They may randomly assign subinterface network addresses, subinterface IDs, and VLAN IDs that do not match each other numerically.

But now a new issue is apparent. How do the subinterfaces get associated with the different VLANs from the switch? This is the power of the **encapsulation dot1q 10** and **encapsulation dot1q 20** commands under these subinterfaces. These commands ensure the subinterfaces can successfully do their job with the 802.1Q tagged traffic.

Notice that IP addressing is also very interesting. The physical interface receives no IP address (more on this later in the chapter), whereas the subinterfaces receive the appropriate IP addresses for the VLANs (subnets). These IP addresses can be used as the Default Gateway addresses hosts will use in the respective subnets.

For the SW1 configuration, things are remarkably straightforward. We configure the interface facing the router as an 802.1Q trunk.

Verification on the router is shown in Example 8.3.

EXAMPLE 8.3 **Verifying the R1 Configuration**

```
R1#show ip interface brief
Interface              IP-Address    OK? Method Status                     Protocol
GigabitEthernet0/0     unassigned    YES unset  administratively down down
GigabitEthernet0/1     unassigned    YES unset  up                         up
GigabitEthernet0/1.10  10.1.10.1     YES manual up                         up
GigabitEthernet0/1.20  10.1.20.1     YES manual up                         up
R1#show vlans

Virtual LAN ID:  1 (IEEE 802.1Q Encapsulation)

   vLAN Trunk Interface:   GigabitEthernet0/1

 This is configured as native Vlan for the following interface(s) :
GigabitEthernet0/1    Native-vlan Tx-type: Untagged

   Protocols Configured:  Address:        Received:      Transmitted:

GigabitEthernet0/1 (1)
        Other                              0              271

   118 packets, 21366 bytes input
   271 packets, 19851 bytes output

Virtual LAN ID:  10 (IEEE 802.1Q Encapsulation)

   vLAN Trunk Interface:   GigabitEthernet0/1.10

   Protocols Configured:  Address:        Received:      Transmitted:

GigabitEthernet0/1.10 (10)
        IP            10.1.10.1          0              0
        Other                            0              2

   0 packets, 0 bytes input
   2 packets, 92 bytes output

Virtual LAN ID:  20 (IEEE 802.1Q Encapsulation)

   vLAN Trunk Interface:   GigabitEthernet0/1.20

   Protocols Configured:  Address:        Received:      Transmitted:

GigabitEthernet0/1.20 (20)
        IP            10.1.20.1          0              0
        Other                            0              2

   0 packets, 0 bytes input
   2 packets, 92 bytes output

R1#
```

Notice I like to first use **show ip interface brief** (as always!) to verify that the physical interface and the subinterfaces are all just fine (UP/UP). You can then use **show vlans** (interesting for a router!) in order to verify the encapsulations you have in place on your subinterfaces.

Example 8.4 shows the verification on SW1.

EXAMPLE 8.4 **Verification on SW1**

```
SW1#show interface trunk

Port        Mode              Encapsulation  Status        Native vlan
Gi0/1       on                802.1q         trunking      1

Port        Vlans allowed on trunk
Gi0/1       1-4094

Port        Vlans allowed and active in management domain
Gi0/1       1,10,20

Port        Vlans in spanning tree forwarding state and not pruned
Gi0/1       1,10,20
SW1#
```

My verification on SW1 is super straightforward. I just like to check the trunking status of my trunk port with **show interface trunk**. This, of course, assumes I have already properly verified my VLANs and interfaces and all of the other infrastructure stuff from earlier chapters.

ExamAlert

In a production environment, or in a robustly constructed exam simulation, you might have the opportunity to move to properly configured host workstations in each VLAN and ensure they can ping each other. Remember, the point of inter-VLAN routing is to permit devices in one VLAN and IP subnet to communicate with devices in another, so always test this if it is possible.

If you are curious like me, you might be wondering about the Native VLAN, that one VLAN that is not tagged with an 802.1Q tag by default. The preceding configurations assume that no Native VLAN is in use by the router. Let me demonstrate two separate methods you can use to handle a Native VLAN. Example 8.5 demonstrates placing the IP address that coordinates with the subnet of the Native VLAN on the physical interface. This makes sense because this traffic is not tagged and requires no recognition of an encapsulated tag, since the encapsulated tag does not exist on the native VLAN!

EXAMPLE 8.5 **The Native VLAN on the Physical Interface**

```
R1#
R1#configure terminal
Enter configuration commands, one per line.  End with CNTL/Z.
R1(config)#interface gi0/1
R1(config-if)#no shutdown
R1(config-if)#
%LINK-3-UPDOWN: Interface GigabitEthernet0/1, changed state to up
%LINEPROTO-5-UPDOWN: Line protocol on Interface GigabitEthernet0/1,
   changed state to up
R1(config-if)#! Notice now the IP address on the physical interface!
R1(config-if)#ip address 10.1.0.1 255.255.255.0
R1(config-if)#interface gi0/1.10
R1(config-subif)#encapsulation dot1q 10
R1(config-subif)#ip address 10.1.10.1 255.255.255.0
R1(config-subif)#exit
R1(config)#interface gi0/1.20
R1(config-subif)#encapsulation dot1q 20
R1(config-subif)#ip address 10.1.20.1 255.255.255.0
R1(config-subif)#end
R1#
%SYS-5-CONFIG_I: Configured from console by console
R1#
```

Example 8.6 show another way to handle the use of a Native VLAN on your ROAS configuration. This time, a subinterface is used for the Native VLAN. Because there is no tagging to identify the VLAN, the **native** keyword must be used in the **encapsulation** command.

EXAMPLE 8.6 **The Native VLAN on a Subinterface**

```
R1#
R1#configure terminal
Enter configuration commands, one per line.  End with CNTL/Z.
R1(config)#interface gi0/1
R1(config-if)#no shutdown
R1(config-if)#
%LINK-3-UPDOWN: Interface GigabitEthernet0/1, changed state to up
%LINEPROTO-5-UPDOWN: Line protocol on Interface GigabitEthernet0/1,
   changed state to up
R1(config-if)#! Notice no IP address on the physical interface
R1(config-if)#interface gi0/1.10
R1(config-subif)#encapsulation dot1q 10
```

```
R1(config-subif)#ip address 10.1.10.1 255.255.255.0
R1(config-subif)#exit
R1(config)#interface gi0/1.20
R1(config-subif)#encapsulation dot1q 20
R1(config-subif)#ip address 10.1.20.1 255.255.255.0
R1(config-subif)#exit
R1(config)#interface gi0/1.777
R1(config-subif)#encapsulation dot1q 777 native
R1(config-subif)#ip address 10.1.0.1 255.255.255.0
R1(config-subif)#end
R1#
%SYS-5-CONFIG_I: Configured from console by console
R1#
```

CramQuiz

1. Examine the configuration of R1 following the depicted network topology. Why is
   ROAS not functioning?

```
Building configuration...
Current configuration : 3056 bytes
!
version 15.6
service timestamps debug datetime msec
service timestamps log datetime msec
no service password-encryption
!
hostname R1
!
boot-start-marker
boot-end-marker
!
!
!
no aaa new-model
ethernet lmi ce
!
!
!
mmi polling-interval 60
no mmi auto-configure
no mmi pvc
```

```
mmi snmp-timeout 180
!
!
!
no ip routing
!
!
!
no ip cef
no ipv6 cef
!
multilink bundle-name authenticated
!
!
!
redundancy
!
!
!
interface GigabitEthernet0/0
 ip address 10.255.0.14 255.255.0.0
 no ip route-cache
 shutdown
 duplex auto
 speed auto
 media-type rj45
!
interface GigabitEthernet0/1
 no ip address
 no ip route-cache
 duplex auto
 speed auto
 media-type rj45
no shutdown
 !
interface GigabitEthernet0/1.10
 encapsulation dot1Q 10
 ip address 10.1.10.1 255.255.255.0
 no ip route-cache
 !
interface GigabitEthernet0/1.20
 encapsulation dot1Q 20
 ip address 10.1.20.1 255.255.255.0
 no ip route-cache
 !
ip forward-protocol nd
 !
 !
```

```
no ip http server
no ip http secure-server
!
!
!
control-plane
!
!
!
line con 0
 exec-timeout 0 0
 logging synchronous
line aux 0
line vty 0 4
 login
 transport input none
!
no scheduler allocate
!
end
```

- ○ **A.** The IP address on the gi0/1.20 interface is the subnet ID
- ○ **B.** Interface gi0/1 has no IP address assigned
- ○ **C.** AAA is disabled
- ○ **D.** IP routing is disabled

2. Examine the configuration of SW1 following the depicted network topology in the figure. Why is ROAS not functioning?

```
Building configuration...
Current configuration : 2688 bytes
!
version 15.2
service timestamps debug datetime msec
service timestamps log datetime msec
no service password-encryption
service compress-config
!
hostname SW1
!
boot-start-marker
boot-end-marker
```

```
!
!
!
no aaa new-model
!
!
!
ip cef
no ipv6 cef
!
!
!
spanning-tree mode rapid-pvst
spanning-tree extend system-id
!
vlan internal allocation policy ascending
!
!
!
interface GigabitEthernet0/0
 media-type rj45
 negotiation auto
!
interface GigabitEthernet0/1
no shutdown
media-type rj45
 negotiation auto
!
ip forward-protocol nd
!
no ip http server
no ip http secure-server
!
!
!
control-plane
!
!
!
line con 0
 exec-timeout 0 0
 logging synchronous
line aux 0
line vty 0 4
 login
!
!
end
```

○ **A.** The trunk is not going to form properly.

○ **B.** The gi0/1 interface is shutdown.

○ **C.** The interface cannot be set to autonegotiate.

○ **D.** The device cannot use CEF.

CramQuiz Answers

1. **D** is correct. On this router, someone has inserted the **no ip routing** command which disabled routing capabilities.

2. **A** is correct. The trunk interface is missing a required command of **switch trunk encapsulation dot1q**. This is required before the use of the command **switch mode trunk**.

Review Questions

1. An RE allows inter-VLAN communication. What is an RE?

   ○ **A.** Routing entity

   ○ **B.** Routing entry

   ○ **C.** Routing engine

   ○ **D.** Register entry

2. What is the virtual interface that makes ROAS possible?

   ○ **A.** Loopback

   ○ **B.** Subinterface

   ○ **C.** TTY

   ○ **D.** VTY

3. What command allows you to verify the ROAS configuration on a router?

   ○ **A. show interface trunk**

   ○ **B. show vlan status**

   ○ **C. show vlan**

   ○ **D. show subinterfaces status**

4. Why might a ROAS configuration have an IP address on the physical interface?

   ○ **A.** The configuration is in error.

   ○ **B.** This is a required configuration.

   ○ **C.** The IP address is associated with the Native VLAN.

   ○ **D.** The IP address is an RFC 1918 address and is not used.

Answers to Review Questions

1. **C** is correct. A routing engine (RE) routes between IPv4 networks and their associated VLANs. In a ROAS configuration, this is a physical router appliance. In modern times, this is a function integrated as part of a multilayer switch.

2. **B** is correct. Subinterfaces are the virtual interfaces that make ROAS able to support multiple IP subnets and their associated VLANs.

3. **C** is correct. You can use the **show vlan** command on a router to help verify ROAS.

4. **C** is correct. You might see an IP address on the physical interface for the Native VLAN. Remember, this VLAN is not 802.1Q tagged.

Additional Resources

Configure Inter-VLAN Routing on Cisco Routers and Switches— http://www.ajsnetworking.com/inter-vlan

Configure InterVLAN Routing on Layer 3 Switches—http://bit.ly/ 1FEll8P

CHAPTER 9

Routing Fundamentals: Static and Dynamic Routing

This chapter covers the following official ICND1 100-105 exam topics:

▶ Compare and contrast static routing and dynamic routing

▶ Configure, verify, and troubleshoot IPv4 and IPv6 static routing

▶ Configure, verify, and troubleshoot RIPv2 for IPv4 (excluding authentication, filtering, manual summarization, redistribution)

This chapter ensures you are ready for the above topic from Routing Fundamentals section of the overall exam blueprint from Cisco Systems. Remember, this is just a section of the Routing Fundamentals area. Chapters Seven and Eight also exist in this grouping. These other chapters deal with general routing concepts and inter-VLAN routing.

Essential Terms and Components

▶ **Static Routing**

▶ **Dynamic Routing**

▶ **Default Route**

▶ **Network Route**

▶ **Host Route**

▶ **Floating Static**

▶ **RIPv2 for IPv4**

Topic: Compare and contrast static routing and dynamic routing

CramSaver

If you can correctly answer these CramSaver questions, save time by skimming the ExamAlerts in this chapter and then completing the CramQuiz at the end of each section and the Review Questions at the end of the chapter. If you are in doubt at all—read EVERYTHING in this chapter!

1. What are the two general categories of how routes are added to a router?

_____

2. What type of dynamic routing protocol is RIP?

_____

3. What is the command to configure a default static route with a next hop of 172.16.1.4?

_____

Answers

1. Static and dynamic
2. RIP is a Distance Vector routing protocol. OSPF is a dynamic link-state routing protocol.
3. **ip route 0.0.0.0 0.0.0.0 172.16.1.4**

When you manually configure your routers with specific routing table entries, you are engaged in **static routing**. It might sound silly considering how much work this would be compared to having the routers dynamically learn routing information themselves, but keep in mind it is extremely common for you to statically configure **default routing** information. Example 9.1 demonstrates the static configuration of a default route.

EXAMPLE 9.1 **The Configuration of a Static Default Route**

```
R1#
R1#configure terminal
Enter configuration commands, one per line.  End with CNTL/Z.
R1(config)#ip route 0.0.0.0 0.0.0.0 10.10.10.2
R1(config)#end
R1#
```

> **ExamAlert**
>
> The next section details static routing configuration in much greater detail—the level of detail (of course) that you need in the exam.

The **default route** indicates the path to take when the router does not have a better matching prefix entry in the routing table. This creates the Gateway of Last Resort as discussed in Chapter 7, "Routing Fundamentals: Routing Concepts."

Dynamic routing protocols share information regarding prefixes in order to dynamically build the routing table. Admins still need to configure these protocols, but the entries in the routing tables auto populate.

Dynamic routing protocols consist of the following categories:

▶ **Distance Vector**: These are the first generation type protocols (RIP is one of them); they periodically share their routing tables with each other.

▶ **Link State**: OSPF is a prime example; these sophisticated protocols build a map of the network.

▶ **Hybrid**: Protocols that feature characteristics of both Distance Vector and Link State; EIGRP is an example.

▶ **Path Vector**: There is one prime example of this type of routing protocol: BGP; this protocol uses an AS-Path attribute to record where the prefix is being learned from.

CramQuiz

1. What is a popular reason for configuring static routing in a modern network?
   - ○ **A.** Remote prefixes in a local area network
   - ○ **B.** Because of the overhead of OSPF
   - ○ **C.** Because static routing has less administrative overhead
   - ○ **D.** Because of the need for a default route

2. OSPF is an example of what type of dynamic routing protocol?
   - ○ **A.** Distance Vector
   - ○ **B.** Link State
   - ○ **C.** Hybrid
   - ○ **D.** Path Vector

CramQuiz Answers

1. **D** is correct. Static routing is a frequent configuration today thanks to the static default route.

2. **B** is correct. OSPF is a link state routing protocol.

Topic: Configure, verify, and troubleshoot IPv4 and IPv6 static routing

CramSaver

1. What is the command to configure a static route to 10.40.40.0/24 with a next hop of 10.10.10.2?

   _____

2. What is the command to configure an IPv6 static route to 2001:aaaa::/64 using the Serial0/0 interface?

   _____

3. What is a floating static route?

   _____

Answers

1. **ip route 10.40.40.0 255.255.255.0 10.10.10.2**
2. **ipv6 route 2001:aaaa::/64 serial 0/0**
3. A floating static route is a static route that is not installed in the routing table initially thanks to an artificially high (untrustworthy) AD.

Using static routing, we can create default routes, **network routes**, and **host routes**. Default routes we have already covered. Network routes are static routes to specific prefixes, whereas host routes are prefixes that have a 32-bit network mask. This means we are specifying the exact address. Example 9.2 shows the configuration of network and host routes using static routing in IPv4.

EXAMPLE 9.2 **Configuring Static Network Routes and Host Routes in IPv4**

```
R1#configure terminal
Enter configuration commands, one per line.  End with CNTL/Z.
R1(config)#ip route 192.168.1.0 255.255.255.0 10.10.10.2
R1(config)#ip route 172.16.1.3 255.255.255.255 10.10.10.2
R1(config)#end
R1#
%SYS-5-CONFIG_I: Configured from console by console
R1#
```

> **Note**
>
> It is a nice timesaver when your link is a point-to-point link to just specify the outgoing interface (also referred to as the exit interface) on the local router, as part of your **ip route** command. For example, **ip route 192.168.1.0 255.255.255.0 serial0/0**, where serial 0/0 is the exit interface of the local router.

Notice how simple the static route creation is. It is the just as easy in an IPv6 environment. Example 9.3 demonstrates this.

EXAMPLE 9.3 **Configuring a Static Route in IPv6**

```
R1#configure terminal
R1(config)#ipv6 route 2001:aaaa::/64 serial 0/0
```

Example 9.4 demonstrates the use of the **show ip route** and **show ipv6 route** commands to verify static routes.

EXAMPLE 9.4 **Verifying Static IPv4 and IPv6 Routes**

```
R1#show ip route
Codes: L—local, C—connected, S—static, R—RIP, M—mobile, B—BGP
       D—EIGRP, EX—EIGRP external, O—OSPF, IA—OSPF inter area
       N1—OSPF NSSA external type 1, N2—OSPF NSSA external type 2
       E1—OSPF external type 1, E2—OSPF external type 2
       i—IS-IS, su—IS-IS summary, L1—IS-IS level-1, L2—IS-IS level-2
       ia-IS-IS inter area, *—candidate default, U—per-user static
route
       o—ODR, P—periodic downloaded static route, +—replicated route

Gateway of last resort is 10.10.10.2 to network 0.0.0.0

S*    0.0.0.0/0 [1/0] via 10.10.10.2
                is directly connected, FastEthernet0/0
      10.0.0.0/8 is variably subnetted, 2 subnets, 2 masks
C        10.10.10.0/24 is directly connected, FastEthernet0/0
L        10.10.10.1/32 is directly connected, FastEthernet0/0
      172.16.0.0/32 is subnetted, 1 subnets
S        172.16.1.3 [1/0] via 10.10.10.2
S     192.168.1.0/24 [1/0] via 10.10.10.2
R1#
R1#show ipv6 route
IPv6 Routing Table—default—2 entries
Codes: C—Connected, L—Local, S—Static, U—Per-user Static route
       B—BGP, M—MIPv6, R—RIP, I1—ISIS L1
       I2—ISIS L2, IA—ISIS interarea, IS—ISIS summary, D—EIGRP
```

```
        EX—EIGRP external, ND—Neighbor Discovery
        O—OSPF Intra, OI—OSPF Inter, OE1—OSPF ext 1, OE2—OSPF ext 2
        ON1—OSPF NSSA ext 1, ON2—OSPF NSSA ext 2
S   2001:AAAA::/64 [1/0]
      via Serial 0/0, directly connected
L   FF00::/8 [0/0]
      via Null0, receive
R1#
```

Another interesting use of a static route is a **floating static** route. A floating static route "floats" above a prefix learned by a dynamic routing protocol. The static route kicks in when the dynamic routing protocol removes the prefix. How does the static route "float"? The answer is administrative distance. To create a floating static route, you set the AD artificially high (numerically higher than other existing routing sources) for the static route. Specifically, you set the AD greater than (less believable than) the dynamic route. Example 9.5 shows the creation of a floating static route that could be used with RIP as the dynamic routing protocol. Notice the AD that is one notch higher (worse) than the default AD of RIP, which is 120. This newly created static router won't be placed in the routing table as long as the same route is being learned via RIP. If the router stops learning of this route via RIP, then the static route, with its AD of 121, will be placed in the routing table.

EXAMPLE 9.5 **Configuring a Floating Static Route**

```
R3#
R3#configure terminal
Enter configuration commands, one per line.   End with CNTL/Z.
R3(config)#ip route 10.60.60.0 255.255.255.0 10.20.20.2 121
R3(config)#end
R3#
```

CramQuiz

1. Which two parameters of a static route are acceptable as part of the **ip route** command to indicate where traffic should be sent? (Choose two.)

   - ○ **A.** Next-hop IP address
   - ○ **B.** RE ID
   - ○ **C.** Destination MAC address
   - ○ **D.** Outgoing interface

2. What command permits the simple verification that a static route is in the routing table?

- ○ **A. show static**
- ○ **B. show ip route**
- ○ **C. show routing table static**
- ○ **D. show admin routes**

3. What feature do you use in order to create a floating static route?

- ○ **A.** Metric
- ○ **B.** Dampening
- ○ **C.** Route suppression
- ○ **D.** Administrative distance

CramQuiz Answers

1. **A** and **D** are correct. You may specify the next hop IP address or the outgoing interface.

2. **B** is correct. The **show ip route** command allows you to view static routes (if they exist) in the routing table.

3. **D** is correct. Administrative distance creates floating static routes. It eliminates the route from appearing through the artificial manipulation of trustworthiness.

Topic: Configure, verify, and troubleshoot RIPv2 for IPv4 (excluding authentication, filtering, manual summarization, redistribution)

CramSaver

1. What command do you use to configure version 2 of RIP in router configuration mode?

   _____

2. What router configuration command enables RIP on specific interfaces?

   _____

Answers

1. **version 2**
2. **network**

RIP version 2 is not a scalable routing protocol, but it does have appeal for small networks because it is simple to understand and configure. Figure 9.1 shows the topology for our configuration, and Example 9.6 shows the relevant configuration on all three devices.

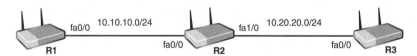

fa0/0   10.10.10.0/24   fa1/0   10.20.20.0/24

R1   fa0/0   **R2**   fa0/0   **R3**

FIGURE 9.1   **The RIPv2 Topology**

EXAMPLE 9.6   **The RIP Version 2 Configuration**

```
R1#
R1#configure terminal
Enter configuration commands, one per line.  End with CNTL/Z.
R1(config)#router rip
R1(config-router)#version 2
R1(config-router)#no auto-summary
```

```
R1(config-router)#network 10.0.0.0
R1(config-router)#end

R2#
R2#configure terminal
Enter configuration commands, one per line.  End with CNTL/Z.
R2(config)#router rip
R2(config-router)#version 2
R2(config-router)#no auto-summary
R2(config-router)#network 10.0.0.0
R2(config-router)#end

R3#
R3#configure terminal
Enter configuration commands, one per line.  End with CNTL/Z.
R3(config)#router rip
R3(config-router)#version 2
R3(config-router)#no auto-summary
R3(config-router)#network 10.0.0.0
R3(config-router)#end
R3#
```

Here are the commands we use in this **RIPv2 for IPv4** configuration:

▶ **router rip**: This global configuration command enters router configuration mode for RIP.

▶ **version 2**: This command ensures we are using the new and improved version of RIP; this version includes many enhancements, including the support for subnet mask advertisement to support Variable Length Subnet Masking (VLSM).

▶ **no auto-summary**: This command ensures that RIP version 2 does not automatically send summary routes for major classful networks.

▶ **network 10.0.0.0**: This command configures RIP on any interfaces on the router that fall within the 10.0.0.0/8 address space; if you have an interface in this range that you do not want to speak RIP you can use the following command—**passive-interface** *interface_name*. This passive interface command is entered in router configuration mode along with the network command. The **passive-interface** command can be used with other routing protocols as well, such as OSPF and EIGRP, and with those protocols it prevents the sending of hello messages on those interfaces.

> **ExamAlert**
>
> The **network** command in RIP must be a classful reference. You can enter something as incredibly specific as a host route (**network 10.10.10.1**), but the router simply converts this entry to the classful entry, based on the 10.x.x.x IPv4 network being a class A address. This fact stems from RIP being a first-generation, originally classful protocol.

Verification of RIP is very simple. Example 9.7 demonstrates the use of the **show ip protocols** command to see the configuration details for RIP.

EXAMPLE 9.7 **Using show IP protocols to Verify RIP**

```
R3#show ip protocols
*** IP Routing is NSF aware ***

Routing Protocol is "rip"
  Outgoing update filter list for all interfaces is not set
  Incoming update filter list for all interfaces is not set
  Sending updates every 30 seconds, next due in 11 seconds
  Invalid after 180 seconds, hold down 180, flushed after 240
  Redistributing: rip
  Default version control: send version 2, receive version 2
    Interface             Send  Recv  Triggered RIP  Key-chain
    FastEthernet0/0        2     2
  Automatic network summarization is not in effect
  Maximum path: 4
  Routing for Networks:
    10.0.0.0
  Passive Interface(s):
    Loopback0
  Routing Information Sources:
    Gateway         Distance      Last Update
    10.20.20.2         120        00:00:24
  Distance: (default is 120)

R3#
```

Example 9.8 shows the use of **show ip route** in order to verify RIP. Note that a RIP route does appear in the routing table for the remote prefix of 10.10.10.0/24.

EXAMPLE 9.8 **Using show ip route to Verify RIP**

```
R3#
R3#show ip route
Codes: L—local, C—connected, S—static, R—RIP, M—mobile, B—BGP
       D—EIGRP, EX—EIGRP external, O—OSPF, IA—OSPF inter area
       N1—OSPF NSSA external type 1, N2—OSPF NSSA external type 2
       E1—OSPF external type 1, E2—OSPF external type 2
       i—IS-IS, su—IS-IS summary, L1—IS-IS level-1, L2—IS-IS level-2
       ia—IS-IS inter area, *—candidate default, U—per-user static
route
       o—ODR, P—periodic downloaded static route, +—replicated route

Gateway of last resort is not set

       10.0.0.0/8 is variably subnetted, 5 subnets, 2 masks
R        10.10.10.0/24 [120/1] via 10.20.20.2, 00:00:11,
FastEthernet0/0
C        10.20.20.0/24 is directly connected, FastEthernet0/0
L        10.20.20.3/32 is directly connected, FastEthernet0/0
R3#
```

CramQuiz

1. Examine the topology and configurations that follow. What is the issue preventing
   the network from functioning properly?

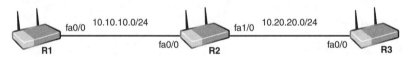

```
R1
Building configuration...
Current configuration : 1346 bytes
!
! Last configuration change at 21:42:50 UTC Sun Aug 21 2016
!
upgrade fpd auto
version 15.0
service timestamps debug datetime msec
service timestamps log datetime msec
no service password-encryption
!
hostname R1
!
boot-start-marker
boot-end-marker
!
```

```
!
no aaa new-model
!
!
!
ip source-route
no ip icmp rate-limit unreachable
ip cef
!
!
!
no ip domain lookup
ipv6 unicast-routing
ipv6 cef
!
multilink bundle-name authenticated
!
!
!
redundancy
!
!
ip tcp synwait-time 5
!
!
!
interface FastEthernet0/0
 ip address 10.10.10.1 255.255.255.0
 duplex half
 ipv6 enable
!
!
interface FastEthernet1/0
 no ip address
 shutdown
 duplex half
!
!
router rip
 version 2
 network 10.0.0.0
!
ip forward-protocol nd
no ip http server
no ip http secure-server
!
!
ip route 0.0.0.0 0.0.0.0 FastEthernet0/0
ip route 0.0.0.0 0.0.0.0 10.10.10.2
```

```
ip route 172.16.1.3 255.255.255.255 10.10.10.2
ip route 192.168.1.0 255.255.255.0 10.10.10.2
!
no cdp log mismatch duplex
ipv6 route 2001:AAAA::/64 FastEthernet0/0
!
!
!
control-plane
!
!
!
mgcp fax t38 ecm
mgcp behavior g729-variants static-pt
!
!
!
gatekeeper
 shutdown
!
!
line con 0
 exec-timeout 0 0
 privilege level 15
 logging synchronous
 stopbits 1
line aux 0
 exec-timeout 0 0
 privilege level 15
 logging synchronous
 stopbits 1
line vty 0 4
```

R2
```
Building configuration...
Current configuration : 1115 bytes
!
! Last configuration change at 20:28:20 UTC Sun Aug 21 2016
!
upgrade fpd auto
version 15.0
service timestamps debug datetime msec
service timestamps log datetime msec
no service password-encryption
!
hostname R2
!
boot-start-marker
boot-end-marker
```

```
!
!
no aaa new-model
!
!
!
ip source-route
no ip icmp rate-limit unreachable
ip cef
!
!
!
no ip domain lookup
no ipv6 cef
!
multilink bundle-name authenticated
!
!
!
redundancy
!
!
ip tcp synwait-time 5
!
!
!
interface FastEthernet0/0
 ip address 10.10.10.2 255.255.255.0
 duplex half
!
!
interface FastEthernet1/0
 ip address 20.20.20.2 255.255.255.0
 duplex half
!
!
router rip
 version 2
 network 10.0.0.0
 no auto-summary
!
ip forward-protocol nd
no ip http server
no ip http secure-server
!
!
!
no cdp log mismatch duplex
!
```

```
!
!
control-plane
!
!
!
mgcp fax t38 ecm
mgcp behavior g729-variants static-pt
!
!
!
gatekeeper
 shutdown
!
!
line con 0
 exec-timeout 0 0
 privilege level 15
 logging synchronous
 stopbits 1
line aux 0
 exec-timeout 0 0
 privilege level 15
 logging synchronous
 stopbits 1
line vty 0 4
 login
!
end
```

R3
```
Building configuration...
Current configuration : 1174 bytes
!
! Last configuration change at 21:52:40 UTC Sun Aug 21 2016
!
upgrade fpd auto
version 15.0
service timestamps debug datetime msec
service timestamps log datetime msec
no service password-encryption
!
hostname R3
!
boot-start-marker
boot-end-marker
!
!
no aaa new-model
```

```
!
!
!
ip source-route
no ip icmp rate-limit unreachable
ip cef
!
!
!
no ip domain lookup
no ipv6 cef
!
multilink bundle-name authenticated
!
!
!
redundancy
!
!
ip tcp synwait-time 5
!
!
!
interface Loopback0
 ip address 10.40.40.3 255.255.255.0
!
!
interface FastEthernet0/0
 ip address 10.20.20.3 255.255.255.0
 duplex half
!
!
router rip
 version 2
 passive-interface Loopback0
 network 10.20.20.3
 no auto-summary
!
ip forward-protocol nd
no ip http server
no ip http secure-server
!
!
ip route 10.60.60.0 255.255.255.0 10.20.20.2 121
!
no cdp log mismatch duplex
!
!
!
```

```
control-plane
 !
 !
 !
mgcp fax t38 ecm
mgcp behavior g729-variants static-pt
 !
 !
 !
gatekeeper
 shutdown
 !
 !
line con 0
 exec-timeout 0 0
 privilege level 15
 logging synchronous
 stopbits 1
line aux 0
 exec-timeout 0 0
 privilege level 15
 logging synchronous
 stopbits 1
line vty 0 4
 login
 !
end
```

    ○ **A.** R3's **network** statement will return an error.

    ○ **B.** R1 must use the **no auto-summary** command.

    ○ **C.** R2 requires the **version 2** command.

    ○ **D.** There is an IP address issue on R2.

2. What command stops an interface that is included by the **network** command to not send RIP information?

    ○ **A.** **disable interface**

    ○ **B.** **passive-interface**

    ○ **C.** **interface-silent**

    ○ **D.** **rip-silent**

CramQuiz Answers

1. **D** is correct. R2 is attempting to use the subnet ID for an IP address.

2. **B** is correct. The **passive-interface** command silences RIP for an interface included in the broad **network** command.

Review Questions

1. What is an example of a hybrid routing protocol?
   - ○ **A.** RIP
   - ○ **B.** OSPF
   - ○ **C.** EIGRP
   - ○ **D.** BGP

2. What is the mask length for a host route?
   - ○ **A.** 0
   - ○ **B.** 64
   - ○ **C.** 16
   - ○ **D.** 32

3. What command permits you to view the IPv6 routing table?
   - ○ **A. show route ipv6**
   - ○ **B. show route new**
   - ○ **C. show ipv6 route**
   - ○ **D. show route**

4. What verification command includes the following?

   Routing for Networks:

   10.0.0.0
   - ○ **A. show ip route**
   - ○ **B. show router rip**
   - ○ **C. show rip config**
   - ○ **D. show ip protocols**

Answers to Review Questions

1. **C** is correct. EIGRP combines some features of Distance Vector and Link State dynamic routing protocols.

2. **D** is correct. A host route in IPv4 features a mask of 32 bits.

3. **C** is correct. The **show ipv6 route** command is the equivalent of **show ip route** but shows the v6 table of course.

4. **D** is correct. The **show ip protocols** command allows you to easily verify the configuration of your dynamic routing protocols.

Additional Resources

RIPv2 Concepts Review—http://www.ajsnetworking.com/ripv2

The Mechanics of Routing Protocols—http://bit.ly/2dcffWU

PART IV

Infrastructure Services

This part of the text deals with one of five overall sections you must master for the ICND1 exam. There are three chapters total that make up Part 4. These three chapters, taken as a whole, represent 15 percent of the exam questions you face in your exam. This means that the Infrastructure Services area is the fourth most important section of the five overall sections that you deal with on your testing day! Remember, even though relatively few questions are from this section, those questions could still easily make the difference between a passing and failing mark on this test.

Here you begin with the critical services of DNS, DHCP, and NTP. You also master ACLS and NAT. For many students, these three chapters prove to be the most challenging!

CHAPTER 10

Infrastructure Services: DNS, DHCP, NTP

This chapter covers the following official ICND1 100-105 exam topics:

▶ Describe DNS lookup operation

▶ Troubleshoot client connectivity issues involving DNS

▶ Configure and verify DHCP on a router (excluding static reservations)

▶ Troubleshoot client- and router-based DHCP connectivity issues

▶ Configure and verify NTP operating in client/server mode

This chapter ensures you are ready for the above topic from the Infrastructure Services section of the overall exam blueprint from Cisco Systems. Remember, this is just a section of the Infrastructure Services area. Chapters Eleven and Twelve also exist in this grouping. These other chapters deal with ACLs and NAT.

Essential Terms and Components

▶ **DNS**

▶ **DNS Lookups**

▶ **Client DNS Configurations**

▶ **DHCP**

▶ **DHCP Server**

▶ **DHCP Relay**

▶ **DHCP Client**

▶ **Other DHCP Assigned Parameters**

▶ **NTP Server**

▶ **NTP Client**

▶ **Stratum**

Topic: Describe DNS lookup operation

CramSaver

If you can correctly answer these CramSaver questions, save time by skimming the ExamAlerts in this chapter and then completing the CramQuiz at the end of each section and the Review Questions at the end of the chapter. If you are in doubt at all—read EVERYTHING in this chapter!

1. What service resolves "friendly names" like www.cbtnuggets.com to an IP address?

   _____

2. Name two types of DNS records.

   _____

Answers

1. The Domain Name System (DNS) resolves friendly names to IP addresses.
2. Common record types include:
   ▶ Start of Authority (SOA)
   ▶ IP Addresses (A and AAAA)
   ▶ SMTP Mail Exchangers (MX)
   ▶ Name Servers (NS)
   ▶ Pointers for Reverse DNS Lookups (PTR)
   ▶ Domain Name Aliases (CNAME)

Imagine a world where we would need to communicate with devices on the Internet (or our company's intranet) using the IP addresses of systems. This would be nearly impossible since IP addresses are so difficult to memorize for the many devices. The **Domain Name System (DNS)** prevents this nightmare.

DNS resolves "friendly" names like www.cbtnuggets.com to the IP address that devices truly need in order to reach the remote system. We use DNS every day, as you might guess. The system can refer to a private RFC 1918 address space inside your organization or to the public, globally routable IPv4 address space on the Internet. You can also have your internal private DNS servers interact with public DNS servers.

The domain name system delegates the responsibility of assigning domain names and mapping those names to Internet resources by designating *authoritative* name servers for each domain. Network administrators may delegate authority over sub-domains of their allocated name space to other name servers. This approach gives us a fault-tolerant design and eliminates the need for everyone to rely on one single huge database.

Remember, when you hear DNS, you are talking about this structure of naming as well as the technical details of the protocol itself (for example, what messages are exchanged and how is data processed in the system).

The Internet maintains the domain name hierarchy and the Internet Protocol (IP) address spaces. DNS maintains the domain name hierarchy and provides translation services between it and the address spaces. A DNS name server is a server that stores the DNS records for a domain; a DNS name server responds with answers to queries against its database.

The most common types of records stored in the DNS database are as follows:

▶ Start of Authority (SOA)

▶ IP Addresses (A and AAAA)

▶ SMTP Mail Exchangers (MX)

▶ Name Servers (NS)

▶ Pointers for Reverse DNS Lookups (PTR)

▶ Domain Name Aliases (CNAME)

DNS databases are traditionally stored in structured zone files.

CramQuiz

1. Which statement about DNS is false?

   ○ **A.** DNS operates thanks to one central master database.

   ○ **B.** DNS resolves domain names to IP addresses.

   ○ **C.** DNS uses many types of records to do its job.

   ○ **D.** Multiple DNS servers are typically available for a client.

2. What device is responsible for each DNS domain?

   ○ **A.** Master DNS

   ○ **B.** Authoritative Name Server

   ○ **C.** Zone File Server

   ○ **D.** DNS Client

CramQuiz Answers

1. **A** is correct. The DNS system creates a distributed database so that one central master database does not need to be relied upon.

2. **B** is correct. Each domain has an authoritative name server that helps manage the domain.

Topic: Troubleshoot client connectivity issues involving DNS

CramSaver

1. What Windows CLI command allows you to see the IP address information configured as well as the DNS server IP address?

   _____

2. What Windows CLI tool allows you to learn information regarding the DNS lookup including the DNS server name, address, non-authoritative response, and resolved addresses and aliases?

   _____

3. What is the command that specifies one or more DNS servers for a Cisco device to use?

   _____

Answers

1. **ipconfig /all**
2. **nslookup**
3. **ip name-server**

Ensuring your clients are properly configured to use DNS is important for full functionality on the Internet today.

On a Windows client system, you can check the DNS settings using **ipconfig** as shown in Example 10.1.

EXAMPLE 10.1 **Examining DNS Settings on a Windows Client**

```
C:\Users\terry>ipconfig /all

Windows IP Configuration

    Host Name . . . . . . . . . . . . : DESKTOP-ABC123
    Primary Dns Suffix  . . . . . . . :
    Node Type . . . . . . . . . . . . : Hybrid
    IP Routing Enabled. . . . . . . . : No
```

```
    WINS Proxy Enabled. . . . . . . . : No
    DNS Suffix Search List. . . . . . : my-router.home

Ethernet adapter Ethernet:

    Connection-specific DNS Suffix  . : my-router.home
    Description . . . . . . . . . . . : Realtek PCIe GBE Family
                                        Controller
    Physical Address. . . . . . . . . : 84-8F-69-F5-5F-3D
    DHCP Enabled. . . . . . . . . . . : Yes
    Autoconfiguration Enabled . . . . : Yes
    Link-local IPv6 Address . . . . . : fe80::bc5e:a448:8dcc:72ce%3
                                        (Preferred)
    IPv4 Address. . . . . . . . . . . : 192.168.1.191(Preferred)
    Subnet Mask . . . . . . . . . . . : 255.255.255.0
    Lease Obtained. . . . . . . . . . : Monday3:33:08 AM
    Lease Expires . . . . . . . . . . : Friday 3:33:19 AM
    Default Gateway . . . . . . . . . : 192.168.1.1
    DHCP Server . . . . . . . . . . . : 192.168.1.1
    DHCPv6 IAID . . . . . . . . . . . : 59019113
    DHCPv6 Client DUID. . . . . . . . : 00-01-00-01-1E-72-89-C7-84-8F-
                                        69-F5-5F-3D
    DNS Servers . . . . . . . . . . . : 192.168.1.1
    NetBIOS over Tcpip. . . . . . . . : Enabled
C:\Users       erry>
```

Notice from the output in Example 10.1 that this client will send DNS requests to 192.168.1.1. This is, of course, a private use only address inside our network. This router receives public DNS server addresses automatically from our ISP so that it can resolve public website names that we want to visit.

Figure 10.1 shows the actual configuration for this Windows client in the graphical user interface of the Control Panel. Notice that the DNS information of 192.168.1.1 is being learned by this client automatically.

FIGURE 10.1   **The DNS Settings Inside of Windows**

What about verifying the Windows client is fine from a DNS perspective? One approach is to ping a known and reachable Web server using the friendly name. Example 10.2 demonstrates this approach.

EXAMPLE 10.2   **Checking DNS Functionality by Using PING**

```
C:\Users\terry>ping www.cisco.com

Pinging e144.dscb.akamaiedge.net [23.202.192.170] with 32 bytes of
data:
Reply from 23.202.192.170: bytes=32 time=35ms TTL=54
Reply from 23.202.192.170: bytes=32 time=37ms TTL=54
Reply from 23.202.192.170: bytes=32 time=36ms TTL=54
Reply from 23.202.192.170: bytes=32 time=35ms TTL=54

Ping statistics for 23.202.192.170:
    Packets: Sent = 4, Received = 4, Lost = 0 (0% loss),
Approximate round trip times in milli-seconds:
    Minimum = 35ms, Maximum = 37ms, Average = 35ms

C:\Users\terry>
```

> **ExamAlert**
>
> You can also configure a Cisco router or switch as a DNS client. We cover this later in this chapter. Do not ignore the Windows Client information, however.

If you would like to receive even more information, however, use the NSLOOKUP command. Example 10.3 demonstrates this powerful tool.

EXAMPLE 10.3 **Using NSLOOKUP to Verify DNS**

```
C:\Users\terry>nslookup www.cisco.com
Server:   ACME_Quantum_Gateway.my-router.home
Address:  192.168.1.1

Non-authoritative answer:
Name:     e144.dscb.akamaiedge.net
Addresses:  2600:1408:10:18c::90
            2600:1408:10:181::90
            23.202.192.170
Aliases:  www.cisco.com
          www.cisco.com.akadns.net
          wwwds.cisco.com.edgekey.net
          wwwds.cisco.com.edgekey.net.globalredir.akadns.net
C:\Users\terry>
```

Just as it can be convenient for your Windows client to use DNS, it can also be beneficial for your Cisco routers and switches. Table 10.1 provides commands available on these devices.

TABLE 10.1 **DNS Related Commands on Cisco Devices**

Cisco Command	Description
ip domain-lookup	This command enables DNS-based host name-to-address translation; note this command is enabled by default on many Cisco devices.
ip name-server	This command specifies the address of one or more name servers for the device to use for DNS resolution.
ip domain-name	This command defines a default domain name that the Cisco IOS software uses to complete unqualified host names (names without a dotted-decimal domain name).

CramQuiz

1. What is a common Windows client setting for IPv4 DNS?

   ○ **A.** The use of only Google DNS public servers

   ○ **B.** To acquire the DNS settings automatically via DHCP

   ○ **C.** To use the public IP address of the ISP's router

   ○ **D.** To use a local loopback address

2. What command enables DNS-based host name translations on a Cisco router and is enabled by default on many Cisco routers?

   ○ **A. ip domain-name**

   ○ **B. ip name-server**

   ○ **C. ip domain-list**

   ○ **D. ip domain-lookup**

CramQuiz Answers

1. **B** is correct. A very common approach for Windows client's DNS is to acquire this information dynamically.

2. **D** is correct. The **ip domain-lookup** command enables DNS-based host name resolution. This command is a default setting.

Topic: Configure and verify DHCP on a router (excluding static reservations)

CramSaver

1. What is the default lease duration on a Cisco DHCP Server?

   _____

2. Which feature allows a router to forward a client's DHCP request to a remote DHCP Server?

   _____

Answers

1. The default lease duration is 1 day, which is 86,400 seconds.
2. The DHCP Relay Agent feature permits this.

Figure 10.2 shows the simple topology we use to configure a Dynamic Host Configuration Protocol (**DHCP**) server using a Cisco router (R1), and also to configure a Cisco router (R2) as a **DHCP client**.

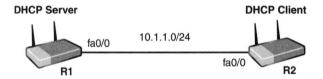

DHCP Server   **DHCP Client**

fa0/0   10.1.1.0/24

fa0/0

R1   **R2**

FIGURE 10.2   **The DHCP Server and Client Topology**

Example 10.4 shows the configuration of R1, the **DHCP Server**.

EXAMPLE 10.4   **The Configuration of the DHCP Server**

```
R1#
R1#configure terminal
Enter configuration commands, one per line.   End with CNTL/Z.
R1(config)#interface fa0/0
R1(config-if)#ip address 10.1.1.1 255.255.255.0
R1(config-if)#no shutdown
```

```
R1(config-if)#exit
R1(config)#
%LINK-3-UPDOWN: Interface FastEthernet0/0, changed state to up
%LINEPROTO-5-UPDOWN: Line protocol on Interface FastEthernet0/0,
changed state to up
R1(config)#ip dhcp excluded-address 10.1.1.1 10.1.1.10
R1(config)#ip dhcp pool ICND1EXAMCRAM
R1(dhcp-config)#default-router 10.1.1.1
R1(dhcp-config)#dns-server 8.8.8.8 4.2.2.2
R1(dhcp-config)#option 150 ip 10.10.10.2
R1(dhcp-config)#network 10.1.1.0 /24
R1(dhcp-config)#end
R1#
```

The commands directly involving DHCP are as follows:

▶ **ip dhcp excluded-address 10.1.1.1 10.1.1.10**: This command tells the DHCP Server *not* to assign the addresses from 10.1.1.1 to 10.1.1.10 to DHCP clients. For example, the 10.1.1.1 address is the static router interface address configured on R1's fa0/0 interface.

▶ **ip dhcp pool ICND1EXAMCRAM**: This command creates our DHCP pool on R1. This pool will contain the specific parameters we want to hand out to clients who lease addresses from the DHCP server.

▶ **default-router 10.1.1.1**: This command assigns the default gateway to clients of this DHCP pool.

▶ **dns-server 8.8.8.8 4.2.2.2**: This command sets a primary and backup DNS server for the clients.

▶ **option 150 ip 10.10.10.2**: This command provides clients with the IP address of a TFTP server.

▶ **network 10.1.1.0 /24**: This command specifies the IP address assignments for the pool. Remember, we excluded a small portion of this network address space. As a result, we expect the first leased address to be 10.1.1.11/24.

ExamAlert

The **network** command used in DHCP configuration accepts a subnet mask or prefix notation in its syntax.

Example 10.5 shows the configuration of a DHCP client function on a Cisco router.

EXAMPLE 10.5 **The Configuration of the DHCP Client**

```
R2#
R2#configure terminal
Enter configuration commands, one per line.  End with CNTL/Z.
R2(config)#interface fa0/0
R2(config-if)#ip address dhcp
R2(config-if)#no shutdown
R2(config-if)#end
R2#
%SYS-5-CONFIG_I: Configured from console by console
R2#
%LINK-3-UPDOWN: Interface FastEthernet0/0, changed state to up
%LINEPROTO-5-UPDOWN: Line protocol on Interface FastEthernet0/0,
changed state to up
R2#
```

Notice here the very simple configuration. The command **ip address dhcp** gets the job done for the client interface.

Next, let's begin our verification on the server. Example 10.6 shows the use of the **show ip dhcp binding** command to verify the server's operation.

EXAMPLE 10.6 **Verifying the DHCP Server**

```
R1#
R1#show ip dhcp binding
Bindings from all pools not associated with VRF:
IP address        Client-ID/             Lease expiration       Type
                  Hardware address/
                  User name
10.1.1.11         0063.6973.636f.2d63.   08:10 PM    Automatic
                  6130.332e.3066.6330.
                  2e30.3030.302d.4661.
                  302f.30
R1#
```

> **ExamAlert**
>
> Notice that the default lease-duration for Cisco DHCP Servers is one day.

Example 10.7 shows a simple verification on the client. The **show ip interface brief** command allows us to quickly view the DHCP learned address on Fa0/0.

EXAMPLE 10.7 **Verifying the DHCP Client**

```
R2#
R2#show ip interface brief
Interface              IP-Address      OK? Method Status                Protocol
FastEthernet0/0        10.1.1.11       YES DHCP   up                    up
FastEthernet1/0        unassigned      YES unset  administratively down down
FastEthernet1/1        unassigned      YES unset  administratively down down
R2#
```

What happens if your DHCP server is not on the same subnet with the clients that need it? One option is to configure a **DHCP Relay** Agent. This is a router that hears the DHCP requests from clients and forwards them to the appropriate DHCP server. It is very simple to configure this Relay Agent. Figure 10.3 and Example 10.8 show a sample topology and configuration. Note that the powerful **ip helper-address** *dhcp-server-ip* command gets the job done. The Relay Agent knows the address of the DHCP Server, so it can successfully forward local DHCP traffic to the DHCP server.

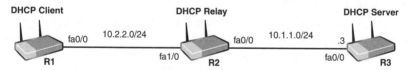

FIGURE 10.3 **The DHCP Relay Agent**

EXAMPLE 10.8 **Configuring the DHCP Relay Agent**

```
R2#
R2#configure terminal
Enter configuration commands, one per line.  End with CNTL/Z.
R2(config)#interface fa1/0
R2(config-if)#ip helper-address 10.1.1.3
R2(config-if)#end
R2#
```

CramQuiz

1. What command ensures your DHCP server does not lease out addresses you have statically configured elsewhere?

   - ○ **A. no dhcp-server assign-address**
   - ○ **B. no dhcp-lease address**
   - ○ **C. ip dhcp no-lease address**
   - ○ **D. ip dhcp excluded-address**

2. What command configures a default gateway in a DHCP Server Pool?

   - ○ **A. ip default-gateway**
   - ○ **B. gateway-of-last-resort**
   - ○ **C. ip domain-server**
   - ○ **D. default-router**

3. What command configures a Cisco device as a DHCP client?

   - ○ **A. ip address auto**
   - ○ **B. ip address dhcp**
   - ○ **C. ip address learn**
   - ○ **D. ip address dynamic**

CramQuiz Answers

1. **D** is correct. Use the **ip excluded-address** command to create a range of excluded addresses from your pool.

2. **D** is correct. Use the **default-router** command in the DHCP Pool to set the default gateway address.

3. **B** is correct. **ip address dhcp**, used in interface configuration mode, sets the Cisco device as a DHCP client.

Topic: Troubleshoot client- and router-based DHCP connectivity issues

1. Examine the figure and the example configurations. Why is the DHCP Client failing to acquire IP address information?

DHCP Server fa0/0 10.1.1.0/24 **DHCP Client** fa0/0

R1 **R2**

```
R1#
R1#show running-config
Building configuration...

Current configuration : 1343 bytes
!
! Last configuration change at 08:30:24 UTC Fri Aug 26 2016
!
upgrade fpd auto
version 15.0
service timestamps debug datetime msec
service timestamps log datetime msec
no service password-encryption
!
hostname R1
!
boot-start-marker
boot-end-marker
!
!
no aaa new-model
!
!
!
ip source-route
no ip icmp rate-limit unreachable
ip cef
!
!
ip dhcp excluded-address 10.1.1.1 10.1.1.10
!
```

```
ip dhcp pool ICND1EXAMCRAM
   network 10.1.2.0 255.255.255.0
   default-router 10.1.1.1
   dns-server 8.8.8.8 4.2.2.2
   option 150 ip 10.10.10.2
!
!
no ip domain lookup
no ipv6 cef
!
multilink bundle-name authenticated
!
!
!
redundancy
!
!
ip tcp synwait-time 5
!
!
!
interface FastEthernet0/0
 ip address 10.1.1.1 255.255.255.0
 duplex half
!
!
interface FastEthernet1/0
 no ip address
 shutdown
 duplex auto
 speed auto
!
!
interface FastEthernet1/1
 no ip address
 shutdown
 duplex auto
 speed auto
!
!
ip forward-protocol nd
no ip http server
no ip http secure-server
!
!
!
no cdp log mismatch duplex
!
```

```
!
!
control-plane
!
!
!
mgcp fax t38 ecm
mgcp behavior g729-variants static-pt
!
!
!
gatekeeper
 shutdown
!
!
line con 0
 exec-timeout 0 0
 privilege level 15
 logging synchronous
 stopbits 1
line aux 0
 exec-timeout 0 0
 privilege level 15
 logging synchronous
 stopbits 1
line vty 0 4
 login
!
ntp master 2
end

R1#


R2#
R2#show running-config
Building configuration...

Current configuration : 1165 bytes
!
! Last configuration change at 08:49:30 UTC Fri Aug 26 2016
!
upgrade fpd auto
version 15.0
service timestamps debug datetime msec
service timestamps log datetime msec
no service password-encryption
!
```

```
hostname R2
!
boot-start-marker
boot-end-marker
!
!
no aaa new-model
!
!
!
ip source-route
no ip icmp rate-limit unreachable
ip cef
!
!
!
no ip domain lookup
no ipv6 cef
!
multilink bundle-name authenticated
!
!
!
redundancy
!
!
ip tcp synwait-time 5
!
!
!
interface FastEthernet0/0
 ip address dhcp
 duplex half
!
!
interface FastEthernet1/0
 no ip address
 shutdown
 duplex auto
 speed auto
!
!
interface FastEthernet1/1
 no ip address
 shutdown
```

```
 duplex auto
 speed auto
!
!
ip forward-protocol nd
no ip http server
no ip http secure-server
!
!
!
no cdp log mismatch duplex
!
!
!
control-plane
!
!
!
mgcp fax t38 ecm
mgcp behavior g729-variants static-pt
!
!
!
gatekeeper
 shutdown
!
!
line con 0
 exec-timeout 0 0
 privilege level 15
 logging synchronous
 stopbits 1
line aux 0
 exec-timeout 0 0
 privilege level 15
 logging synchronous
 stopbits 1
line vty 0 4
 login
!
ntp server 10.1.1.1
end

 R2#
```

2. What command allows you to easily verify the lease assignments from the DHCP Server?

_____

Answers

1. The subnet for lease assignments is incorrect for the DHCP Server Pool; the correct subnet should be configured with **network 10.1.1.0 /24.**

2. show ip dhcp server bindings

There can be many issues to prevent proper DHCP connectivity. Here are just some issues you should be aware of:

▶ Errors in router or switch configurations

▶ DHCP Server configuration

▶ DHCP Relay Agent configuration

▶ DHCP Server scope configuration or software defect

ExamAlert

Although there are many possible errors in your ICND1 exam, watch out for server or client misconfigurations because these will be the most common.

The four steps of the DHCP process that must succeed for a successful DHCP lease are as follow:

1. Discover (from the client)

2. Offer (from the server)

3. Request (from the client)

4. Acknowledgement (from the server)

Remember the key verification commands for DHCP. **show ip dhcp binding** is critical for the server, and **show ip interface brief** works well for the client.

CramQuiz

1. Examine the configuration shown. DHCP clients in the 10.1.1.0/24 subnet are
    complaining that they cannot access Internet resources. What is the most
    likely issue?

```
R1#show running-config
Building configuration...

Current configuration : 1312 bytes
!
! Last configuration change at 08:57:10 UTC Fri Aug 26 2016
!
upgrade fpd auto
version 15.0
service timestamps debug datetime msec
service timestamps log datetime msec
no service password-encryption
!
hostname R1
!
boot-start-marker
boot-end-marker
!
!
no aaa new-model
!
!
!
ip source-route
no ip icmp rate-limit unreachable
ip cef
!
!
ip dhcp excluded-address 10.1.1.1 10.1.1.10
!
ip dhcp pool ICND1EXAMCRAM
   network 10.1.1.0 255.255.255.0
   default-router 10.1.1.1
   option 150 ip 10.10.10.2
!
!
no ip domain lookup
no ipv6 cef
!
multilink bundle-name authenticated
!
!
redundancy
!
!
```

```
ip tcp synwait-time 5
!
!
!
interface FastEthernet0/0
 ip address 10.1.1.1 255.255.255.0
 duplex half
!
!
interface FastEthernet1/0
 no ip address
 shutdown
 duplex auto
 speed auto
!
!
interface FastEthernet1/1
 no ip address
 shutdown
 duplex auto
 speed auto
!
!
ip forward-protocol nd
no ip http server
no ip http secure-server
!
!
!
no cdp log mismatch duplex
!
!
!
control-plane
!
!
!
mgcp fax t38 ecm
mgcp behavior g729-variants static-pt
!
!
!
gatekeeper
 shutdown
!
!
line con 0
 exec-timeout 0 0
```

```
    privilege level 15
    logging synchronous
    stopbits 1
line aux 0
    exec-timeout 0 0
    privilege level 15
    logging synchronous
    stopbits 1
line vty 0 4
    login
    !
ntp master 2
end

R1#
```

- O **A.** The scope of addresses in the pool is not correct.
- O **B.** There is no lease duration set.
- O **C.** There are no DNS servers assigned to the clients.
- O **D.** The default gateway is incorrect.

2. What is the second step of the four steps of the DHCP process?

- O **A.** Acknowledgement
- O **B.** Request
- O **C.** Offer
- O **D.** Discover

CramQuiz Answers

1. **C** is correct. This configuration is missing the assignment of DNS servers for the clients.

2. **C** is correct. The second step of the process is an Offer.

Topic: Configure and verify NTP operating in client/server mode

CramSaver

1. What command configures your Cisco router to be an authoritative reference clock source with a stratum of 3?

   _____

2. What command confirms your NTP client to server relationship in tabular form?

   _____

Answers

1. **ntp master 3**
2. **show ntp association**

It is critical for many reasons to have accurate time on your network devices. In order to automate this process, we have Network Time Protocol (NTP). NTP uses the transport layer protocol of UDP and port 123. NTP uses the concept of a **stratum** value to gauge the accuracy of time values carried by NTP. A lower stratum value is preferred. You can think of stratum like a hop count from the authoritative reference clock source. Ideally, this time source should be an atomic clock, or at least linked to one. Example 10.9 configures R1 to act as a reference clock source for the network. Notice we select a stratum value of 2.

EXAMPLE 10.9 **Configuring the NTP Master in the Network**

```
R1#configure terminal
Enter configuration commands, one per line.   End with CNTL/Z.
R1(config)#ntp master ?
  <1-15>  Stratum number
  <cr>

R1(config)#ntp master 2
R1(config)#end
R1#
```

ExamAlert

The default stratum value for the **ntp master** command is **8**.

How do you configure an **NTP Client** to receive the correct time from your **NTP Server** (Master)? The command is **ntp server** *ntp-server-ip-address*. Example 10.10 shows this configuration.

EXAMPLE 10.10   **Configuring the NTP Client**

```
R2#
R2#configure terminal
Enter configuration commands, one per line.   End with CNTL/Z.
R2(config)#ntp server 10.1.1.1
R2(config)#end
R2#
```

ExamAlert

There are several other NTP configuration options available (such as broadcasting NTP updates), but these are not required at the ICND1 level.

There are two key commands for verifying NTP. Example 10.11 shows one of them, the **show ntp associations** command. Note how this allows us to easily verify our association with the configured NTP Master device.

EXAMPLE 10.11   **Verifying the NTP Configuration with Show NTP Associations**

```
R2#show ntp associations

  address          ref clock       st   when   poll reach  delay
offset    disp
 *~10.1.1.1        127.127.1.1      2      0      64   275 19.784
40129.7 68.951
 * sys.peer, # selected, + candidate, - outlyer, x falseticker, ~
configured
R2#
```

Example 10.12 shows another frequently used verification option of **show ntp status**.

EXAMPLE 10.12 **Using Show NTP Status to Verify NTP**

```
R2#show ntp status
Clock is synchronized, stratum 3, reference clock is 10.1.1.1
nominal freq is 250.0000 Hz, actual freq is 250.0000 Hz, precision is
2**24
reference time is DA5E7147.56CADEA7 (19:54:31.339 EST Thu Feb 4 2016)
clock offset is 0.0986 msec, root delay is 2.46 msec
root dispersion is 16.27 msec, peer dispersion is 5.33 msec
loopfilter state is 'CTRL' (Normal Controlled Loop), drift is
0.000000009 s/s
system poll interval is 64, last update was 530 sec ago.
R2#
```

CramQuiz

1. What is a stratum in NTP?

   ○ **A.** A measure of the proximity to the reference clock

   ○ **B.** A key value for authentication

   ○ **C.** The number of total NTP clients

   ○ **D.** A measurement for the number of NTP queries per minute

2. What command configures your Cisco device as an NTP client of 10.1.1.1?

   ○ **A. ntp client 10.1.1.1**

   ○ **B. ntp master 10.1.1.1**

   ○ **C. ntp server 10.1.1.1**

   ○ **D. ntp 10.1.1.1**

CramQuiz Answers

1. **A** is correct. The stratum indicates how far a device is from the reference clock.

2. **C** is correct. The **ntp server** command is used on a client.

Review Questions

1. What type of record is used in DNS for a mail server?

   ○ **A.** SOA

   ○ **B.** MX

   ○ **C.** NS

   ○ **D.** CNAME

2. Your junior network admin issues a ping to www.cisco.com, which is successful. What has been verified?

   ○ **A.** WINS

   ○ **B.** DNS

   ○ **C.** NTP

   ○ **D.** DHCP

3. What command sets the DHCP scope to 192.168.1.0/24?

   ○ **A. scope 192.168.1.0 /24**

   ○ **B. network 192.168.1.0 255.255.255.0**

   ○ **C. subnet 192.168.1.0 /24**

   ○ **D. addresses 192.168.1.0**

4. What command configures a DHCP Relay Agent?

   ○ **A. ip dhcp relay-agent**

   ○ **B. ip dhcp relay-agent enable**

   ○ **C. ip forward-address**

   ○ **D. ip helper-address**

Answers to Review Questions

1. **B** is correct. The MX record is for a mail server.

2. **B** is correct. DNS name resolution has been verified.

3. **B** is correct. The **network** command sets this.

4. **D** is correct. To configure a Relay Agent, we use **ip helper-address**.

Additional Resources

Configuring a Cisco Router as a DHCP Server—http://www.ajsnet working.com/dhcp-server

Network Time Protocol—http://www.ajsnetworking.com/network-time-protocol

CHAPTER 11

Infrastructure Services: ACLs

This chapter covers the following official ICND1 100-105 exam topics:

▶ Configure, verify, and troubleshoot IPv4 standard numbered and named access list for routed interfaces

This chapter ensures you are ready for the above topic from the Infrastructure Services section of the overall exam blueprint from Cisco Systems. Remember, this is just a section of the Infrastructure Services area. Chapters Ten and Twelve also exist in this grouping. These other chapters deal with DNS, DHCP, NTP, and NAT.

Essential Terms and Components

    ▶ **Access Control List (ACL)**

    ▶ **Numbered ACL**

    ▶ **Named ACL**

    ▶ **Standard ACL**

    ▶ **Extended ACL**

    ▶ **Access Control Entry (ACE)**

    ▶ **Wildcard (Inverse) Mask**

    ▶ **Implicit Deny All**

Topic: Configure, verify, and troubleshoot IPv4 standard numbered and named access list for routed interfaces

CramSaver

If you can correctly answer these CramSaver questions, save time by skimming the ExamAlerts in this chapter and then completing the CramQuiz at the end of each section and the Review Questions at the end of the chapter. If you are in doubt at all—read EVERYTHING in this chapter!

1. What are the ranges possible for a standard numbered Access Control List (ACL)?

   _____

2. What is implied at the end of every ACL?

   _____

3. Examine the topology and configurations shown. Why is R3 unable to ping R1? Be as specific as possible.

   _____

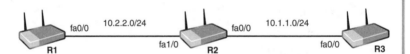

```
R1#show running-config
Building configuration...

Current configuration : 1296 bytes
!
! Last configuration change at 17:41:54 UTC Fri Aug 26 2016
!
upgrade fpd auto
version 15.0
service timestamps debug datetime msec
service timestamps log datetime msec
no service password-encryption
!
hostname R1
!
```

```
boot-start-marker
boot-end-marker
!
!
no aaa new-model
!
!
!
ip source-route
no ip icmp rate-limit unreachable
ip cef
!
!
!
no ip domain lookup
no ipv6 cef
!
multilink bundle-name authenticated
!
!
!
redundancy
!
!
ip tcp synwait-time 5
!
!
!
interface FastEthernet0/0
 ip address 10.2.2.1 255.255.255.0
 ip access-group 1 in
 duplex half
!
!
interface FastEthernet1/0
 no ip address
 shutdown
 duplex auto
 speed auto
!
!
interface FastEthernet1/1
 no ip address
 shutdown
 duplex auto
 speed auto
!
!
```

```
router rip
 version 2
 network 10.0.0.0
 no auto-summary
!
ip forward-protocol nd
no ip http server
no ip http secure-server
!
!
!
access-list 1 permit 10.1.1.0 0.0.0.255
access-list 1 permit 10.2.2.0 0.0.0.255
no cdp log mismatch duplex
!
!
!
control-plane
!
!
!
mgcp fax t38 ecm
mgcp behavior g729-variants static-pt
!
!
!
gatekeeper
 shutdown
!
!
line con 0
 exec-timeout 0 0
 privilege level 15
 logging synchronous
 stopbits 1
line aux 0
 exec-timeout 0 0
 privilege level 15
 logging synchronous
 stopbits 1
line vty 0 4
 login
!
end

R1#
```

```
R2#show running-config
Building configuration...

Current configuration : 1281 bytes
!
! Last configuration change at 17:28:48 UTC Fri Aug 26 2016
!
upgrade fpd auto
version 15.0
service timestamps debug datetime msec
service timestamps log datetime msec
no service password-encryption
!
hostname R2
!
boot-start-marker
boot-end-marker
!
!
no aaa new-model
!
!
!
ip source-route
no ip icmp rate-limit unreachable
ip cef
!
!
!
no ip domain lookup
no ipv6 cef
!
multilink bundle-name authenticated
!
!
!
redundancy
!
!
ip tcp synwait-time 5
!
!
!
interface FastEthernet0/0
 ip address 10.1.1.2 255.255.255.0
 ip access-group 1 in
!
!
```

```
interface FastEthernet1/0
 ip address 10.2.2.2 255.255.255.0
 duplex auto
 speed auto
!
!
interface FastEthernet1/1
 no ip address
 shutdown
 duplex auto
 speed auto
!
!
router rip
 version 2
 network 10.0.0.0
 no auto-summary
!
ip forward-protocol nd
no ip http server
no ip http secure-server
!
!
!
access-list 1 deny    10.1.1.3
access-list 1 permit any
no cdp log mismatch duplex
!
!
!
control-plane
!
!
!
mgcp fax t38 ecm
mgcp behavior g729-variants static-pt
!
!
!
gatekeeper
 shutdown
!
!
line con 0
 exec-timeout 0 0
 privilege level 15
 logging synchronous
 stopbits 1
```

```
line aux 0
 exec-timeout 0 0
 privilege level 15
 logging synchronous
 stopbits 1
line vty 0 4
 login
!
end

R2#

R3#show running-config
Building configuration...

Current configuration : 1194 bytes
!
! Last configuration change at 17:25:44 UTC Fri Aug 26 2016
!
upgrade fpd auto
version 15.0
service timestamps debug datetime msec
service timestamps log datetime msec
no service password-encryption
!
hostname R3
!
boot-start-marker
boot-end-marker
!
!
no aaa new-model
!
!
!
ip source-route
no ip icmp rate-limit unreachable
ip cef
!
!
!
no ip domain lookup
no ipv6 cef
!
multilink bundle-name authenticated
!
!
!
```

```
redundancy
!
!
ip tcp synwait-time 5
!
!
!
interface FastEthernet0/0
 ip address 10.1.1.3 255.255.255.0
 duplex half
!
!
interface FastEthernet1/0
 no ip address
 shutdown
 duplex auto
 speed auto
!
!
interface FastEthernet1/1
 no ip address
 shutdown
 duplex auto
 speed auto
!
!
router rip
 version 2
 network 10.0.0.0
 no auto-summary
!
ip forward-protocol nd
no ip http server
no ip http secure-server
!
!
!
no cdp log mismatch duplex
!
!
!
control-plane
!
!
!
mgcp fax t38 ecm
mgcp behavior g729-variants static-pt
!
!
!
```

```
     gatekeeper
      shutdown
     !
     !
     line con 0
      exec-timeout 0 0
      privilege level 15
      logging synchronous
      stopbits 1
     line aux 0
      exec-timeout 0 0
      privilege level 15
      logging synchronous
      stopbits 1
     line vty 0 4
      login
     !
     end

     R3#
```

Answers

1. Numbered standard ACLs use 1–99 or 1300–1999.
2. An implicit deny all ends an ACL.
3. There is an inbound ACL on R2 Fa0/0 explicitly denying R3 source traffic.

Access Control Lists (ACLs) are powerful methods of identifying traffic. In this chapter, a specific usage is explored per the exam objectives. Here we examine applying ACLs as a security filter to a routed interface.

There are also two types of ACLs you need to be aware of—standard and extended. Here is a breakdown of each:

▶ **Standard ACLs**: These lists can be named or numbered to identify them. If numbered, you must use 1–99 or 1300–1999. Standard ACLs can only match on source IP address. As a result of this very limited matching criteria, Cisco recommends that, in general, standard ACLs be placed as close to the destination of your filtering as possible.

▶ **Extended ACLs**: These lists can be named or numbered. If numbered, you must use 100–199 or 2000–2699. Extended ACLs can match on a wide variety of criteria including source and destination IP addresses, protocol type, and specific port numbers. Because there is such a vast amount of filtering criteria, Cisco recommends that, in general, extended ACLs be placed as close to the source of traffic as possible.

> ### ExamAlert
>
> Although our exam objective in this topic specifies standard ACLs used as filters on routed interfaces, you might be tempted to skip the preceding information about Extended ACLs. Please do not do this because you are expected to know this general information about them.

Entries in an ACL are called **Access Control Entries (ACEs).** The order of these entries is critical because packets are processed in a top-down fashion, with a match resulting in the processing of the permit or deny action and the termination of further processing. Example 11.1 shows an example of the construction of a standard ACL that would function as desired if properly assigned to a routed interface (this configuration is demonstrated later in this topic).

EXAMPLE 11.1   **Building a Standard Numbered ACL**

```
R1#
R1#configure terminal
Enter configuration commands, one per line.  End with CNTL/Z.
R1(config)#access-list 1 deny host 172.16.1.100
R1(config)#access-list 1 deny host 172.16.1.101
R1(config)#access-list 1 permit 172.16.1.0 0.0.0.255
R1(config)#end
R1#
```

Notice in this example the more specific entries are located above the more general entry so the desired effect of blocking these two specific host source addresses would be achieved by the filter. Notice also the use of a **wildcard (or inverse) mask** in an Access Control List. This functions as the opposite of a subnet mask. So, in the entry **access-list 1 permit 172.16.1.0 0.0.0.255**, we match on the 172.16.1 portion of the address, and any value can appear in the fourth octet.

Notice the use of the keyword **host** in Example 11.1. This eliminates the requirement of the longer entry of **access-list 1 deny 172.16.1.100 0.0.0.0.** Another shortcut keyword we use frequently is **any**. This eliminates entries such as **access-list 1 permit 0.0.0.0 255.255.255.255.** Typing **access-list 1 permit any** is much easier.

> **ExamAlert**
>
> All ACLs end with an implicit deny all entry that we cannot see. For this reason, when using an ACL as a routing interface filter, you must have at least one permit state-ment. Notice also in our Example 11.1 that traffic sourced from 10.10.10.1 would be denied as a result of this implicit deny all entry that truly ends this ACL. Many times you will see an entry of **deny any log** to end an ACL. This is because the administra-tor wants to track how many packets are reaching the end of the ACL!

Verifying the creation of your ACL is simple, as you can see in Example 11.2.

EXAMPLE 11.2 **Verifying a Standard ACL**

```
R1#
R1#show access-list
Standard IP access list 1
    20 deny    172.16.1.101
    10 deny    172.16.1.100
    30 permit 172.16.1.0, wildcard bits 0.0.0.255
R1#
```

> **Note**
>
> You see from this output that the Cisco router numbers the entries for you even though you did not specify line numbers during the ACL's construction. This makes it easier for you to potentially edit an ACL layer. The order shown in the output (with line 20 first, followed by line 10, and then 30), doesn't negatively impact the results of the ACL created. The IOS adds an entry by descending order of the IP address.

Example 11.3 demonstrates the configuration of a standard **named ACL**.

EXAMPLE 11.3 **Configuring a Standard Named ACL**

```
R1#
R1#configure terminal
Enter configuration commands, one per line.  End with CNTL/Z.
R1(config)#ip access-list standard MYACL
R1(config-std-nacl)#deny 10.0.0.0 0.255.255.255
R1(config-std-nacl)#permit 192.168.1.0 0.0.0.255
R1(config-std-nacl)#end
R1#
```

Well-constructed ACLs are wonderful, but they're useless as routing filters unless they are applied to an interface. Example 11.4 demonstrates the assignment of numbered and named ACLs to interfaces.

EXAMPLE 11.4 **Assigning Standard ACLs to Interfaces**

```
R1#
R1#configure terminal
Enter configuration commands, one per line.  End with CNTL/Z.
R1(config)#interface fa0/0
R1(config-if)#ip access-group 1 in
R1(config-if)#exit
R1(config)#interface fa1/0
R1(config-if)#ip access-group MYACL out
R1(config-if)#end
R1#
```

As shown in Example 11.4, the **ip access-group** command is key regardless of named or **numbered ACL** assignment. Notice how you must assign the filter for inbound traffic or for outbound traffic on the interface.

> **ExamAlert**
>
> By default, an ACL does not impact traffic generated by the local router. So even if you place an ACL outbound on an interface, by default this ACL does not impact local router generated packets such as routing protocol updates. Remember, it is other devices' routed traffic, moving through a router, that ACLs can filter.

Is there a verification command you can use to see if an ACL is applied to an interface (other than **show run** of course)? There is, as demonstrated in Example 11.5.

EXAMPLE 11.5 **Verifying ACL Interface Assignment**

```
R1#
R1#show ip interface fa0/0
FastEthernet0/0 is up, line protocol is up
  Internet address is 10.1.1.1/24
  Broadcast address is 255.255.255.255
  Address determined by setup command
  MTU is 1500 bytes
  Helper address is not set
  Directed broadcast forwarding is disabled
  Outgoing access list is not set
  Inbound  access list is 1
```

```
Proxy ARP is enabled
Local Proxy ARP is disabled
...
```

Here, the **show ip interface** command verifies that there is an inbound access list set numbered 1. Notice that I trimmed the rest of this command's output for brevity's sake.

Although Example 11.5 is great, what about verifying that an ACL is actually filtering traffic? This is possible with the **show access-list** command after the filter is assigned to an interface. Example 11.6 shows this. Notice the matches are being logged.

EXAMPLE 11.6 **The Use of show access-list for Verification of Matches**

```
R2#
R2#show access-list
Standard IP access list 1
    10 deny   10.1.1.3 (10 matches)
    20 permit any
R2#
```

ExamAlert

Even though this topic deals with the specific case of standard ACLs used as filters, you actually revisit ACLs in Chapter 12, "Infrastructure Services: NAT," which deals with NAT. In the case of NAT, ACLs are used to simply identify traffic, not filter it. As stated earlier, there are many additional uses for ACLs that are not covered in ICND1.

CramQuiz

1. What ACL correctly denies traffic from 192.168.1.1 while permitting all other traffic?

   ○ **A.** **access-list 1 permit 192.168.1.1 0.0.0.0**

   access-list 1 permit 192.168.1.0 0.0.0.255

   ○ **B.** **access-list 1 deny 192.168.1.1 0.0.0.0**

   access-list 1 permit 192.168.1.0 0.0.0.255

   ○ **C.** **access-list 1 deny 192.168.1.1 0.0.0.0**

   access-list 1 permit any

   ○ **D.** **access-list 1 permit any**

   access-list 1 deny host 192.168.1.1

2. What command would you use to see the matches that an ACL would have?

   ○ **A. show ip interface**

   ○ **B. show ip interface brief**

   ○ **C. show access-list hits**

   ○ **D. show access-list**

3. What keyword can you use in place of a four-zeroes wildcard mask?

   ○ **A. device**

   ○ **B. system**

   ○ **C. host**

   ○ **D. entry**

CramQuiz Answers

1. **C** is correct. This entry denies 192.168.1.1 and then permits all other traffic.

2. **D** is correct. The **show access-list** command displays matches once the filter is in place.

3. **C** is correct. The **host** keyword allows you to eliminate the wildcard mask entry of 0.0.0.0.

Review Questions

1. What field can a standard ACL filter on?

   ○ **A.** Protocol

   ○ **B.** Port

   ○ **C.** Dest IP

   ○ **D.** Source IP

2. Why might **deny any log** appear at the end of an ACL?

   ○ **A.** To track traffic matching no previous ACL entries.

   ○ **B.** It is required as the final ACE.

   ○ **C.** To ensure fast packet processing.

   ○ **D.** To send emails to security team members.

3. What command assigns a standard ACL for filtering on an interface?

   ○ **A.** ip access-group in|out

   ○ **B.** ip-access bind in|out

   ○ **C.** ip-access assign in|out

   ○ **D.** ip-access track in|out

4. What command permits you to verify that an access list is assigned to an interface in a specific direction?

   ○ **A.** show access-list

   ○ **B.** show access-list interface

   ○ **C.** show ip interface

   ○ **D.** show access-list assign

Answers to Review Questions

1. **D** is correct. A standard ACL can filter on source IP address only.

2. **A** is correct. This is matched before the implicit deny all. An explicit deny all is used for tracking entries that match the end of the list.

3. **A** is correct. The **ip access-group** command is what we use.

4. **C** is correct. We use **show ip interface** to verify assignment of ACLs to interfaces.

Additional Resources

Configuring Standard ACLs on Cisco Routers—http://www.ajsnet working.com/standard-acls

Configuring IP Access Lists—http://bit.ly/2d2SC3P

CHAPTER 12

Infrastructure Services: NAT

This chapter ensures you are ready for the above topic from the Infrastructure Services section of the overall exam blueprint from Cisco Systems. Remember, this is just a section of the Infrastructure Services area. Chapters Ten and Eleven also exist in this grouping. These other chapters deal with DNS, DHCP, NTP, and standard ACLs.

Essential Terms and Components

▶ **NAT**

▶ **Source NAT**

▶ **Static NAT**

▶ **Unidirectional NAT**

▶ **Bidirectional NAT**

▶ **NAT Pools**

▶ **Dynamic NAT**

▶ **PAT**

Topic: Configure, verify, and troubleshoot inside source NAT

CramSaver

If you can correctly answer these CramSaver questions, save time by skimming the ExamAlerts in this chapter and then completing the CramQuiz at the end of each section and the Review Questions at the end of the chapter. If you are in doubt at all—read EVERYTHING in this chapter!

1. What is a classic example of using unidirectional (or one-way) NAT?

    _____

2. With inside source dynamic NAT, what is the pool used for?

    _____

3. Examine the topology and configuration shown. 10.2.2.0/24 is the inside segment. 10.1.1.0/24 is the outside segment. R1 (10.2.2.1) cannot trigger a NAT translation on R2 when pinging R3. The configuration should also permit PAT if needed. What are four issues with the NAT configuration on R2?

    _____

    _____

    _____

    _____

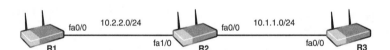

```
R2#
R2#show running-config
Building configuration...
Current configuration : 1406 bytes
!
! Last configuration change at 16:00:36 UTC Sun Aug 28 2016
!
upgrade fpd auto
version 15.0
service timestamps debug datetime msec
service timestamps log datetime msec
no service password-encryption
```

```
!
hostname R2
!
boot-start-marker
boot-end-marker
!
!
no aaa new-model
!
!
!
ip source-route
no ip icmp rate-limit unreachable
ip cef
!
!
!
no ip domain lookup
no ipv6 cef
!
multilink bundle-name authenticated
!
!
!
redundancy
!
!
ip tcp synwait-time 5
!
!
!
interface FastEthernet0/0
 ip address 10.1.1.2 255.255.255.0
 ip nat inside
 ip virtual-reassembly
!
!
interface FastEthernet1/0
 ip address 10.2.2.2 255.255.255.0
 ip nat outside
 ip virtual-reassembly
!
!
interface FastEthernet1/1
 no ip address
 shutdown
 duplex auto
```

```
  speed auto
 !
 !
router rip
 version 2
 network 10.0.0.0
 no auto-summary
 !
ip forward-protocol nd
no ip http server
no ip http secure-server
 !
 !
ip nat inside source list 10 interface FastEthernet0/0
 !
access-list 1 permit host 10.2.1.1
access-list 1 permit host 10.2.1.100
no cdp log mismatch duplex
 !
 !
 !
control-plane
 !
 !
 !
mgcp fax t38 ecm
mgcp behavior g729-variants static-pt
 !
 !
 !
gatekeeper
 shutdown
 !
 !
line con 0
 exec-timeout 0 0
 privilege level 15
 logging synchronous
 stopbits 1
line aux 0
 exec-timeout 0 0
 privilege level 15
```

```
    logging synchronous
    stopbits 1
   line vty 0 4
    login
    !
   end

   R2#
```

Answers

1. To allow a large number of private IP addresses on an inside network to dynamically access public IP addresses on an outside Internet network

2. The NAT pool is used to specify the outside addresses to be used in the translation.

3. The **inside** and **outside** interface commands are reversed.

   The access-list is specifying the incorrect internal device.

   The NAT statement is missing the **overload** keyword.

   The incorrect list is specified in the NAT statement.

The RFC 1918 address space we reviewed in our chapter on IPv4 addressing helped delay the depletion of IPv4 address space. But private addresses that aren't routable over the Internet necessitated another change—the introduction of **Network Address Translation (NAT)**. A private IP address must be converted to a public IP address for proper communication on the public Internet. Specifically, the inside source IP address must be converted to one that is valid on the Internet.

Although there are many different variations of NAT, notice the ICND1 exam focus is very specific to inside **source NAT**. Again, we are taking inside devices and translating the source IP address for public communication.

ExamAlert

Unidirectional NAT, or *one-way NAT,* permits devices on the inside to initiate connections and communicate to devices on the public network, but devices on the public network cannot initiate a connection with a device on the inside network. If you configure NAT to permit connections initiated from the Internet as well, you are configuring **bidirectional NAT**.

The first approach we examine is static NAT. Static NAT has you configure a manual mapping from an inside address to an outside address. Figure 12.1 shows the topology used in our example. This bidirectional translation would allow initial connections to be sourced by devices on the inside or outside.

FIGURE 12.1 **The NAT Topology**

The configuration begins by identifying the inside network. We will pretend that 10.2.2.0/24 is the inside segment. Next, identify the outside segment. We will pretend the outside network is the 10.1.1.0/24 segment. We are now ready for the configuration shown in Example 12.1.

EXAMPLE 12.1 **Configuring Inside Source Static NAT**

```
R2#
R2#configure terminal
Enter configuration commands, one per line.   End with CNTL/Z.
R2(config)#interface fa1/0
R2(config-if)#ip nat inside
R2(config-if)#exit
R2(config)#interface fa0/0
R2(config-if)#ip nat outside
R2(config-if)#exit
R2(config)#ip nat inside source static 10.2.2.1 10.1.1.100
R2(config)#end
R2#
```

Notice the commands this configuration requires:

▶ **ip nat inside**: Configures the inside interface for the device and enables NAT there.

▶ **ip nat outside**: Configures the outside interface for the device and enables NAT there.

▶ **ip nat inside source static 10.2.2.1 10.1.1.100**: Provides the static instructions for translation;10.2.2.1 is the source IP address from the inside for translation and 10.1.1.100 is the new source IP address for the translated packet.

For verification of this configuration, we **ping** from R1 (10.2.2.1) to R3 (10.1.1.3). This creates the translation on R2 that we can view with **show ip nat translation**. Example 12.2 demonstrates this.

EXAMPLE 12.2 **Verifying the Inside Source Static NAT Configuration**

```
R1#
R1#ping 10.1.1.3
Type escape sequence to abort.
Sending 5, 100-byte ICMP Echos to 10.1.1.3, timeout is 2 seconds:
!!!!!
Success rate is 100 percent (5/5), round-trip min/avg/max =
200/221/244 ms
R1#


R2#
R2#show ip nat translation
Pro Inside global       Inside local       Outside local       Outside
global
icmp 10.1.1.100:0       10.2.2.1:0         10.1.1.3:0
10.1.1.3:0
--- 10.1.1.100          10.2.2.1           ---                 ---
R2#
```

Notice from the output that our exact NAT instructions were followed. The inside local source address of 10.2.2.1 was translated to global address of 10.1.1.100.

> **Note**
>
> It is interesting that the ping succeeds because there is actually no device with the IP address of 10.1.1.100 in our topology! This is because when the traffic returns to R2 (the NAT device), it sees that 10.1.1.100 actually maps to the device at 10.2.2.1, and it replaces the original source address.

In addition to static NAT, there is also **dynamic NAT**. Example 12.3 demonstrates this new configuration on R2 from our topology in Figure 12.1. Note that all previous NAT commands have been removed from R2 before Example 12.3 is presented.

> **ExamAlert**
>
> A simple method to check for NAT configurations in a running configuration is to use **show run | include nat**. This returns any commands, including the term NAT.

EXAMPLE 12.3 **Configuring Inside Source Dynamic NAT**

```
R2#
R2#configure terminal
Enter configuration commands, one per line.  End with CNTL/Z.
R2(config)#interface fa1/0
R2(config-if)#ip nat inside
R2(config-if)#exit
R2(config)#interface fa0/0
R2(config-if)#ip nat outside
R2(config-if)#exit
R2(config)#access-list 1 permit 10.2.2.1
R2(config)#access-list 1 permit 10.2.2.100
R2(config)#ip nat pool MYNATPOOL 10.1.1.100 10.1.1.101 netmask
255.255.255.0
R2(config)#ip nat inside source list 1 pool MYNATPOOL
R2(config)#end
R2#
```

Notice what is unique about this configuration:

▶ **access-list 1**: This access list defines the inside source addresses that can be translated.

▶ **ip nat pool MYNATPOOL**: This **NAT pool** defines the starting IP address and ending IP address that R2 will translate the source address to.

▶ **ip nat inside source list 1 pool MYNATPOOL**: The NAT instructions that tie the access list to the NAT pool we created.

Verification is identical to the output shown in Example 12.2. A ping from R1 to R3 results in the translation of 10.2.2.1 to 10.1.1.100. Of course, this time there is a dynamic element to the translation. For example, if there were another host on the inside network at 10.2.2.100, and if this device were to communicate first across the R2 device, it could translate to 10.1.1.100, which is the first address in the pool.

But even inside source dynamic NAT is not the most popular form of NAT! What is, then? It is **Port Address Translation (PAT)**, also sometimes termed NAT overloading.

Here we permit many inside devices to all communicate on the outside network using the single public address on the outside address. The IP address on the outside interface can even be used. How is this possible? It is a result of unique port numbers being assigned to each translation entry. Example 12.4 shows this configuration based on the topology shown in Figure 12.1. Again, all previous NAT configurations have been removed.

EXAMPLE 12.4 **The Inside Source Dynamic PAT Configuration**

```
R2#
R2#configure terminal
Enter configuration commands, one per line.  End with CNTL/Z.
R2(config)#interface fa1/0
R2(config-if)#ip nat inside
R2(config-if)#exit
R2(config)#interface fa0/0
R2(config-if)#ip nat outside
R2(config-if)#exit
R2(config)#access-list 1 permit 10.2.2.1
R2(config)#access-list 1 permit 10.2.2.100
R2(config)#ip nat inside source list 1 interface fa0/0 overload
R2(config)#end
R2#
```

What is unique about this configuration from inside source dynamic NAT? Not much, really. Notice the **ip nat inside source** command now specifies the **interface fa0/0 overload**. This instructs NAT to translate source addresses to the IP address that is on the physical outside interface, and allows it to be used over and over again for the source address translation of multiple inside devices.

Example 12.5 shows the verification. The IP address on R2 fa0/0 is 10.1.1.2.

EXAMPLE 12.5 **Verifying the Inside Source Dynamic PAT Configuration**

```
R1#
R1#ping 10.1.1.3
Type escape sequence to abort.
Sending 5, 100-byte ICMP Echos to 10.1.1.3, timeout is 2 seconds:
!!!!!
Success rate is 100 percent (5/5), round-trip min/avg/max =
200/221/244 ms
R1#
R2#
R2#show ip nat translation
Pro Inside global      Inside local      Outside local      Outside
global
icmp 10.1.1.2:2        10.2.2.1:2        10.1.1.3:2
10.1.1.3:2
R2#
```

Notice this time R1's source address of 10.2.2.1 is translated to 10.1.1.2. Other inside hosts could translate to this same address. This type of configuration and functionality is the one that helped hold off the public IPv4 address shortage. This is also the common configuration of NAT in home networks today.

What about NAT troubleshooting? What can commonly go wrong? Here are some important things to watch out for:

▶ Failure to assign NAT inside and outside interfaces

▶ Incorrect assignment of inside versus outside interfaces

▶ With static inside NAT, ensure the **ip nat inside source static** command lists the inside and outside addresses in the correct order

▶ With dynamic NAT, ensure the IP address is constructed properly and matches the appropriate source addresses for translation

▶ With PAT, ensure the **overload** keyword is not forgotten

CramQuiz

1. What was the main motivation for NAT?

   ○ **A.** To increase the number of possible IP v4 addresses

   ○ **B.** To allow the RFC1918 private address space to communicate on the internet

   ○ **C.** To secure private networks from outside attackers

   ○ **D.** To increase the visibility possible with Internet connections

2. What is the purpose of static NAT?

   ○ **A.** To ensure the destination IP address remains unchanged during translation

   ○ **B.** To translate a single specific inside address to a single specific outside address

   ○ **C.** To ensure that multiple inside addresses can translate to a single outside address

   ○ **D.** To pull inside addresses for translation from a pool of addresses

3. What is another name commonly used for unidirectional NAT?

   ○ **A.** One-way

   ○ **B.** Synchronous

   ○ **C.** Dual

   ○ **D.** Static

CramQuiz Answers

1. **B** is correct. The primary motivation for NAT was to allow RFC1918 addresses to be used on inside network while providing them with Internet connectivity.

2. **B** is correct. Inside source static NAT translates a single specific inside address to a single specific outside address.

3. **A** is correct. One-way and unidirectional NAT terms are used interchangeably.

Review Questions

1. What command identifies the inside NAT interface?

   ○ **A. nat inside**

   ○ **B. nat ip inside**

   ○ **C. inside**

   ○ **D. ip nat inside**

2. What command allows you to view the NAT translations at the CLI?

   ○ **A. show ip nat translation**

   ○ **B. show nat usage**

   ○ **C. show nat statistics**

   ○ **D. show nat all**

3. Examine the following command: **ip nat inside source list 1 interface fa0/0 overload** What is the inside global address for translation?

   ○ **A.** The IP address on interface fa0/0

   ○ **B.** The virtual address on interface fa0/0

   ○ **C.** The address in access-list 1

   ○ **D.** The address in the NAT pool named **interface**

Answers to Review Questions

1. **D** is correct. The **ip nat inside** command identifies the inside NAT interface.

2. **A** is correct. The **show ip nat translation** command allows you to see all of the translations currently on the device.

3. **A** is correct. The IP address on the interface specified here is the inside global address.

Additional Resources

What is N.A.T. (Network Address Translation)—
http://www.ajsnetworking.com/nat-2

NAT FAQ—http://bit.ly/2cIyHaF

PART V

Infrastructure Maintenance

This part of the text deals with one of five overall sections you must master for the ICND1 exam. There are five chapters total that make up Part 5. These five chapters, taken as a whole, represent 14 percent of the exam questions you face in your exam. This means that the Infrastructure Maintenance area is the fifth most important section of the five overall sections that you deal with on your testing day! Remember, even though relatively few questions are from this section, those questions could still easily make the difference between a passing and failing mark on this test.

These chapters prove critical for your success in production networks. If you cannot successfully manage your complex infrastructure, you are in for big trouble, especially when things inevitably go wrong.

CHAPTER 13

Infrastructure Maintenance: Syslog and Device Management

This chapter covers the following official ICND1 100-105 exam topics:

▶ Configure and verify device-monitoring using syslog

▶ Configure and verify device management

This chapter ensures you are ready for the above topic from the Infrastructure Maintenance section of the overall exam blueprint from Cisco Systems. Remember, this is just a section of the Infrastructure Maintenance area. Chapters Fourteen through Seventeen also exist in this grouping. These other chapters deal with initial device configuration, device hardening, device maintenance, and IOS troubleshooting tools.

Essential Terms and Components

▶ **Syslog**

▶ **Backup Configurations**

▶ **Restoring Configurations**

▶ **Running Configuration**

▶ **Startup Configuration**

▶ **Cisco Discovery Protocol (CDP)**

▶ **Link Layer Discovery Protocol (LLDP)**

▶ **Licensing**

▶ **Logging**

▶ **Timezones**

▶ **Loopbacks**

Topic: Configure and verify device-monitoring using syslog

Network devices typically engage in system logging capabilities commonly termed **syslog**. Cisco devices are no exception. System logging allows devices to report on their health and important events that might be transpiring. In Cisco networking, we commonly call syslog simply **logging**. These messages can vary from the mundane to the critical. Example 13.1 shows the default logging configuration on a Cisco router.

EXAMPLE 13.1 **The Default Logging Configuration of a Cisco Router**

```
R2#
R2#show logging
Syslog logging: enabled (0 messages dropped, 2 messages rate-limited,
                0 flushes, 0 overruns, xml disabled, filtering
disabled)

No Active Message Discriminator.

No Inactive Message Discriminator.

    Console logging: level debugging, 16 messages logged, xml
disabled,
```

```
                         filtering disabled
      Monitor logging: level debugging, 0 messages logged, xml disabled,
                         filtering disabled
      Buffer logging:  level debugging, 16 messages logged, xml
disabled,
                         filtering disabled
      Logging Exception size (8192 bytes)
      Count and timestamp logging messages: disabled
      Persistent logging: disabled

No active filter modules.

ESM: 0 messages dropped

      Trap logging: level informational, 19 message lines logged

Log Buffer (8192 bytes):

*Aug 28 15:54:56.991: %LINEPROTO-5-UPDOWN: Line protocol on Interface
VoIP-Null0, changed state to up
*Aug 28 15:54:56.995: %LINK-3-UPDOWN: Interface FastEthernet0/0,
changed state to up
*Aug 28 15:54:57.003: %LINK-3-UPDOWN: Interface FastEthernet1/0,
changed state to up
...
```

Notice that by default logging is enabled and that syslog messages are being stored in a buffer for later analysis. Specifically, notice there are three forms of logging that are enabled by default: console logging, monitor logging, and buffer logging. Console logging is why you see console syslog messages like this **%LINK-3-UPDOWN: Interface FastEthernet0/0, changed state to up** when you are configuring the device. Monitor logging allows remote users connected via SSH or Telnet to see log messages as well, whereas buffer logging permits viewing messages at a later date, as Example 13.1 demonstrates.

ExamAlert

Just because a feature like console logging is typically on by default, never make assumptions in the exam environment. Console logging might be disabled in a running configuration.

Notice from the last example log message shown in Example 13.1 that these messages follow a specific format with fields that include:

▶ **A timestamp**: *Aug 28 15:54:57.003:

▶ **A facility that generated the message**: %LINK

▶ **A severity level**: 3

▶ **A mnemonic for the message**: UPDOWN

▶ **A description**: Interface FastEthernet1/0, changed state to up

The possible severity levels for messages are very important, especially because you can filter the logging to the various destinations using these levels. Table 13.1 shows the syslog severity levels used by most Cisco equipment.

TABLE 13.1 **The Syslog Severity Levels**

Keyword	Level	Description
Emergency	0	System unusable, or unstable
Alert	1	Immediate action needed
Critical	2	Critical event
Error	3	Error event
Warning	4	Warning event
Notification	5	Normal but significant condition
Informational	6	Informational messages only
Debug	7	Debugging messages, requested by administrator

Example 13.2 shows a sample configuration involving logging on a Cisco router.

EXAMPLE 13.2 **A Sample Syslog Configuration on a Cisco Router**

```
R2#
R2#configure terminal
Enter configuration commands, one per line.  End with CNTL/Z.
R2(config)#logging console 6
R2(config)#logging buffered 4
R2(config)#logging monitor warning
R2(config)#logging host 10.1.1.3
R2(config)#end
R2#
```

The commands in Example 13.2 have the following effect:

▶ **logging console 6**: Console syslog messages are limited to levels 6 through 0.

▶ **logging buffered 4**: Buffer syslog messages are limited to levels 4 through 0.

▶ **logging monitor warning**: Monitor syslog messages are limited to levels 4 through 0; note that you can use the keyword or level number.

▶ **logging host 10.1.1.3**: Send syslog messages to a recipient network device for storage; this device is located at 10.1.1.3.

CramQuiz

1. What level of logging is for an event where an immediate action is required?

   ○ **A.** Emergency

   ○ **B.** Critical

   ○ **C.** Error

   ○ **D.** Alert

2. How can you configure your Cisco router so that level 5 through 0 log messages appear in a buffer?

   ○ **A. logging buffered 5**

   ○ **B. logging level 5 buffer**

   ○ **C. logging 5 buffer**

   ○ **D. logging buffered 5 0**

CramQuiz Answers

1. **D** is correct. The Alert level of syslog in Cisco is to indicate an immediate action is required.

2. **A** is correct. The command logging buffered 5 allows you to filter the buffer for log messages at a level of 0 through 5.

Topic: Configure and verify device management

CramSaver

1. What is the "backup" configuration called on a Cisco router?

   _____

2. How do you globally disable CDP on a Cisco router?

   _____

3. What is a virtual/logical interface called that is often used for management purposes?

   _____

Answers

1. startup-config
2. **no cdp run**
3. A loopback interface

Remember that the **running configuration** is the device configuration currently in use and stored in RAM on the device. In order to view this configuration, we issue the command **show running-config**, as in Example 13.3.

EXAMPLE 13.3 **Viewing the Running Configuration on a Cisco Router**

```
R2#
R2#show running-config
Building configuration...

Current configuration : 1474 bytes
!
! Last configuration change at 17:43:08
!
upgrade fpd auto
version 15.4
service timestamps debug datetime msec
service timestamps log datetime msec
```

```
no service password-encryption
!
hostname R2
!
...
```

In order to backup this configuration to nonvolatile RAM (NVRAM) on the device, use the command **copy running-config startup-config**, as shown in Example 13.4.

EXAMPLE 13.4 **Backing Up a Router Configuration to NVRAM**

```
R3#
R3#copy running-config startup-config
Destination filename [startup-config]?
Overwrite the previous NVRAM configuration?[confirm]
Building configuration...
[OK]
R3#
```

> **ExamAlert**
>
> Remember which configuration you need to view when in a lab-based exam environment. For example, **show running-config** shows the configuration currently in use, but **show startup-config** shows the saved configuration that would be in place after a reboot of the device.

Cisco Discovery Protocol (CDP) is a built-in device management protocol that is at times a convenience and other times a requirement. For example, if you are configuring a network that you did not install and for which you have no documentation, you might need to discover the IP address of a directly connected neighboring device. CDP makes this possible, as shown in Example 13.5.

EXAMPLE 13.5 **Obtaining Information About a Neighboring Cisco Device**

```
R3#
R3#show cdp neighbor detail
-------------------------
Device ID: R2
Entry address(es):
  IP address: 10.1.1.2
Platform: Cisco 7206VXR,  Capabilities: Router
Interface: FastEthernet0/0,  Port ID (outgoing port): FastEthernet0/0
Holdtime : 157 sec
Version :
```

```
Cisco IOS Software, 7200 Software (C7200-ADVIPSERVICESK9-M), Version
15.8(1)M, RELEASE SOFTWARE (fc2)
Technical Support: http://www.cisco.com/techsupport
Copyright (c) 1986-2009 by Cisco Systems, Inc.
Compiled Wed 30-Sep-16 07:48 by prod_rel_team
advertisement version: 2
Duplex: half
R3#
```

CDP is required in some situations. For example, Cisco IP Phones use it in order to discover and communicate key capabilities with a switch.

At times, administrators do not want CDP running on an interface or even an entire device. Example 13.6 shows how to disable CDP on an interface or an entire device. The output also allows you to confirm CDP is disabled.

EXAMPLE 13.6 **Disabling CDP on an Interface or an Entire Device**

```
R3#
R3#configure terminal
Enter configuration commands, one per line.  End with CNTL/Z.
R3(config)#interface fa0/0
R3(config-if)#no cdp enable
R3(config-if)#exit
R3(config)#no cdp run
R3(config)#end
R3#
R3#show cdp
% CDP is not enabled
R3#
```

Link Layer Discovery Protocol (LLDP) is an open standard protocol that provides similar functionality as Cisco proprietary CDP. The command structure and usage is nearly identical to that of CDP as follows:

► **show lldp neighbors**: See a table of LLDP neighbors

► **show lldp entry R2**: Obtain detailed information about a specific neighbor, including IP information

► **lldp run**: Enables LLDP globally on the router

► **lldp transmit** and **lldp receive**: Interface level commands for controlling the sending and receiving of LLDP information

Another aspect of device management you should be familiar with is **licensing**. Be aware of the following commands:

▶ **show license**: This command allows you to view the license state on your device; information shown includes type of license and time period left.

▶ **show license feature**: This command allows you to see the specific features you might be permitted to use and whether they are enabled.

▶ **show version**: This command provides information about the license in use on the device.

▶ **license install**: This command allows you to install a license on a Cisco device.

ExamAlert

Remember, when logging appears in your ICND1 exam blueprint, it can mean two things: the syslog configurations from earlier in this chapter or the specific aspect of logging termed debugging (logging level 7). We review debugging in a later chapter.

From a device management perspective, you should also review how to set the time and **timezone** on a device. This is simple, as shown in Example 13.7. Remember, you might engage in this configuration so that you can see the correct local time on the device when using NTP.

EXAMPLE 13.7   **Setting the Clock and Time Settings on a Cisco Device**

```
R3#
R3#configure terminal
Enter configuration commands, one per line.  End with CNTL/Z.
R3(config)#clock timezone EST -5
R3(config)#
%SYS-6-CLOCKUPDATE: System clock has been updated from 18:19:36 UTC
Sun Aug 28 2016 to 13:19:36 EST Sun Aug 28 2016, configured from
console by console.
R3(config)#clock summer-time EDT recurring
R3(config)#
%SYS-6-CLOCKUPDATE: System clock has been updated from 13:19:52 EST
Sun Aug 28 2016 to 14:19:52 EDT Sun Aug 28 2016, configured from
console by console.
R3(config)#exit
R3#clock set 19:23:23 15 November 2018
R3#
%SYS-6-CLOCKUPDATE: System clock has been updated from 14:20:35 EDT
Sun Aug 28 2016 to 19:23:23 EST Thu Nov 15 2018, configured from
console by console.
R3#show clock
19:31:49.679 EST Thu Nov 15 2018
R3#
```

The final device management component here to review is the frequent use of **loopback** interfaces on Cisco devices. Many management features need a stable interface on the device to function. A virtual interface known as a loopback interface can be created on the device. Example 13.8 demonstrates the creation and verification of three loopback interfaces.

EXAMPLE 13.8 **The Configuration and Verification of Loopback Interfaces**

```
R3#
R3#configure terminal
Enter configuration commands, one per line.  End with CNTL/Z.
R3(config)#interface loopback 0
R3(config-if)#ip address 10.3.3.3 255.255.255.0
R3(config-if)#exit
R3(config)#interface loopback 1
R3(config-if)#ip address 10.4.4.3 255.255.255.0
R3(config-if)#exit
R3(config)#interface loopback 3
R3(config-if)#ip address 10.5.5.3 255.255.255.0
R3(config-if)#end
R3#
%SYS-5-CONFIG_I: Configured from console by console
R3#show ip interface brief
Interface              IP-Address      OK? Method Status
Protocol
FastEthernet0/0        10.1.1.3        YES NVRAM  up                     up
FastEthernet1/0        unassigned      YES NVRAM  administratively down down
FastEthernet1/1        unassigned      YES NVRAM  administratively down down
Loopback0              10.3.3.3        YES manual up                     up
Loopback1              10.4.4.3        YES manual up                     up
Loopback3              10.5.5.3        YES manual up                     up
R3#R3#
```

CramQuiz

1. How do you save the running configuration?

   ○ **A. copy run star**

   ○ **B. copy star run**

   ○ **C. copy run backup**

   ○ **D. copy run wr**

2. What is an open standard protocol with features similar to CDP?

   ○ **A.** SLARP

   ○ **B.** LLDP

   ○ **C.** NTP

   ○ **D.** ARP

3. What license verification command can be used for verifying the status of certain features?

   ○ **A. show license all**

   ○ **B. show license detail**

   ○ **C. show license feature**

   ○ **D. show license full**

4. What command sets the time zone on a Cisco router to EST?

   ○ **A. timezone EST**

   ○ **B. timezone EST -5**

   ○ **C. clock timezone EST -5**

   ○ **D. set clock timezone EST -5**

CramQuiz Answers

1. **A** is correct. The command **copy run star** copies the running configuration in RAM to NVRAM.

2. **B** is correct. LLDP has a similar function to CDP and is an open standard.

3. **C** is correct. The **show license feature** command provides this information.

4. **C** is correct. Use **clock timezone EST -5** in order to set the time zone to EST.

Review Questions

1. What command allows you to see the logging configuration currently in place on your Cisco router?

   - ○ **A. show syslog**
   - ○ **B. show logging**
   - ○ **C. show logging enable**
   - ○ **D. show logging detail**

2. Given the syslog message of ***Nov 16 00:23:23.003: %SYS-6-CLOCKUPDATE: System clock has been updated from 14:20:35 EDT Sun Aug 28 2017 to 19:23:23 EST Thu Nov 15 2018**, configured from console by console what is the facility that produced the message?

   - ○ **A. % 6-CLOCKUPDATE**
   - ○ **B. CLOCKUPDATE**
   - ○ **C. %SYS**
   - ○ **D. 6**

3. What command permits you to send log messages to a device at 10.1.1.3?

   - ○ **A. logging 10.1.1.3**
   - ○ **B. logging trap level 2 10.1.1.3**
   - ○ **C. logging host 10.1.1.3**
   - ○ **D. logging host send 7 host 10.1.1.3**

4. What command allows you to retrieve the IP address of your neighbor?

   - ○ **A. show cdp**
   - ○ **B. show cdp neighbor**
   - ○ **C. show cdp neighbor detail**
   - ○ **D. show cdp all**

5. What two commands are used on an interface in order to ensure LLDP is functioning properly? (Choose two.)

   ○ **A. lldp transmit**

   ○ **B. lldp enable**

   ○ **C. lldp run**

   ○ **D. lldp receive**

6. What command do you use to verify your time settings on the local router?

   ○ **A. show time**

   ○ **B. show calendar**

   ○ **C. show counter**

   ○ **D. show clock**

Answers to Review Questions

1. **B** is correct. Use the simple **show logging** command to verify syslog settings.

2. **C** is correct. The facility precedes the severity level.

3. **C** is correct. Use **logging host 10.1.1.3**.

4. **C** is correct. Use the **show cdp neighbor detail** command to see the IP address information. **show cdp** and **show cdp neighbor** are also valid commands but do not provide enough details on neighbors.

5. **A** and **D** are correct. The **lldp transmit** and **lldp receive** commands permit this.

6. **D** is correct. The **show clock** command verifies your time settings.

Additional Resources

Troubleshooting and Fault Management—http://bit.ly/2buThbJ

Configuring Cisco Discovery Protocol—http://bit.ly/1TaK8s9

CHAPTER 14

Infrastructure Maintenance: Initial Device Configuration

> **This chapter covers the following official ICND1 100-105 exam topics:**
>
> ▶ Configure and verify initial device configuration

This chapter ensures you are ready for the above topic from the Infrastructure Maintenance section of the overall exam blueprint from Cisco Systems. Remember, this is just a section of the Infrastructure Maintenance area. Chapters Thirteen and Fifteen through Seventeen also exist in this grouping. These other chapters deal with syslog, device management, device hardening, device maintenance, and troubleshooting tools.

Essential Terms and Components

▶ **Initial Device Configuration**

▶ **Interfaces**

▶ **Loopbacks**

▶ **Console**

▶ **VTY (Virtual Terminal Lines)**

Topic: Configure and Verify Initial Device Configuration

CramSaver

If you can correctly answer these CramSaver questions, save time by skimming the ExamAlerts in this chapter and then completing the CramQuiz at the end of each section and the Review Questions at the end of the chapter. Notice the CramSaver is also broken down by section, so perhaps you just need to review a certain area. If you are in doubt at all—read EVERYTHING in this chapter!

1. Name at least three common factory default configurations for a Cisco router.

   _____

   _____

   _____

2. What command stops the console line timing out after inactivity?

   _____

Answers

1. Physical interfaces are shutdown

   The hostname is Router

   IPv6 routing is disabled

   Service timestamps are in place for logging

   No Telnet access is possible

2. **no exec-timeout** or **exec-timeout 0 0**

ExamAlert

Many of the initial device configuration features deal with hardening (securing) a Cisco device. These are not covered in this chapter; they're covered in the next chapter. This chapter prepares you for what you need to know for ICND1 about initial device configuration outside of these security features.

Figure 14.1 shows the topology for our **initial device configuration** in this chapter. We will configure the R1 device together from its completely factory default configuration from Cisco. Notice that initial device configuration in this chapter means the initial config that we provide above and beyond the factory default configuration from Cisco Systems.

ExamAlert

A factory default router initially offers the use of a setup script to apply an initial configuration. Declining this option results in the configuration shown in Figure 14.1. Factory defaults might vary slightly between versions of Cisco IOS Software.

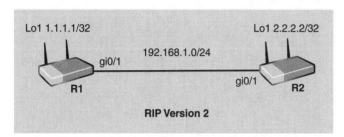

FIGURE 14.1   **The Topology for the Initial Device Configuration**

Example 14.1 provides a look at the factory default configuration from Cisco before we provide our own additions:

EXAMPLE 14.1   **The Initial Factory Default Configuration of a Cisco Router**

```
Router#show run
Building configuration...
Current configuration : 2667 bytes
!
version 15.6
service timestamps debug datetime msec
service timestamps log datetime msec
no service password-encryption
!
hostname Router
!
boot-start-marker
boot-end-marker
!
!
!
no aaa new-model
ethernet lmi ce
!
!
!
```

```
mmi polling-interval 60
no mmi auto-configure
no mmi pvc
mmi snmp-timeout 180
!
!
!
ip cef
no ipv6 cef
!
multilink bundle-name authenticated
!
!
!
redundancy
!
!
!
interface GigabitEthernet0/0
 no ip address
 shutdown
 duplex auto
 speed auto
 media-type rj45
!
interface GigabitEthernet0/1
 no ip address
 shutdown
 duplex auto
 speed auto
 media-type rj45
!
ip forward-protocol nd
!
!
no ip http server
no ip http secure-server
!
!
!
control-plane
!
!
line con 0
line aux 0
line vty 0 4
```

```
 login
 transport input none
 !
no scheduler allocate
 !
end
```

Our initial device configuration of R1 seeks to accomplish many things, including:

▶ Enable synchronous logging for the **console** port

▶ Ensure we are not timed out of the console port in this lab environment

▶ Configure the correct router hostname

▶ Establish all IP addressing shown in the diagram

▶ Establish a RIP dynamic routing relationship with R2

▶ Allow remote access from R2 using Telnet

Example 14.2 demonstrates the required initial device configuration in this case.

EXAMPLE 14.2 **The Initial Configuration of the R1 Router**

```
Router>enable
Router#configure terminal
Enter configuration commands, one per line.  End with CNTL/Z.
Router(config)#line console 0
Router(config-line)#logging synchronous
Router(config-line)#exec-timeout 0 0
Router(config-line)#exit
Router(config)#hostname R1
R1(config)#interface lo1
R1(config-if)#ip address 1.1.1.1 255.255.255.255
R1(config-if)#exit
R1(config)#interface gi0/1
R1(config-if)#ip address 192.168.1.1 255.255.255.0
R1(config-if)#no shutdown
R1(config-if)#exit
R1(config)#router rip
R1(config-router)#version 2
R1(config-router)#no auto-summary
R1(config-router)#network 192.168.1.0
R1(config-router)#network 1.0.0.0
R1(config-router)#exit
R1(config)#line vty 0 4
```

```
R1(config-line)#password cisco
R1(config-line)#login
R1(config-line)#transport input telnet
R1(config-line)#end
R1#
```

Here is a review of the commands that we use in this initial device configuration:

- **enable**: This command moves us from user mode to privileged mode; note that a key distinguishing feature is the prompt change; a > indicates user mode, whereas the # symbol indicates privileged mode.

- **configure terminal:** This command places the device in a mode where global parameters can be configured; for example, this mode allows providing the device with a unique hostname; this mode is easy to spot because the prompt includes (config); this mode is also a launching pad for many other modes; for example, interface configuration mode.

- **line console 0**: This global configuration command enters line configuration mode for the console port; the prompt is (config-line); this mode allows you to apply important parameters for the console connection to the device; many of these impact your experience with the local command line interface (CLI).

- **logging synchronous:** This command is considered a necessity by almost every administrator; this line configuration command ensures that console messages do not interrupt your entry of commands at the command line interface.

- **exex-timeout 0 0**: This line configuration command sets the inactivity timeout in minutes and seconds for the console port (in our case); while in actual production, you would want your console port to time out when inactive; in a lab environment, we love **exec-timeout 0 0** because security is not a concern.

- **exit:** This command allows you to move from the configuration mode that you are in to one level higher.

- **hostname R1**: This global configuration command sets the host name of the router.

ExamAlert

Do not expect case to be preserved with all of your Cisco hostnames. The name must also follow strict rules—it must start with a letter, end with a letter or digit, and have as interior characters only letters, digits, and hyphens. Names must be 63 characters or fewer. Creating an all numeric hostname is not recommended.

▶ **interface lo1**: This command creates a virtual interface named Loopback 1; loopback interfaces automatically achieve the status of UP/UP once an IP address is assigned.

▶ **ip address 1.1.1.1 255.255.255.255**: This interface level command assigns the IP address and subnet mask.

▶ **no shutdown:** This command enables an interface, notice that most Cisco router interfaces are in a shutdown state by default and require this command.

ExamAlert

The RIP commands shown in our configuration here are not explicitly covered because they were covered in detail Chapter 9, "Routing Fundamentals: Static and Dynamic Routing." They are shown here because most administrators consider this a key part of the initial configuration.

▶ **line vty 0 4**: This command enters the configuration mode for the first five **virtual terminal lines (vty)**; these lines allow remote connections like Telnet and SSH.

▶ **password cisco**: This line command sets the password of **cisco** for incoming Telnet connections.

▶ **login:** This line command requires a login and indicates the local password setting (**cisco**) should be checked upon Telnet login.

▶ **transport input telnet:** This line command indicates that Telnet sessions are permitted into this device.

▶ **end:** This command exits all configuration levels and returns the administrator to the privileged mode prompt.

CramQuiz

1. What command requires authentication for Telnet connections?

   - ○ **A.** local
   - ○ **B.** login
   - ○ **C.** check
   - ○ **D.** aaa-local

2. What configuration creates a loopback 10 interface and assigns the IP address 10.10.10.1/19?

   - ○ **A. interface loopback 10**

     ip address 10.10.10.1/19
   - ○ **B. interface loopback 10**

     ip address 10.10.10.1 255.255.255.0
   - ○ **C. interface loopback 10**

     ip address 10.10.10.1 255.255.248.0
   - ○ **D. interface loopback 10**

     ip address 10.10.10.1 255.255.224.0

CramQuiz Answers

1. **B** is correct. The **login** command requires authentication for Telnet connections.

2. **D** is correct. The correct mask here is 255.255.224.0. Note that prefix notation is now accepted on some Cisco devices, but for this exam, D is the best answer.

Review Questions

1. What is the default configuration of a Cisco router from the factory?

   ○ **A.** There is no default configuration—you must enter commands through a setup script.

   ○ **B.** All interfaces are assigned 192.168.1.0/24 addresses and Telnet is enabled.

   ○ **C.** Layer 3 physical interfaces are in the shutdown state.

   ○ **D.** Basic RIP routing is configured.

2. What command in line configuration mode specifically permits Telnet?

   ○ **A. transport input none**

   ○ **B. transport input**

   ○ **C. transport input telnet**

   ○ **D. transport input no ssh**

Answers to Review Questions

1. **C** is correct. Layer 3 interfaces are disabled by default on most Cisco routers.
2. **C** is correct. The **transport input telnet** command permits Telnet access.

Additional Resource

Configuration Fundamentals Configuration Guide—http://bit.ly/2c5Oy0g

CHAPTER 15

Infrastructure Maintenance: Device Hardening

This chapter covers the following official ICND1 100-105 exam topics:

▶ Configure, verify, and troubleshoot basic device hardening

This chapter ensures you are ready for the above topic from the Infrastructure Maintenance section of the overall exam blueprint from Cisco Systems. Remember, this is just a section of the Infrastructure Maintenance area. Chapters Thirteen, Fourteen, Sixteen, and Seventeen also exist in this grouping. These other chapters deal with Syslog, Device Management, Initial Configuration, Device Maintenance, and IOS Troubleshooting Tools.

Essential Terms and Components

▶ **Local Authentication**
▶ **Secure Passwords**
▶ **Device Access**
▶ **Source Addressing**
▶ **Telnet**
▶ **SSH**
▶ **Login Banners**

Topic: Configure, Verify, and Troubleshoot Basic Device Hardening

CramSaver

If you can correctly answer these CramSaver questions, save time by skimming the ExamAlerts in this chapter and then completing the CramQuiz at the end of each section and the Review Questions at the end of the chapter. Notice the CramSaver is also broken down by section, so perhaps you just need to review a certain area. If you are in doubt at all—read EVERYTHING in this chapter!

1. What single command allows you to create a local user account named **JOHNS** with an MD5 hashed password of **cisco123** and a privilege level of 15? This command should be entered as efficiently as possible.

   _____

2. What password is used for backward compatibility with very old Cisco devices?

   _____

3. What command can you use to place a weak hashing on the clear text passwords in a configuration?

   _____

4. What two parameters must be set before you generate an RSA key for SSH usage?

   _____

   _____

5. Examine the configuration that follows. Name at least seven things wrong with this configuration from a device-hardening standpoint.

```
R1#
R1#show running-config
Building configuration...

Current configuration : 1113 bytes
!
version 15.4
service timestamps debug datetime msec
service timestamps log datetime msec
no service password-encryption
!
hostname R1
```

```
!
boot-start-marker
boot-end-marker
!
enable password cisco123
!
no aaa new-model
memory-size iomem 5
no ip icmp rate-limit unreachable
ip cef
!
!
!
no ip domain lookup
!
multilink bundle-name authenticated
!
!
!
archive
 log config
  hidekeys
!
!
!
!
ip tcp synwait-time 5
!
!
!
!
interface FastEthernet0/0
 ip address 10.10.10.1 255.255.255.0
 duplex auto
 speed auto
!
interface Serial0/0
 no ip address
 shutdown
 clock rate 2000000
!
interface FastEthernet0/1
 no ip address
 shutdown
 duplex auto
 speed auto
!
interface Serial0/1
 no ip address
 shutdown
```

```
 clock rate 2000000
!
ip forward-protocol nd
!
!
no ip http server
no ip http secure-server
!
no cdp log mismatch duplex
!
!
!
control-plane
!
!
line con 0
 exec-timeout 0 0
 privilege level 15
 logging synchronous
line aux 0
 exec-timeout 0 0
 privilege level 15
 logging synchronous
line vty 0 4
 password cisco
 login
 transport input telnet
!
!
end
R1#
```

Answers

1. **username JOHNS privilege 15 secret cisco123**

2. **enable password**

3. **service password-encryption**

4. A device hostname other than router and a domain name.

5. There is no enable secret configured.

   Telnet is allowed

   There is no banner message.

   There is no service password-encryption.

   The console port never times out from inactivity.

   Simple passwords are in use.

   Privilege level 15 is granted at the console without authentication.

Your ICND1 exam is concerned with **local authentication** on your Cisco device exclusively. This means that AAA is not extensively tested at this level. We will want to ensure that local authentication can be used to enforce user accounts on the device.

We begin with Example 15.1, which demonstrates configuring a local user account for access to the device.

EXAMPLE 15.1 **Configuring Local Authentication for the Console Line**

```
R1#
R1#configure terminal
Enter configuration commands, one per line.  End with CNTL/Z.
R1(config)#aaa new-model
R1(config)#username JOHNS privilege 15 secret 1L0v3C1sc0Systems
R1(config)#line con 0
R1(config-line)#login local
R1(config-line)#end
R1#
```

The commands are as follows:

▶ **aaa new-model**: This command enables the AAA system on the router.

▶ **username JOHNS secret privilege 15 1L0v3C1sc0Systems**: This command creates a local user account with a name of **JOHNS**; the password is hashed using MD5 so it does not display as clear text in the configuration; note the **password** keyword used in place of **secret** would not accomplish this hashing; the password itself for this user is **1L0v3C1sc0Systems**. The **privilege 15** portion of the command provides that level of access for the user. The default privilege level for a user is privilege level 1.

▶ **login local**: This command requires authentication (based on the local configuration of user accounts), for a user to access this router through line console 0.

ExamAlert

Obviously, configurations of this nature are critical (misconfiguration can actually lead to device lock out), so be careful and always verify. Example 15.2 walks through our verification.

EXAMPLE 15.2 **Verifying the Local Authentication Configuration**

```
R1#
R1#exit
R1 con0 is now available
Press RETURN to get started.
! Note: pressing enter will prompt for a username and password
User Access Verification

Username: JOHNS
Password:
R1#
```

ExamAlert

When creating local user accounts, you can assign privilege levels to those accounts with the **privilege** keyword. The default privilege for local users is 1, which is commonly referred to as *user mode*.

Consideration must also be given to **secure passwords** on all of your Cisco devices. Note that in our Example 15.1 we use simple character substitution and a mix of case in order to set a fairly strong password. Your organization should set password length and complexity requirements. These are easily enforced using commands on modern Cisco Operating Systems now.

What about passwords that might appear in plain text in the configuration, however? Cisco provides the **service password-encryption** feature to help with this. Example 15.3 shows the configuration and verification of this feature.

EXAMPLE 15.3 **Configuring and Verifying the Service Password-Encryption Feature**

```
R1#
R1#configure terminal
Enter configuration commands, one per line.  End with CNTL/Z.
R1(config)#enable password ThisIsmyPassw0rd
R1(config)#line vty 0 4
R1(config-line)#password ThisIsMyT3ln3tPassword
R1(config-line)#login
R1(config-line)#end
R1#
R1#show run
Building configuration...
Current configuration : 1370 bytes
...
```

```
enable password ThisIsmyPassw0rd
!
line vty 0 4
 password ThisIsMyT3ln3tPassword
 login
 transport input telnet
!
end
R1#configure terminal
Enter configuration commands, one per line.  End with CNTL/Z.
R1(config)#service password-encryption
R1(config)#end
R1#show run
Building configuration...
Current configuration : 1413 bytes
...
service password-encryption
enable password 7 02320C52182F1C2C557E080A1600421908
!
line vty 0 4
 password 7 15260305170338093107662E1D54023300454A4F5C460A
!
end
R1#
```

The **enable password** is used for backward compatibility for very old Cisco
devices that do not support the enable secret or other MD5 hashes. Passwords
stored in clear text are a security risk. Examples include the **enable password** and passwords used on VTY and console lines. Note that the **service
password-encryption** command places a very weak level 7 Cisco proprietary
hashing on these passwords. Although this is not a strong method of protecting
them, it does at least prevent them from appearing in clear text.

ExamAlert

If you use this **service password-encryption** command and then issue **no service
password-encryption**, no future clear text passwords are protected, but your existing passwords remain in their hashed form.

Remember, the modern alternative to the **enable password** command is the
enable secret command. This protects privileged mode using a securely
hashed version of the password. If using both of these commands, the password
must be different between the two.

Another important consideration with proper device hardening is physical security (**device access**). If someone can gain physical access to your Cisco equipment, they can fairly easily reset the equipment, never mind the fact they could easily physical damage it as well.

Another important consideration for device hardening is **source addressing** specific traffic, such as management traffic. Often we source traffic from a loopback address to improve reliability, consistency, and security by allowing access only from those loopback addresses. Example 15.4 provides an example.

EXAMPLE 15.4　**Setting a Source Address for Network Communications**

```
R1#
R1#configure terminal
Enter configuration commands, one per line.  End with CNTL/Z.
R1(config)#interface loopback 1
R1(config-if)#ip address 192.168.1.1 255.255.255.0
R1(config-if)#exit
R1(config)#snmp-server source-interface traps loopback 1
R1(config)#end
R1#
```

Notice here we use the **source-interface** keyword to ensure that Simple Network Management Protocol (SNMP) traps are sent from a source address of our loopback interface.

It is interesting that Telnet exists in this section because it is an insecure protocol. We should only really use it in a lab environment because it sends information in clear text.

Example 15.5 reviews the configuration of Telnet for you. This is, of course, review since we examined it in our chapter on initial device setup. Notice this time that the **service password-encryption** command helps with security on the password, as we have seen in this chapter.

EXAMPLE 15.5　**The Configuration of Telnet**

```
R1#
R1#configure terminal
Enter configuration commands, one per line.  End with CNTL/Z.
R1(config)#line vty 0 4
R1(config-line)#password C1sc0I$Aw3some
R1(config-line)#login
R1(config-line)#transport input telnet
R1(config-line)#exit
R1(config)#service password-encryption
```

```
R1(config)#end
R1#
*Mar  1 00:01:34.131: %SYS-5-CONFIG_I: Configured from console by
console
R1#
```

> **ExamAlert**
>
> All of our configuration examples have shown manipulation of the default VTY 0 4
> lines. Remember, other lines are available depending on your exact device. This
> enables you to provide alternate configurations to different lines. Specifying **line vty
> 5 10**, for example, applies a specific configuration to VTY lines 5 through 10. Most
> Cisco switches have VTY lines 0–15 by default, so if you are configuring security on
> VTY lines, apply it to all of them, not just the first five lines.

Since Telnet is insecure, there must be a secure remote access protocol
alternative . . . and there is—it is Secure Shell (**SSH**). Example 15.6 shows
the SSH configuration.

EXAMPLE 15.6 **The Configuration of SSH**

```
R2#
R2#configure terminal
Enter configuration commands, one per line.  End with CNTL/Z.
R2(config)#ip domain-name lab.cbtnuggets.com
R2(config)#crypto key generate rsa
The name for the keys will be: R2.lab.cbtnuggets.com
Choose the size of the key modulus in the range of 360 to 2048 for your
  General Purpose Keys. Choosing a key modulus greater than 512 may take
  a few minutes.
How many bits in the modulus [512]: 768
% Generating 768 bit RSA keys, keys will be non-exportable...[OK]
R2(config)#
%SSH-5-ENABLED: SSH has been enabled
R2(config)#ip ssh version 2
R2(config)#line vty 0 4
R2(config-line)#transport input ssh
R2(config-line)#end
R2#
%SYS-5-CONFIG_I: Configured from console by console
R2#
```

These configuration commands are as follows:

▶ **ip domain-name lab.cbtnuggets.com**: The setting of a domain name on the device is required for the generation of the RSA key used for the SSH security; note that a hostname configuration is also required, but this is not shown here because it has been done (R2).

▶ **crypto key generate rsa**: This command triggers the generation of the RSA key for security; notice that you must specify how many bits are in the modulus; this controls the strength of the security where more is better; **768** is used here in order to later specify SSH version 2 because at least 768 is required.

▶ **ip ssh version 2**: This command specifies that version 2 of SSH should be used.

▶ **transport input ssh**: This command locks down the VTY lines to the use of SSH and excludes the use of other protocols such as Telnet.

ExamAlert

Take note that you can configure multiple protocols with the **transport input** command. For example, **transport input ssh telnet** specifies that SSH or Telnet may be used. It is not ideal for security because Telnet is never considered acceptable regarding security owing to the fact that it sends and receives information in plain text.

Another aspect of device hardening is the configuration of a **login banner**. This is a text message displayed to users when they log in to the device. It appears just before the username and password prompt. The typical use of this banner is to provide a legal disclaimer that access is restricted. Example 15.7 shows the configuration and verification of a login banner. Note that because your author is not an attorney, be sure to check with your own lawyer regarding the exact language of your banner!

EXAMPLE 15.7 The Configuration and Verification of a Login Banner Message

```
R2#
R2#configure terminal
Enter configuration commands, one per line.  End with CNTL/Z.
R2(config)#banner login #
Enter TEXT message.  End with the character '#'.
This router is for the exclusive use of ACME.INC employees.
```

```
Any other use is strictly prohibited.
Violators will be prosecuted to the full extent of the law.#
R2(config)#exit
R2#exit

R2 con0 is now available

Press RETURN to get started.

This router is for the exclusive use of ACME.INC employees.
Any other use is strictly prohibited.
Violators will be prosecuted to the full extent of the law.
User Access Verification

Username: JOHNS
Password:
R2#
```

Notice how simple the configuration is. The **banner login #** command gets the job done. Notice the **#** symbol is a character chosen by the administrator, and when used again in the configuration of the banner—it triggers the end of the banner text. This allows you to do carriage returns and even ASCII art, should you desire. The character or symbol used as part of the banner message doesn't have to be the "#" character.

ExamAlert

The login banner is only one type of banner possible on the Cisco device. For example, the **banner motd** command configures a Message of the Day Banner. This MOTD banner is displayed to all terminals connected and is useful for sending messages that affect all users (such as impending system shutdowns). When a user connects to the router, the MOTD banner appears.

CramQuiz

1. What is wrong with the command **username JOHNS password cisco123?**
   (Choose two.)

   ○ **A.** The password is in clear text if **service password-encryption** is not
   in use.

   ○ **B.** The **username** command must be separate from the password
   assignment.

   ○ **C.** The password is too simple.

   ○ **D.** The privilege level must be set.

2. What command dictates the use of AAA on a Cisco device?

   ○ **A. aaa enable**

   ○ **B. aaa run**

   ○ **C. aaa authentication**

   ○ **D. aaa new-model**

3. What command under the VTY lines allows the checking of a local password?

   ○ **A. check-password**

   ○ **B. enable**

   ○ **C. login local**

   ○ **D. test**

4. What is the effect of the command **transport input ssh telnet?**

   ○ **A.** SSH is used instead of Telnet

   ○ **B.** Telnet is used instead of SSH

   ○ **C.** Telnet and SSH are restricted

   ○ **D.** SSH and Telnet are allowed

5. What is true about banner messages on Cisco routers? (Choose two.)

   ○ **A.** You must always use a # symbol to indicate the end of the banner.

   ○ **B.** There are various types of banner messages that appear at different
   times or conditions.

   ○ **C.** You can use ASCII art in them.

   ○ **D.** They typically are not used for legal warnings.

CramQuiz Answers

1. **A** and **C** are correct. The password here will be in clear text and the password that is selected is much too simple.

2. **D** is correct. The **aaa new-model** command enables the use of AAA on the device.

3. **C** is correct. The **login local** command requires authentication using the local configuration. The command **no login** on a VTY line (when **aaa new-model** is not enabled globally) disables password checking and results in open access

4. **D** is correct. **tranport input ssh telnet** permits Telnet and SSH.

5. **B** and **C** are correct. There are various types of banner messages used for different purposes. They can contain carriage returns and even ASCII art.

Review Questions

1. What is an alternative to using local authentication on a Cisco router?

   ○ **A.** Centralized AAA

   ○ **B.** A remote Telnet database

   ○ **C.** SNMP for authentication

   ○ **D.** FTP for authentication

2. What happens if you issue the command—**no service password-encryption**?

   ○ **A.** Hashed passwords are reversed.

   ○ **B.** The device no longer hashes future passwords.

   ○ **C.** The device removes all hashed passwords.

   ○ **D.** This command is not valid.

3. Why might you set the source interface in traffic? (Choose two.)

   ○ **A.** In order to increase reliability

   ○ **B.** In order to enhance processing speed

   ○ **C.** In order to enhance security

   ○ **D.** In order to eliminate the use of send buffers

4. What command do you use to create the RSA key for SSH?

   ○ **A.** **crypto key ssh create**

   ○ **B.** **crypto key generate ssh**

   ○ **C.** **crypto key ssh**

   ○ **D.** **crypto key generate rsa**

Answers to Review Questions

1. **A** is correct. The most common and most powerful configuration for authentication is to centralize this with AAA.

2. **B** is correct. This command has no effect on passwords that have already been hashed on the device. No future passwords created will be hashed.

3. **A** and **C** are correct. Source address control is often used for enhanced reliability and or security.

4. **D** is correct. This command creates the keying material needed for SSH security.

Additional Resources

Setting Up SSH on a Cisco IPv6 Router—
http://www.ajsnetworking.com/setting-ssh-ipv6

Managing Connections Menus and System Banners—http://bit.ly/
2bU7wGL

CHAPTER 16

Infrastructure Maintenance: Device Maintenance

This chapter covers the following official ICND1 100-105 exam topics:

▶ Perform device maintenance

This chapter ensures you are ready for the above topic from the Infrastructure Maintenance section of the overall exam blueprint from Cisco Systems. Remember, this is just a section of the Infrastructure Maintenance area. Chapters Thirteen, Fourteen, Fifteen, and Seventeen also exist in this grouping. These other chapters deal with Syslog, Device Management, Initial Configuration, Device Hardening, and IOS Troubleshooting Tools.

Essential Terms and Components

▶ IOS upgrade

▶ IOS Recovery

▶ password recovery

▶ SCP

▶ FTP

▶ TFTP

▶ MD5 Verify

▶ File System Management

Topic: Perform Device Maintenance

CramSaver

If you can correctly answer these CramSaver questions, save time by skimming the ExamAlerts in this chapter and then completing the CramQuiz at the end of each section and the Review Questions at the end of the chapter. Notice the CramSaver is also broken down by section, so perhaps you just need to review a certain area. If you are in doubt at all—read EVERYTHING in this chapter!

1. What command would you use to transfer an IOS image from a TFTP server to a local device's Flash memory?

   _____

2. What step begins the typical password recovery process for a router?

   _____

3. What transport protocol does TFTP use?

   _____

4. What process can you use on a router to check the integrity of the IOS upgrade image?

   _____

Answers

1. **copy tftp flash**
2. Boot the router into ROMMON
3. UDP
4. MD5 Verify

Inevitably you are going to want an **IOS upgrade** to experience new features, or perhaps to fix issues with your current IOS. Here is an overview of how this process works:

1. Obtain your new IOS. You typically accomplish this using a browser and going to Cisco.com. Make note of the MD5 hash that Cisco provides. Later in this chapter, we review how you can confirm the integrity of your new ISO using this hash value.

2. Place this new IOS in a location that is accessible to the device that you want to upgrade. Common examples would be a TFTP server, FTP server, or even a USB stick for insertion into a USB capable Cisco device.

3. Use the **copy** command to move the new IOS to the file system on your Cisco device. We review the file systems later in this chapter.

Example 16.1 demonstrates the use of the **copy** command. In this example, we copy the new IOS from a TFTP server on the network to the local Flash system of the device.

EXAMPLE 16.1 **Using the copy Command to Upgrade your IOS**

```
R2#
R2# copy tftp flash
Address or name of remote host [ ]? 10.10.10.100
Source filename [ ]? c2900-universalk9-mz.SPA.152-4.M1.bin
Destination filename [c2900-universalk9-mz.SPA.152-4.M1.bin ]?
Accessing tftp://10.10.10.100/c2900-universalk9-mz.SPA.152-4.M1.bin ...
Loading c2900-universalk9-mz.SPA.152-4.M1.bin from 2.2.2.1 (via
GigabitEthernet0/2): !!!!!!!!!!!!!!!!!!!!!!!!!!!!!!!!!!!!!!!!!!!!!!!!!!!!!!!
!!!!!!!!!!!!!!!!!!!!!!!!!!!!!!!!!!!!!!!!!!!!!!!!!!!!!!!!!!!!!!!!!!!!!!!!!!!!!
!!!!!!!!!!!!!!!!!!!!!!!

!!!!!!!!!!!!!!!!!!!!!!!!!!!!!!!!!!!!!!!!!!!!!!!!!!!!!!!!!!!!!!!!!!!!!!!!!!!!!
!!!!!!!!!!!!!!!!!!!!!!!!!!!!!!!!!!!!!!!!!!!!!!!!!!!!!!!!!!!!!!!!!!!!!!!!!!!!!
!!!!!!!!!!!!!!
[OK - 97794040 bytes]

97794040 bytes copied in 187.876 secs (396555 bytes/sec)
R2#
```

How can you verify this copy operation was a success? It is simple—**show flash**. Example 16.2 demonstrates an example of the **show flash** command.

EXAMPLE 16.2 **Using the show flash Command**

```
R2#
R2# show flash
-#- --length-- -----date/time------ path 1
84193476 Jul 21 2015 13:38:06 +00:00 c2900-universalk9-mz.SPA.151-1.
  M1.bin
3        3000320 Jul 10 2015 00:05:44 +00:00 cpexpress.tar
4           1038 Jul 10 2015 00:05:52 +00:00 home.shtml
5         122880 Jul 10 2015 00:06:02 +00:00 home.tar
6        1697952 Jul 10 2015 00:06:16 +00:00 securedesktop-ios-3.1.1.
  45-k9.pkg
7         415956 Jul 10 2015 00:06:28 +00:00 sslclient-win-1.1.4.176.pkg
```

```
8          1153 Aug 16 2015 18:20:56 +00:00 wo-lic-1
9       97794040 Oct 10 2017 21:06:38 +00:00 c2900-universalk9-mz.
SPA.152-4.M1.bin
49238016 bytes available (207249408 bytes used)
R2#
```

It is very typical for network administrators today to keep that downloaded copy of the new IOS on that accessible TFTP server. Why? **IOS recovery** of course! Should issues arise with the local router or switch copy of the IOS, you will still have a copy of the IOS on the TFTP server if needed in the future.

> **ExamAlert**
>
> There are many options for transfer of the IOS image to your local device. For the exam, you should understand the fundamentals of TFTP, FTP, and SCP. We detail these protocols for you later in this chapter.

What about forgetting the enable secret for your device? Or perhaps you purchase used equipment for lab practice and the passwords are in place, completely unknown to you? Thankfully, there is a **password recovery** process on most Cisco devices. To be fair, it is not really password recovery, it is password reset. Also, keep in mind this requires physical access to the device. This assists us in being more secure against attacks from remote users.

> **ExamAlert**
>
> Password recovery procedures vary from Cisco device to Cisco device. For the ICND1 exam, obviously be familiar with the typical procedure covered here. The Additional Resources section of this chapter provides a master document link for specific devices.

Here is the password recovery process:

1. Boot the device into ROMMON mode; this is accomplished with a break key during boot, or the removal of Flash memory.

2. The configuration register of the device is then set to ignore the startup-config file (a common configuration register setting for this is 0x2142); a sample ROMMON command for this is **confreg 0x2142**. There are other methods for setting this within ROMMON, depending on the device.

3. Reboot the router, which is now ignoring the startup-config.

4. Enter privileged mode.

5. If the previous startup-config is desired, issue the command **copy startup-config running-config.**

6. Change the **enable secret** password to your own new one.

7. Set the configuration register back with **config-reg 0x2102.**

8. Copy the running-config to the startup-config with **copy running-config startup-config.**

Secure Copy Protocol (SCP), as its name implies, is a secure method of moving configuration files or IOS images through the network. SCP uses Secure Shell (SSH) for data transfer and uses authentication and encryption. This ensures the authenticity and confidentiality of the information in transit. SCP runs over TCP port 22 by default.

File Transfer Protocol (FTP) is an insecure method for moving files or IOS images through the network. FTP may run in active or passive mode, which determines how the data connection is established. In both cases, the client creates a TCP control connection to the FTP server command port at TCP 21.

Trivial File Transfer Protocol (TFTP) is an insecure method for moving files or IOS images through the network. Unlike FTP, it is lighter weight and uses UDP port 69.

As mentioned earlier in this section, it is important that you verify images that you download from Cisco have not been tampered with. A simple way to do this is using **MD5 Verify.** Technically, when you use this feature, you ensure the integrity of the image. Integrity checks verify that the original image is the image you acquired. Example 16.3 demonstrates the use of the **verify /md5** command.

EXAMPLE 16.3 **Using the Verify MD5 Feature**

```
R1# verify /md5 flash0:c2900-universalk9-mz.SPA.154-3.M3.bin
a79e325e6c498b70829d4db0afba2011
...................................................................
...................................................................
...................................
.....MD5 of flash0:c2900-universalk9-mz.SPA.154-3.M3.bin Done!
Verified (flash0:c2900-universalk9-mz.SPA.154-3.M3.bin)
=a79e325e6c498b70829d4db0afba2011
```

Notice this command has you specify your IOS image and the MD5 hash you acquired from Cisco. Here we see the match of the hash value and successful integrity checking!

Throughout this text in various spots, we have actually been dealing with the last topic in this section—**File System Management**. This is actually another area on Cisco devices where technologies can vary from device to device, therefore possibilities abound. With that said, there are command examples that you should fully understand as follows:

- ▶ **copy running-config startup-config**: Here we take the configuration running in RAM and "back it up" to the NVRAM; when rebooted, a Cisco device clears the RAM and loads it with the NVRAM configuration.

- ▶ **copy startup-config usbflash1:copy_config**: This command demonstrates how the **copy** command could also be used to make a backup of your startup-config and place this for safekeeping on a USB device; note here that **copy_config** is the name we provide for this USB-stored version.

ExamAlert

Although the copy functionality has been with us for a long time in Cisco networking, there are more modern methods you should be aware of. For example, there is an **archive** command that provides you with the ability to automate the archiving of configuration files on set intervals. There is also the **configure replace** command that allows the enactment of a new running-config without a reload of the device. Note this could work well when used in conjunction with the **archive** command to restore a previous version of the device's configuration.

CramQuiz

1. What command can you use to verify the contents of Flash on your device?

   ○ **A. show flash**

   ○ **B. show memory**

   ○ **C. show usb**

   ○ **D. show nvram**

2. What value do you change to have a router ignore its own startup-config on boot?

   ○ **A.** flash-boot

   ○ **B.** system.ini

   ○ **C.** configuration register

   ○ **D.** boot.ini

3. Which transfer option is secure?

   ○ **A.** TFTP

   ○ **B.** FTP

   ○ **C.** Telnet

   ○ **D.** SCP

4. What command would you use in order to perform an integrity check of an upgrade IOS?

   ○ **A. config verify**

   ○ **B. config check**

   ○ **C. ios check**

   ○ **D. verify /md5**

CramQuiz Answers

1. **A** is correct. The **show flash** command allows you to view the contents of Flash.

2. **C** is correct. The configuration register value controls this, among other router behaviors.

3. **D** is correct. The Secure Copy Protocol uses SSH and is secure.

4. **D** is correct. The **verify /md5** command provides a valuable integrity check.

Review Questions

1. What command can transfer a file from your local device to a USB device?

   ○ **A. transfer**

   ○ **B. move**

   ○ **C. dirsync**

   ○ **D. copy**

2. Where might you typically store a downloaded IOS upgrade image from the Cisco Systems website for future deployment to your local router?

   ○ **A.** DNS

   ○ **B.** A TFTP server

   ○ **C.** A DHCP server

   ○ **D.** An SNMP server

3. From what mode do you initially configure the configuration register value during password recovery?

   ○ **A.** Global Confi

   ○ **B.** ROMMON

   ○ **C.** TFTP

   ○ **D.** Interface Config

4. What command can periodically backup your running-configuration to an external location?

   ○ **A. replace**

   ○ **B. backup**

   ○ **C. archive**

   ○ **D. store**

Answers to Review Questions

1. **D** is correct. The **copy** command does this transfer.

2. **B** is correct. Images are often copied to a TFTP server for deployment to devices.

3. **B** is correct. You initially set the configuration register to ignore the startup-config from ROMMON mode.

4. **C** is correct. You can use the **archive** command to automate the periodic archiving of a configuration.

Additional Resources

Password Recovery on a Cisco Router—
http://www.ajsnetworking.com/password-recovery

Password Recovery Procedures—http://bit.ly/2cAQuim

CHAPTER 17

Infrastructure Maintenance: IOS Troubleshooting Tools

> **This chapter covers the following official ICND1 100-105 exam topics:**
>
> ▶ Use Cisco IOS tools to troubleshoot and resolve problems

This chapter ensures you are ready for the above topic from the Infrastructure Maintenance section of the overall exam blueprint from Cisco Systems. Remember, this is just a section of the Infrastructure Maintenance area. Chapters Thirteen through Sixteen also exist in this grouping. These other chapters deal with Syslog, Device Management, Initial Configuration, Device Hardening, and Device Maintenance.

Essential Terms and Components

▶ IOS Tools

▶ ping

▶ traceroute

▶ extended options

▶ terminal monitor

▶ log events

Topic: Use Cisco IOS tools to troubleshoot and resolve problems

CramSaver

If you can correctly answer these CramSaver questions, save time by skimming the ExamAlerts in this chapter and then completing the CramQuiz at the end of each section and the Review Questions at the end of the chapter. Notice the CramSaver is also broken down by section, so perhaps you just need to review a certain area. If you are in doubt at all—read EVERYTHING in this chapter!

1. What protocol does ping use in its operation?

   _____

2. How many packets are sent by the ping command on a Cisco router by default?

   _____

3. What is the default IP source address for ping packets?

   _____

4. What does DF stand for in an extended ping?

   _____

5. If there is a timeout experienced for a Traceroute probe, what character is displayed?

   _____

6. What is the default maximum TTL for a Traceroute probe?

   _____

7. What is the command to see debug messages at the CLI while you are using Telnet to access a remote router?

   _____

8. What command disables all debugging on a Cisco router?

   _____

Answers

1. ICMP
2. 5
3. The exit interface of the device sending the Ping
4. Don't Fragment
5. *
6. 30
7. **terminal monitor**
8. **undebug all**

There are many powerful **IOS tools** you can use to successfully troubleshoot problems with your Cisco devices. Fortunately, the ICND1 exam focuses on just a handful of the main methods we use today.

First, let's examine **ping**. You can use it to verify and troubleshoot connectivity in your networks.

Figure 17.1 shows the topology we use in this section. The last octet of the IP addresses has been configured to match the router number. For example, the IP addresses on R1 all have .1 for the last octet. RIP version 2 is running on all devices for all networks. In addition to the physical networks shown, each router possesses a loopback 0 interface with an IP address in the format of 1.1.1.1/24, 2.2.2.2/24, and so on.

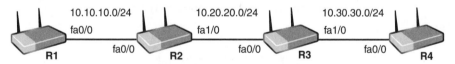

FIGURE 17.1   **Our IOS Tools Troubleshooting Topology**

We begin with just a simple, basic-but-important ping test. A quick and easy way to see if we have full reachability in our topology is to perform a test from R1 to R4 using ping. Example 17.1 shows this test.

ExamAlert

Remember, ping uses an ICMP echo (sometimes referred to as an Echo Request) and an ICMP Echo Reply in its operation.

EXAMPLE 17.1 **Performing a Simple Ping Test**

```
R1#
R1#ping 10.30.30.4

Type escape sequence to abort.
Sending 5, 100-byte ICMP Echos to 10.30.30.4, timeout is 2 seconds:
!!!!!
Success rate is 100 percent (5/5), round-trip min/avg/max = 52/61/72
ms
R1#
```

Note that this test was 100 percent successful. Five ping (ICMP echo request) packets were sent by default, and five responses (ICMP echo replies) were received. Notice also that the output shows a round-trip time of an average of 61 milliseconds.

What have we confirmed exactly? We have confirmed the physical Fa0/0 interface of R1 can reach the physical interface (Fa0/0) of R4. This means that all of the physical connectivity between these devices appears to be functioning normally. It also indicates that *most* of our logical configuration appears correct. For example, our IP addressing assignments and RIP configuration appear to be correct. But what about the loopbacks that exist in this scenario? Are they properly configured, both from an IP addressing standpoint and from a RIP standpoint? We need to perform a more elaborate ping test for this information. We should also combine this with a **show ip route** command, as demonstrated in Example 17.2.

EXAMPLE 17.2 **Testing the Loopback Connectivity Using ping**

```
R1#
R1#show ip route
Codes: L—local, C—connected, S—static, R—RIP, M—mobile, B—BGP
       D—EIGRP, EX—EIGRP external, O—OSPF, IA—OSPF inter area
       N1—OSPF NSSA external type 1, N2—OSPF NSSA external type 2
       E1—OSPF external type 1, E2—OSPF external type 2
       i—IS-IS, su—IS-IS summary, L1—IS-IS level-1, L2—IS-IS level-2
       ia—IS-IS inter area, *—candidate default, U—per-user static
route
       o—ODR, P—periodic downloaded static route, +—replicated route

Gateway of last resort is not set

      1.0.0.0/8 is variably subnetted, 2 subnets, 2 masks
C        1.1.1.0/24 is directly connected, Loopback0
L        1.1.1.1/32 is directly connected, Loopback0
      2.0.0.0/24 is subnetted, 1 subnets
R        2.2.2.0 [120/1] via 10.10.10.2, 00:00:17, FastEthernet0/0
      3.0.0.0/24 is subnetted, 1 subnets
```

```
R          3.3.3.0 [120/2] via 10.10.10.2, 00:00:17, FastEthernet0/0
      4.0.0.0/24 is subnetted, 1 subnets
R          4.4.4.0 [120/3] via 10.10.10.2, 00:00:17, FastEthernet0/0
      10.0.0.0/8 is variably subnetted, 4 subnets, 2 masks
C          10.10.10.0/24 is directly connected, FastEthernet0/0
L          10.10.10.1/32 is directly connected, FastEthernet0/0
R          10.20.20.0/24 [120/1] via 10.10.10.2, 00:00:17,
FastEthernet0/0
R          10.30.30.0/24 [120/2] via 10.10.10.2, 00:00:18,
FastEthernet0/0
R1#
R1#ping 4.4.4.4 source loopback 0

Type escape sequence to abort.
Sending 5, 100-byte ICMP Echos to 4.4.4.4, timeout is 2 seconds:
Packet sent with a source address of 1.1.1.1
!!!!!
Success rate is 100 percent (5/5), round-trip min/avg/max = 40/56/64 ms
R1#
```

Notice that our routing table indicates we have reachability to the networks for the loopback interfaces of R2, R3, and R4 learned through RIP. We then perform a ping, this time with a destination address of the loopback 0 on R4 of 4.4.4.4, and we source this ping from the R1 loopback 0 interface. The five packets are successful. What if we want to perform this test again, but this time with 100 packets? Example 17.3 demonstrates how easy this is.

EXAMPLE 17.3 **Running a Ping Test with More Packets**

```
R1#
R1#ping 4.4.4.4 source loopback 0 repeat 100

Type escape sequence to abort.
Sending 100, 100-byte ICMP Echos to 4.4.4.4, timeout is 2 seconds:
Packet sent with a source address of 1.1.1.1
!!!!!!!!!!!!!!!!!!!!!!!!!!!!!!!!!!!!!!!!!!!!!!!!!!!!!!!!!!!!!!!!!!!!!!!!!!!
!!!!!!!!!!!!!!!!!!!!!!!!!!!!!!!
Success rate is 100 percent (100/100), round-trip min/avg/max =
44/60/68 ms
R1#
```

Let's review what a ping looks like when things are broken in the network. In this example, we disable the physical interface on R4 and retry our ping (with five packets). Example 17.4 shows the results.

EXAMPLE 17.4 **A ping with Failures in the Network**

```
R4#
R4#configure terminal
Enter configuration commands, one per line.  End with CNTL/Z.
R4(config)#interface fa0/0
R4(config-if)#shutdown
R4(config-if)#end
R4#
%SYS-5-CONFIG_I: Configured from console by console
%LINK-5-CHANGED: Interface FastEthernet0/0, changed state to adminis-
tratively down
R4#
%LINEPROTO-5-UPDOWN: Line protocol on Interface FastEthernet0/0,
changed state to down
R4#


R1#
R1#ping 4.4.4.4 source loopback 0

Type escape sequence to abort.
Sending 5, 100-byte ICMP Echos to 4.4.4.4, timeout is 2 seconds:
Packet sent with a source address of 1.1.1.1
.....
Success rate is 0 percent (0/5)
R1#
```

Note the exclamation point usage for success on the ping packets versus the period for failure. Table 17.1 provides a few of the ping return codes for a Cisco router, regarding IPv4. Not all of these return codes are supported or used on all Cisco router IOS versions and platforms.

TABLE 17.1 **The Ping Return Codes**

Character	Description
!	Reply success
.	Server timed out
U	Destination unreachable error received
Q	Source quench (destination too busy)
M	Could not fragment
?	Unknown packet type
&	Packet lifetime exceeded

Although features like source and repeat count seem impressive with ping, things get even more impressive when we do a ping with **extended options**.

Example 17.5 demonstrates what most engineers term an extended ping. For this example, the fa0/0 interface on R4 has been brought up since the previous example.

EXAMPLE 17.5 **Running an Extended Ping in the Network**

```
R1#
R1#ping
Protocol [ip]: ip
Target IP address: 4.4.4.4
Repeat count [5]: 8
Datagram size [100]: 1600
Timeout in seconds [2]: 4
Extended commands [n]: y
Source address or interface: 1.1.1.1
Type of service [0]: 1
Set DF bit in IP header? [no]: no
Validate reply data? [no]: no
Data pattern [0xABCD]: 0xAAAA
Loose, Strict, Record, Timestamp, Verbose[none]: none
Sweep range of sizes [n]: n
Type escape sequence to abort.
Sending 8, 1600-byte ICMP Echos to 4.4.4.4, timeout is 4 seconds:
Packet sent with a source address of 1.1.1.1
Packet has data pattern 0xAAAA
!!!!!!!!
Success rate is 100 percent (8/8), round-trip min/avg/max = 56/64/76 ms
R1#
```

Notice the incredible variations and detail we can add here including:

▶ **Protocol [ip]**: Our example uses the default IPv4.

▶ **Target IP address**: We use our earlier target IP of the loopback on R4 (4.4.4.4).

▶ **Repeat count [5]**: How many packets we want to send; we decide to send 8.

▶ **Datagram size [100]**: The size of the packets we are sending; we chose 1600 bytes.

▶ **Timeout in seconds [2]**: The timeout value in seconds; we change from the default of 2 and select a second timeout.

▶ **Extended commands [n]**: Whether or not we want to perform an extended ping with additional options; of course, we choose yes.

- ▶ **Source address or interface**: The source address or interface of the ping packets; we choose 1.1.1.1 as the source IPv4 address.

- ▶ **Type of service [0]**: The ToS value for QoS we want marked in the packets; we choose 1.

- ▶ **Set DF bit in IP header? [no]**: Whether we want the Don't Fragment setting in the packets; we choose no.

- ▶ **Validate reply data? [no]**: This checks the reply packets to see if the data pattern sent is the exact data pattern received; we choose no.

- ▶ **Data pattern [0xABCD]**: This allows you to set the exact data pattern in the payload of the ping packets; we choose 0xAAAA.

- ▶ **Loose, Strict, Record, Timestamp, Verbose[none]**: This permits you to set specific options in the ping packets, like whether or not a specific path should be selected; we choose none of these options.

- ▶ **Sweep range of sizes [n]**: This dictates whether the router will generate packets in a range of sizes up to the datagram size value set earlier; we choose no.

ExamAlert

Remember, in the Cisco CLI, values in brackets represent the default value inserted should we press Enter on the keyboard.

What about tracing the path of traffic as it traverses the network? With ping, we can see that 1.1.1.1 can reach 4.4.4.4, but without an extended ping, and using the record option, we get no information about the Layer 3 routers that were traversed for this to take place. **traceroute** is the tool that can provide this path information. traceroute on a Cisco router uses a combination of UDP and ICMP in order to provide this information. It also uses a Time to Live (TTL) value in the IP header.

When using traceroute on a Cisco router, three UDP segments are sent, each with a Time-to-Live (TTL) field value set to one ("1") in the IPv4 Layer 3 header of each packet. The TTL value of 1 causes these packets to "timeout" as soon as they hit the first router in the path, and that router then replies back with ICMP Time Exceeded Messages indicating that the packets were dropped (one ICMP message per dropped packet). These ICMP responses include the source IP address of the router, and that source address is how we learn about that specific router in the path to the final destination.

Three more UDP segments are then sent, each with the TTL value set to 2, which causes the second router to return ICMP time exceeded messages. This reveals the IP address of the second router in the path. The process of increasing the TTL by one and sending out three more UDP packets continues until the packets reach the final destination.

The purpose of traceroute is to record the source of each ICMP Time Exceeded Message packet in order to provide a trace of the path the packet took to reach the final destination.

Example 17.6 shows a simple (non-extended) use of traceroute.

EXAMPLE 17.6 **Using a Simple traceroute**

```
R1#
R1#traceroute 4.4.4.4

Type escape sequence to abort.
Tracing the route to 4.4.4.4

  1 10.10.10.2 16 msec 16 msec 20 msec
  2 10.20.20.3 16 msec 44 msec 40 msec
  3 10.30.30.4 68 msec 52 msec 64 msec
R1#
```

Here we see that the journey to 4.4.4.4 from the physical interface of R1 (Fa0/0 10.10.10.1) begins with a next hop of 10.10.10.2 (R2 Fa0/0); then the packet reaches the next hop of 10.20.20.3 (R3 Fa0/0), and then 10.30.30.4 (R4 Fa0/0).

Notice that three test packets are sent to produce these results, and Traceroute provides us with time values similar to how ping does. Should a packet time out, a * displays for that packet. This often occurs when tracing paths to Internet destinations because delay can cause issues as well with devices in the path that are configured not to respond with ICMP messages. Example 17.7 shows an example of performing a Traceroute from a Windows system to an external destination. Note that on a Windows system, the command is **tracert**. When using **tracert** on Windows, be aware that the packets sent out are ICMP-based, as opposed to a Cisco router, which sends out UDP-based segments when doing a traceroute. In both cases, the intention is that the Layer 3 devices in the path reply back with ICMP Time Exceeded Messages when the TTL expires for the packets.

EXAMPLE 17.7 **Performing a traceroute on Windows System to an Internet Destination**

```
C:\Users\terry>tracert www.cnn.com

Tracing route to prod.turner.map.fastlylb.net [151.101.4.73]
over a maximum of 30 hops:

  1    <1 ms    <1 ms    <1 ms   FIOS_Quantum_Gateway.fios-router.home
[192.168.1.1]
  2     8 ms     6 ms     6 ms   71.99.214.1
  3     6 ms     7 ms     8 ms   172.99.45.136
  4    12 ms    11 ms    11 ms   ae7---0.scr01.mias.fl.frontiernet.net
[74.40.3.69]
  5    10 ms    11 ms    12 ms   ae0---0.cbr01.mias.fl.frontiernet.net
[74.40.1.22]
  6     *       13 ms    11 ms   lag-101.ear3.Miami2.Level3.net
[4.15.156.29]
  7    15 ms    14 ms    14 ms   Cogent-level3-40G.Miami2.Level3.net
[4.68.110.170]
  8     *        *        *      Request timed out.
  9    11 ms    11 ms    12 ms   151.101.4.73

Trace complete.


C:\Users\terry>
```

What about extended traceroute? Example 17.8 demonstrates this capability on a Cisco router from our Figure 17.1 topology.

EXAMPLE 17.8 **Using Extended traceroute Options**

```
R1#
R1#traceroute
Protocol [ip]: ip
Target IP address: 4.4.4.4
Source address: 1.1.1.1
Numeric display [n]: y
Timeout in seconds [3]: 1
Probe count [3]: 5
Minimum Time to Live [1]: 1
Maximum Time to Live [30]: 10
Port Number [33434]: 33000
Loose, Strict, Record, Timestamp, Verbose[none]: none
Type escape sequence to abort.
Tracing the route to 4.4.4.4

  1 10.10.10.2 40 msec 16 msec 20 msec 20 msec 16 msec
  2 10.20.20.3 24 msec 36 msec 36 msec 72 msec 20 msec
  3 10.30.30.4 72 msec 60 msec 64 msec 60 msec 64 msec
R1#
```

Notice how remarkably similar this is to the extended ping capabilities. Here we manipulate the following:

▶ **Protocol [ip]**: Set the protocol to trace; we set IPv4.

▶ **Target IP address**: Set the target IP address; we set R4 loopback (4.4.4.4).

▶ **Source address**: Now we can set the specific source address; we set R1 loopback (1.1.1.1).

▶ **Numeric display [n]**: The default is to have both a symbolic and numeric display; however, you can suppress the symbolic display with yes; we set yes.

▶ **Timeout in seconds [3]**: Set the number of seconds to wait for a response to a probe packet; we set 1 second.

▶ **Probe count [3]**: Set the number of probe packets; we set 5.

▶ **Minimum Time to Live [1]**: Set the TTL value for the first probes; the default is 1, but it can be set to a higher value to suppress the display of known hops. We choose the default of 1.

▶ **Maximum Time to Live [30]**: Set the largest TTL value that can be used; the default is 30. The **traceroute** command terminates when the destination is reached or when this value is reached; we set a non-default value of 10.

▶ **Port Number [33434]**: Set the destination port used by the UDP probe messages; the default on this router is 33434. We set the non-default of 33000.

▶ **Loose, Strict, Record, Timestamp, Verbose[none]**: Set the IP options; here we choose the default of none.

To end this section shortly, we discuss a very important feature of **log events** called debug messages. Before we cover those fully, however, let's remind ourselves of a feature we initially discussed in an earlier chapter: the **terminal monitor** feature.

> **ExamAlert**
>
> The terminal monitor feature permits you to view syslog messages at the CLI while you are accessing a device using a remote access protocol like Telnet or SSH. If you are connected to multiple remote routers using a Telnet or SSH application, you can suspend a session with one of the routers using the keystroke sequence of **Ctrl+Shift+6**, and then pressing the **x** key. When you later resume that session on the router, and if that session hasn't timed out, you would expect see the exact prompt you had before you suspended that session with that router. For example, if you were in user mode, you would return to user mode. If you were in configuration mode, you would return to configuration mode.

Example 17.9 shows the use of the **terminal monitor** feature.

EXAMPLE 17.9 **Using the terminal monitor Feature**

```
R1#
R1#telnet 2.2.2.2
Trying 2.2.2.2 ... Open


User Access Verification

Password:
R2>enable
Password:
R2#debug ip rip
RIP protocol debugging is on
R2#terminal monitor
R2#
RIP: received v2 update from 10.10.10.1 on FastEthernet0/0
1.1.1.0/24 via 0.0.0.0 in 1 hops
RIP: sending v2 update to 224.0.0.9 via FastEthernet0/0 (10.10.10.2)
RIP: build update entries
2.2.2.0/24 via 0.0.0.0, metric 1, tag 0
3.3.3.0/24 via 0.0.0.0, metric 2, tag 0
4.4.4.0/24 via 0.0.0.0, metric 3, tag 0
10.20.20.0/24 via 0.0.0.0, metric 1, tag 0
10.30.30.0/24 via 0.0.0.0, metric 2, tag 0
RIP: sending v2 update to 224.0.0.9 via FastEthernet1/0 (10.20.20.2)
RIP: build update entries
1.1.1.0/24 via 0.0.0.0, metric 2, tag 0
2.2.2.0/24 via 0.0.0.0, metric 1, tag 0
10.10.10.0/24 via 0.0.0.0, metric 1, tag 0
R2#undebug all
All possible debugging has been turned off
R2#exit

[Connection to 2.2.2.2 closed by foreign host]
R1#
```

Notice in Example 17.9 the following steps:

1. We use Telnet to connect to R2 using its loopback address of 2.2.2.2.

2. We access privileged mode on R2.

3. We issue the **debug ip rip** command in order to initiate syslog messages.

4. These messages do not appear at our CLI as we are accessing R2 via remote access (Telnet).

5. We issue the **terminal monitor** privileged mode command.

6. We see syslog messages (debug) at the CLI.

7. We turn off debugging with the **undebug all** command.

8. We exit the router.

Enabling debugging and terminal monitoring is important to see log messages when connected via SSH or Telnet. To turn off monitoring, use the command **terminal no monitor**. Viewing logging and debugging messages allows us to see events in almost real time on the device and can be critical when troubleshooting or verifying features.

Notice in Example 17.9 that we can get valuable details regarding the functioning of RIP on the devices thanks to the **debug ip rip** command.

Example 17.10 shows another example of debugging at work. Here, we turn on ICMP debugging on R4. Then from R1, we issue a ping to R4. Notice the messages that appear on R4 about this ping. Here we see confirmation, for example, that the source address is the physical interface address of R1 (10.10.10.1).

EXAMPLE 17.10 **Performing a Debug of ICMP Traffic**

```
R4#
R4#debug ip icmp
ICMP packet debugging is on
R4#


R1#
R1#ping 4.4.4.4

Type escape sequence to abort.
Sending 5, 100-byte ICMP Echos to 4.4.4.4, timeout is 2 seconds:
!!!!!
Success rate is 100 percent (5/5), round-trip min/avg/max = 96/104/112
ms
R1#
```

```
R4#
19:14:19.822: ICMP: echo reply sent, src 4.4.4.4, dst 10.10.10.1,
topology BASE, dscp 0 topoid 0
19:14:19.922: ICMP: echo reply sent, src 4.4.4.4, dst 10.10.10.1,
topology BASE, dscp 0 topoid 0
19:14:20.042: ICMP: echo reply sent, src 4.4.4.4, dst 10.10.10.1,
topology BASE, dscp 0 topoid 0
19:14:20.142: ICMP: echo reply sent, src 4.4.4.4, dst 10.10.10.1,
topology BASE, dscp 0 topoid 0
19:14:20.242: ICMP: echo reply sent, src 4.4.4.4, dst 10.10.10.1,
topology BASE, dscp 0 topoid 0
R4#
```

Example 17.11 demonstrates how to turn off a specific debug (in this case, our ICMP debugging). Keep in mind you can turn all debugging off quickly with the **undebug all** or **no debug all** commands.

EXAMPLE 17.11 **Disabling the Debug of ICMP Traffic**

```
R4#
R4#no debug ip icmp
ICMP packet debugging is off
R4#
```

ExamAlert

Be very specific and careful when debugging. You can overwhelm the device by creating too much debug traffic.

You can control where debug messages appear, and you can control syslog message logging. Example 17.12 demonstrates us eliminating log messages of level 7 from being sent to the console. By default, these level 7 messages are still being stored in memory (in the buffer) on the router. We then turn on RIP debugging and confirm these messages are appearing in the logging buffer. This example also demonstrates how to clear the logging buffer with **clear logging**.

EXAMPLE 17.12 **Controlling Debug Messages**

```
R1#
R1#configure terminal
Enter configuration commands, one per line.  End with CNTL/Z.
R1(config)#logging console 6
R1(config)#exit
R1#
```

```
%SYS-5-CONFIG_I: Configured from console by console
R1#clear logging
Clear logging buffer [confirm]
R1#debug ip rip
RIP protocol debugging is on
R1#show logging
Syslog logging: enabled (0 messages dropped, 2 messages rate-limited,
                0 flushes, 0 overruns, xml disabled, filtering
disabled)

No Active Message Discriminator.



No Inactive Message Discriminator.


    Console logging: level informational, 22 messages logged, xml
disabled,
                    filtering disabled
    Monitor logging: level debugging, 0 messages logged, xml disabled,
                    filtering disabled
    Buffer logging:  level debugging, 118 messages logged, xml
disabled,
                    filtering disabled
    Logging Exception size (8192 bytes)
    Count and timestamp logging messages: disabled
    Persistent logging: disabled

No active filter modules.

ESM: 0 messages dropped

    Trap logging: level informational, 25 message lines logged

Log Buffer (8192 bytes):

20:07:26.658: RIP: sending v2 update to 224.0.0.9 via FastEthernet0/0
(10.10.10.1)
20:07:26.658: RIP: build update entries
20:07:26.658:   1.1.1.0/24 via 0.0.0.0, metric 1, tag 0
20:07:29.638: RIP: sending v2 update to 224.0.0.9 via Loopback0
(1.1.1.1)
20:07:29.638: RIP: build update entries
20:07:29.638:   2.2.2.0/24 via 0.0.0.0, metric 2, tag 0
20:07:29.638:   3.3.3.0/24 via 0.0.0.0, metric 3, tag 0
20:07:29.638:   4.4.4.0/24 via 0.0.0.0, metric 4, tag 0
```

```
20:07:29.638:    10.10.10.0/24 via 0.0.0.0, metric 1, tag 0
20:07:29.638:    10.20.20.0/24 via 0.0.0.0, metric 2, tag 0
20:07:29.638:    10.30.30.0/24 via 0.0.0.0, metric 3, tag 0
20:07:29.638: RIP: ignored v2 packet from 1.1.1.1 (sourced from one of
our addresses)
R1#no debug ip rip
RIP protocol debugging is off
R1#
```

There is an incredible number of debug commands that exist on Cisco equipment. The "Additional Resources" section of this chapter leads you to the command references for the IOS. These command references include several dedicated to debug commands.

CramQuiz

1. What ICMP packets are used with ping packets? (Choose two.)

   ○ **A.** Return

   ○ **B.** Send

   ○ **C.** Echo

   ○ **D.** Echo-Reply

2. What command sends ping packets to 4.4.4.4 from the source IP address assigned to the Loopback 10 interface?

   ○ **A.** ping 4.4.4.4 source loopback 10

   ○ **B.** ping 4.4.4.4 source-interface loopback 10

   ○ **C.** ping 4.4.4.4 source-address loopback 10

   ○ **D.** ping 4.4.4.4 address loopback 10

3. What symbol indicates a timeout with a ping packet?

   ○ **A.** !

   ○ **B.** ?

   ○ **C.** *

   ○ **D.** .

4. What is the default ToS in an Extended ping?

   ○ **A.** 0

   ○ **B.** 1

   ○ **C.** 2

   ○ **D.** 3

5. Name three elements that allow traceroute to function in a Cisco network? (Choose three.)

   ○ **A.** TCP

   ○ **B.** UDP

   ○ **C.** TTL

   ○ **D.** ICMP

   ○ **E.** FTP

6. How many traceroute probes are used by default with the same TTL?

   ○ **A.** 4

   ○ **B.** 1

   ○ **C.** 5

   ○ **D.** 3

7. What is the default port used by traceroute by default on a Cisco router?

   ○ **A.** 32340

   ○ **B.** 33434

   ○ **C.** 36534

   ○ **D.** 32114

8. What level of syslog messages are debug messages?

   ○ **A.** Level 0

   ○ **B.** Level 5

   ○ **C.** Level 1

   ○ **D.** Level 7

CramQuiz Answers

1. **C** and **D** are correct. The ping sends an Echo (sometimes called an Echo Request) and then there is an Echo-Reply.

2. **A** is correct. The **source** keyword in ping allows you to set the source IP address.

3. **D** is correct. The . symbol allows ping to communicate a timeout condition.

4. **A** is correct. The default ToS is 0.

5. **B, C**, and **D** are correct. traceroute uses a TTL, as well as UDP and ICMP in its operation in a Cisco network.

6. **D** is correct. traceroute uses three probes by default.

7. **B** is correct. The default initial port for traceroute is 33434 on a Cisco router.

8. **D** is correct. Debug messages are a Level 7.

Review Questions

1. What is sent in response to a ping probe?

   ○ **A.** A ping Echo-Reply

   ○ **B.** A ping Response

   ○ **C.** A ping Ack

   ○ **D.** A ping TTL

2. Ping also provides latency information. What is the measurement value for this?

   ○ **A.** usecs

   ○ **B.** ms

   ○ **C.** parsecs

   ○ **D.** mms

3. What is the syntax for sending 1000 ping packets?

   ○ **A. count 1000**

   ○ **B. try 1000**

   ○ **C. send 1000**

   ○ **D. repeat 1000**

4. What is the code for a destination unreachable returned in ping?

   ○ **A.** .

   ○ **B.** Q

   ○ **C.** U

   ○ **D.** ?

5. What is the default minimum TTL with traceroute?

   ○ **A.** 0

   ○ **B.** 1

   ○ **C.** 2

   ○ **D.** 5

6. What feature permits additional viewing of syslog information by remote clients?

   ○ **A. terminal copy**

   ○ **B. terminal monitor**

   ○ **C. terminal send**

   ○ **D. terminal test**

7. What is the command to negate the **debug ip rip** feature?

   ○ **A.** **debug ip rip disable**

   ○ **B.** **debug ip rip stop**

   ○ **C.** **no debug ip rip**

   ○ **D.** **debug ip rip terminate**

8. What does the following command do: **logging console 6**?

   ○ **A.** It places only level 6 messages on the console.

   ○ **B.** It places log messages 0 through 6 to the console.

   ○ **C.** It places all log messages to the console.

   ○ **D.** It returns an error, you must log to the console.

Answers to Review Questions

1. **A** is correct. A ping Echo-Reply is the response

2. **B** is correct. ping uses Milliseconds in order to communicate latency information.

3. **D** is correct. Use repeat 1000 in order to send 1000 ping echo request packets.

4. **C** is correct. The U symbol indicates a destination unreachable.

5. **B** is correct. traceroute uses a default minimum TTL of 1.

6. **B** is correct. The **terminal monitor** command/feature permits this.

7. **C** is correct. **no debug ip rip** is the correct command.

8. **B** is correct. This command omits level 7 messages to the console.

Additional Resources

Finding Your Way with Traceroute—http://www.ajsnetworking.com/trace-route

Debug Command References—http://bit.ly/2cu06OO

Command Reference, Practice Exams, and Glossary

This part of the book provides both reference study material and two intense practice exams to help prepare you for the actual exam. The Command Reference defines commands that are relevant for your CCENT (ICND1) Exam. The two practice exams are followed by their answer keys with explanations to help with remediation on those questions you missed. Finally, the Glossary provides definitions for all of the essential terms and components highlighted in all of the chapters.

Part 6 includes the following elements:

COMMAND REFERENCE

PRACTICE EXAM 1

PRACTICE EXAM 2

ANSWER KEY TO PRACTICE EXAM 1

ANSWER KEY TO PRACTICE EXAM 2

GLOSSARY

Command Reference

This Command Reference permits you to quickly brush up on any commands that might be relevant for your CCENT Exam. Use this as a reference, or if you prefer, run through all of the commands from A to Z to help further prepare you for exam day!

A

access-list 1 permit 172.16.1.0 0.0.0.255: This global configuration command creates a standard ACL; note here the number is 1 and the permitted source addresses are 172.16.1.0 0.0.0.255

B

banner login #: This command is done in global configuration mode, and it sets a banner message to display before the username: login prompt; note that the special character is your choice and will end the banner entry

C

cdp enable: This interface-level command enables CDP on an interface

cdp run: This global configuration command enables CDP on the local device

clear logging: This command clears the contents of the logging buffer; you run this from privileged mode

clock set 19:23:23 15 November 2018: This command sets the time and date on your Cisco device

clock summer-time EDT recurring: This global configuration command sets the Daylight Savings Time settings

clock timezone EST -5: This global configuration command sets the time zone for your device

copy running-config startup-config: This command saves your configuration in RAM to the NVRAM of the system

copy tftp flash: This command retrieves files from a TFTP server and copies them into the local Flash memory of your system; this command could be used to upgrade or restore an IOS image

crypto key generate rsa: This global configuration mode command creates the RSA keys material needed for SSH encryption

---

D

debug ip icmp: This command enables the syslog (level 7 debug) information to be produced for ICMP traffic on the device

debug ip rip: This command enables the syslog (level 7 debug) information to be produced for RIP traffic to and from the device

default-router 10.1.1.1: This DHCP pool configuration command sets the default gateway for DHCP clients; in this example, the clients will use 10.1.1.1 as their default gateway

dns-server 8.8.8.8 4.2.2.2: This DHCP pool configuration command sets the DNS server addresses for the clients; in this example, the DNS servers used by clients would be 8.8.8.8 and 4.2.2.2

E

enable: This user mode command allows you to enter privileged mode

enable password ThisIsmyPassw0rd: This global configuration command sets an unencrypted password; it is used for backward compatibility with very old Cisco devices

end: This command sends you back to the privileged mode prompt regardless of how deep you are in the configuration hierarchy

exec-timeout 0 0: This command is typically performed in the console port—it configures an inactivity timer in minutes and seconds; this example will never cause a timeout on the line where it is configured

exit: This command exits the current configuration mode and sends you back one level

---

H

hostname R1: This global configuration command sets the network name of the local device; here we set a name of R1

I

ip nat inside source static 10.2.2.1 10.1.1.100: This global configuration command configures inside static source NAT; the first IP listed is the inside local and the second is the inside global

interface fastethernet0/0: This global configuration command enters interface configuration mode for the referenced interface

interface gi0/1.10: This command creates a subinterface; in this example, its ID is 10

ip access-group 1 in: This interface-level command assigns a numbered standard ACL as a network filter in the inbound direction

ip access-group 40 out: This interface-level command sets the outbound filtering ACL to 40 (in this example)

ip access-list standard MYACL: This global configuration command creates a named access list; the ACL is a standard type; in this example, we use the name MYACL

ip address 10.10.10.1 255.255.255.0: This command configures the IPv4 address and subnet mask under an interface

ip address dhcp: This interface-level command instructs the device to obtain its interface IP address using DHCP; this is DHCP client functionality

ip dhcp excluded-address 10.1.1.1 10.1.1.10: This global configuration command excludes a range of IP addresses from the DHCP pool scope

ip dhcp pool ICND1EXAMCRAM: This global configuration command begins the DHCP pool configuration mode; note that it also creates the pool specified

ip domain-list: This global configuration command defines a list of domains, each to be tried in turn; if there is no domain list, the domain name that you specified with the **ip domain-name** global configuration command is used; if there is a domain list, the default domain name is not used

ip domain-lookup: This global configuration command sets the router to request DNS resolution as a client

ip domain-name: This global configuration command sets the domain name for the local device; note that this command is required for using SSH

ip helper-address 10.1.1.3: This interface-level command instructs the router to forward DHCP broadcasts as directed unicasts to the address listed, which is the address of your DHCP server

ip name-server: This global configuration command is used to specify a DNS server that the router can use to resolve names to IP addresses

ip nat inside: This interface-level command sets the inside interface for NAT

ip nat inside source list 1 interface fa0/0 overload: This global configuration command configures PAT; note the source list is ACL 1

ip nat inside source list 1 pool MYNATPOOL: This global configuration command configures dynamic source NAT; note the ACL 1 is for the devices to be translated (inside local); the pool represents IP address(es) that will be used for the translation(s)

ip nat outside: This interface-level command sets the outside interface for NAT

ip nat pool MYNATPOOL 10.1.1.100 10.1.1.101 netmask 255.255.255.0: This global configuration command configures a NAT pool used in dynamic NAT; the IP addresses are the starting IP and the ending IP of a range

ip route 0.0.0.0 0.0.0.0 10.10.10.2: This global configuration command configures a static route; in this case, it is a static default route; note that the next-hop is 10.10.10.2; in certain cases (such as point to point serial interfaces), you can also exit interfaces instead of the next-hop router address

ip route 10.60.60.0 255.255.255.0 10.20.20.2 121: This global configuration command configures a static route

ip ssh version 2: This global configuration command sets the version of SSH to be used

ipv6 address 2001:aaaa:bbbb::1/64: This command assigns an IPv6 address under an interface; notice here the mask is 64-bits and the user is assigning a specific host portion; the user is also taking advantage of the IPv6 address notation shortcuts

ipv6 address 2001:AAAA:BBBB::/64 eui-64: This command assigns an IPv6 address under an interface; note here that the modified EUI-64 format is used for the automatic host portion assignment

ipv6 address autoconfig: This interface-level command instructs the local device to acquire its IPv6 address through the Stateless Autoconfiguration process

ipv6 route 2001:aaaa::/64 serial 0/0: This global configuration command configures a static route for IPv6

L

line console 0: This global configuration command enters the configuration for the console 0 port

line vty 0 4: This global configuration mode command allows you to enter the virtual terminal lines for configuration on a router. The default for most switches are vty lines 0–15

lldp run: This global configuration command enables LLDP on the local device

lldp receive: This interface-level command configures settings for the receiving of LLDP messages

lldp transmit: This interface-level command configures the settings for the sending of LLDP messages

logging buffered 4: This global configuration command sends syslog messages of level 4 through 0 to the buffer

logging console 6: This global configuration command sends syslog messages of level 6 through 0 to the console line

logging host 10.1.1.3: This command sets the sending of syslog messages to the specified destination address

logging synchronous: This line configuration mode command ensures that syslog output does not interrupt your command input at the CLI

login: This line configuration command causes a local password check for access

login local: This line configuration command causes authentication to use the local accounts database

---

N

name EAST: This VLAN configuration mode command provides a name for your VLAN; this command is optional

network 10.0.0.0: This router configuration mode command sets the interfaces on which to run RIP

network 10.1.1.0 /24: This DHCP pool configuration command sets the addresses to be leased to clients; note that any excluded-addresses are not included; here the addresses to lease are set to 10.1.1.0 255.255.255.0

no shutdown: This interface-level command enables the interface

no auto-summary: This router configuration mode command sets RIP to not perform automatic summarization on major network boundaries

ntp master 2: This global configuration command sets the local device to be the authoritative time source; the stratum set here is 2; the default stratum is 8

ntp server 10.1.1.1: This global configuration command configures the local device to be a client of a remote NTP server; here the NTP server is located at 10.1.1.1

O

option 150 ip 10.10.10.2: This DHCP pool configuration command allows DHCP to function in conjunction with VoIP TFTP servers for the downloading of configurations to IP Phones

P

passive-interface: This command, when used as part of routing protocol configuration, can cause interfaces to not send routing updates

password ThisIsMyT3ln3tPassword: This line configuration mode command provides a password for access via that line

ping: This command allows you to begin a Ping with extended options

ping 10.1.1.3: This command allows you to perform a Ping to the IP address specified

ping 4.4.4.4 source loopback 0: This command performs a Ping setting the source address to the interface you specify

ping 4.4.4.4 source loopback 0 repeat 100: This command performs a Ping and sets the source address as well as sets the Ping packet count (packets sent) to 100

R

router rip: This global configuration command enters RIP configuration mode

S

service password-encryption: This command ensures that passwords do not appear as clear text in the running and startup configurations; a weak Cisco hashing is used

show access-list: This command allows you to see the access lists that are configured on the device; note that this command also would allow you to see hits on the access list; this command does not indicate interface assignments for filtering, however

show cdp: This command shows global CDP settings for the device

show cdp entry *: This command shows detailed neighbor information for CDP; this includes the IP address of the neighboring device or devices

show cdp neighbor: This command shows general information about the neighbors in a tabular format; note that this command does not show detailed information like IP address information

show cdp neighbor detail: Like **show cdp entry ***, this command shows detailed information about CDP neighbors

show clock: This command shows the current time and date settings for the router

show flash: This command shows the contents of Flash memory on the Cisco device; remember, the Flash is typically where the IOS is stored

show interface gi0/1: This command shows the statistics and health information for an interface

show interface gi0/2 switchport: This command is very useful on a switch in order to see details of the Layer 2 configuration such as the data and voice VLAN assignments; this is also very useful to see details regarding trunking on the port, should trunking be configured

show interface trunk: This command shows details for all of the trunk ports that exist on the Cisco switch

show ip dhcp binding: This command shows the lease information that clients possess from the local DHCP server where this command is run

show ip interface brief: This command shows a tabular summary of the status of interfaces as well as the IP address information that is assigned; note this command does not show subnet mask information

show ip interface fa0/0: This command shows important Layer 3 characteristics for an interface; this includes the assignment of access-lists that might be used as incoming or outgoing filters

show ip nat translation: This command shows NAT translations that exist on the local device performing NAT

show ip protocols: This command shows details about the routing protocols that are running on the local device

show ip route: This command shows the IP routing database

show ipv6 interface brief: This command shows brief tabular information about the status and IPv6 address information on interfaces; note it is the IPv6 equivalent of **show ip interface brief**

show ipv6 interface fa0/0: This command shows IPv6 details on the referenced interface

show ipv6 route: This command shows the IPv6 routing table; note that it is the IPv6 equivalent of **show ip route**

show logging: This command shows the logging (syslog) settings for the local device; note that this command also shows the logging buffer and its contents

show mac address-table: This command allows you to view the CAM (or MAC) table on your local switch; note that by default you see both static and dynamic entries

show ntp associations: This command permits you to see the NTP devices that you are synchronized with

show ntp status: This command provides you information on your local NTP sync status; this command is critical to ensure you are receiving accurate time from a time source

show port-security interface gi0/1: This command provides valuable status information regarding the Port Security settings for a particular interface; it is an excellent way to check your configured settings, as well as the defaults in place

show running-config: This command permits you to view the commands that make up the configuration in RAM on the device; this is the configuration that is currently being used by your local device

show startup-config: This command allows you to see the configuration stored in NVRAM; this config is the one that is activated upon a reboot of your device; it is often thought of as the "saved" or backed up" config

show vlan brief: This command shows you a tabular summary of the VLAN information on your switch

show vlan: This command shows you detailed information about the VLANs that exist on your device; it is rarely used, compared to **show vlan brief**

show vtp status: This command allows you to confirm the VTP settings on your local switch; remember, there are different VTP versions and VTP modes; these, among other things, are confirmed with this command

shutdown: This interface-level command disables an interface; the resulting status is Administratively Disabled

switchport access vlan 20: This interface-level switch command assigns the data VLAN on the interface; this example sets data VLAN 20

switchport mode access: This interface-level switch command sets the local interface to access mode as opposed to trunk mode. Port Security requires that ports are not dynamic. They must be configured manually either as an access or trunk port

switchport mode trunk: This interface-level switch command sets the local interface to trunk mode as opposed to access mode; note that this command allows multiple data VLANs on the port

switchport port-security: This interface-level switch command enables Port Security on the interface; if this is the only command used, all settings use the default

switchport port-security mac-address fa16.3e20.58f1: This interface-level switch command sets a static MAC address for Port Security; here the MAC address is fa16.3e20.58f1

switchport port-security mac-address sticky: This interface-level switch command causes MAC addresses to be learned dynamically, then static entries to be written in the running config; it is a Port Security optional configuration

switchport port-security maximum 2: This interface-level switch command sets the maximum number of MAC addresses for Port Security; in this example, two MAC addresses are permitted

switchport trunk encapsulation dot1q: This interface-level switch command sets the local interface to use 802.1Q encapsulation; on some switches, specifying the trunking protocol is a requirement before setting the mode to trunk

switchport voice vlan 50: This interface-level switch command sets the local interface to use a specific Voice VLAN; this example uses VLAN 50 for this

---

T

telnet 2.2.2.2: This command is used to Telnet to the address specified

terminal monitor: This command permits a client to see syslog information while remotely accessing a device

traceroute: This command shows you the path taken to reach a specific destination; note that this variation allows you to use extended options. **traceroute** uses the TTL in the IP header, and ICMP response messages for its functionality

traceroute 4.4.4.4: This command shows the path to the specified destination

transport input ssh: This line configuration mode command permits the specific remote access protocols you are allowing; note that you can list multiple protocols

---

U

undebug all: This command disables any enabled debugging on the local system; you run this command from privileged mode

username JOHNS secret 1L0v3C1sc0Systems: This command is done in global configuration mode; it creates a user account on the system for local access, with an MD5 stored password for that user; the default privilege level is 1

V

verify /md5 flash0:c2900-universalk9-mz.SPA.154-3.M3.bin a79e325e6c 498b70829d4db0afba2011: This command verifies the IOS image referenced has not been altered since download from Cisco

version 2: This router configuration command sets RIP to use version 2

vlan 20: This command is performed in VLAN configuration mode and creates a VLAN on the device; in this example VLAN 20; this creation of a new VLAN does not take effect until you exit from VLAN configuration mode

Practice Exam 1

Are you ready to assess your preparedness for the actual ICND1 exam? Practice Exam 1 and then Practice Exam 2 are here for this purpose.

As you take this practice exam, please consider the following test-taking tips:

▶ **Read each question twice if necessary:** Be sure to read each question carefully so that you can fully understand the question. Sometimes this will necessitate reading the question twice.

▶ **Read the answers starting from the bottom:** When you read the answers from the bottom, you force yourself to carefully read each answer. If you read the answers from the top, you might find yourself quickly selecting an answer that looks right and skipping over the other answers. This is dangerous since there might be a better answer later in the options.

▶ **Time yourself:** The CCENT exam is a 90-minute exam. Time yourself during this practice exam to make sure that you stay within this time limit.

▶ **If you do not know the answer to a question, make a note of it:** Go back and review any trouble areas later. Be sure that you are mastering the topic area, not just looking up the answer to this one question. If you are unsure about one aspect of a topic, chances are you might be unsure about other areas related to that same topic. The Answer Key provides a chapter reference for you to make looking up trouble spots much easier for you.

▶ **Prepare mentally to take a test:** To properly assess yourself, take this practice exam as you would take the real exam. This means that you should find a quiet place without any distractions so that you can focus on each question. Provide scratch paper and a pen and pencil for yourself. No other tools (such as calculators) may be used in your actual exam or in your practice here.

▶ **If you cannot determine the correct answer(s), begin by eliminating incorrect answer(s):** If there are four options and you know that three are absolutely wrong, the fourth option has to be the correct one.

▶ **Consider taking this practice exam, as well as the next one, multiple times until you get perfect scores:** When you can consistently score high on these practice exams, the better you are likely to perform in the actual exam.

▶ **Pay close attention to the Answer Key:** You will note that many exam answers lie in store for you in our explanations to questions as well!

▶ **Enjoy the fill-in-the-blank style questions:** Although these question types are rare for the actual exam, we use them here to make this exam much tougher! These questions also provide me with the ability to test you in a simulation style manner—where you must provide correct configurations.

▶ **Use the CD-ROM materials:** There are even more practice exams waiting for you on the CD-ROM that accompanies this text. Be sure to use those materials as well.

▶ **Don't despair:** Do not be overly upset if on your first attempt at this practice exam, you do not score well. It only means that you need to continue studying. Be glad that you are able to spot your weak areas now and not after taking the actual exam. Go back through and review your problem areas now to ensure you are ready!

Congratulations in your pursuit of this valued IT certification!

1. What transport layer protocol features the use of sequencing and synchronization methods?

- ○ **A.** ICMP
- ○ **B.** TCP
- ○ **C.** UDP
- ○ **D.** ARP

2. Examine the figure. If devices 1, 2, and 3 are all Cisco Layer 2 switches in their default configuration, how many collision domains exist in this network?

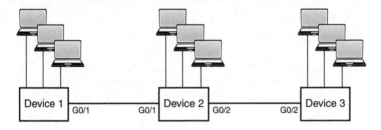

3. You have configured your gi0/1 Cisco switch port as follows:

```
interface gi0/1
switchport mode access
switchport port-security
```

Which of the following statements is true?

- ○ **A.** The default violation mode is Restrict.
- ○ **B.** The mode must be trunk for port security to be used.

    ○ **C.** The default number of dynamic MAC addresses is 1.

    ○ **D.** This configuration prevents the logging of Port Security violations.

    ○ **E.** The violation mode in use here is Protect

4. What is the possible range for the stratum value in Cisco NTP?

_____

5. What is the default administrative distance for iBGP?

    ○ **A.** 20

    ○ **B.** 120

    ○ **C.** 110

    ○ **D.** 200

    ○ **E.** 90

6. What is the following IPv4 address range used for? 224.0.0.0 to 239.255.255.255

    ○ **A.** To send a packet to all systems

    ○ **B.** To send a packet to a group of systems

    ○ **C.** To send a packet to a single, specific system

    ○ **D.** To send multiple packets to only a single specific system

7. What is the default range for TTL in Cisco's implementation of extended Traceroute?

    ○ **A.** 1–20

    ○ **B.** 0–30

    ○ **C.** 1–30

    ○ **D.** 1–10

8. What is the privilege level for the user given the following command? **username johns secret cisco123**

    ○ **A.** 0

    ○ **B.** 1

    ○ **C.** 15

    ○ **D.** 8

9. How are IPv6 addresses typically allocated to computers at a company connected to the Internet?

    ○ **A.** By an ISP

    ○ **B.** Using an EUI-64 Server

    ○ **C.** Using an NATv6 device

    ○ **D.** Using Unique Local Addressing (ULA)

10. Examine the figure. What is the Layer 2 destination address?

```
⊟ Ethernet II, Src: ca:00:1a:a4:00:1c (ca:00:1a:a4:00:1c), Dst: IntelCor_12:34:56 (00:1b:77:12:34:56)
  ⊞ Destination: IntelCor_12:34:56 (00:1b:77:12:34:56)
  ⊞ Source: ca:00:1a:a4:00:1c (ca:00:1a:a4:00:1c)
    Type: IP (0x0800)
⊞ Internet Protocol Version 4, Src: 198.133.219.25 (198.133.219.25), Dst: 10.0.0.2 (10.0.0.2)
⊞ Transmission Control Protocol, Src Port: http (80), Dst Port: d-cinema-rrp (1173), Seq: 0, Ack: 1, Len: 0
```

---

11. Which of the following is an error-free valid hostname for a Cisco switch running version 12.x of Cisco IOS?

- ○ **A.** 12345
- ○ **B.** 1SW-2
- ○ **C.** SW1-4501
- ○ **D.** 1SW12

12. What technology permits a switch port to support multiple data VLANs?

- ○ **A.** Voice VLAN
- ○ **B.** Port Security
- ○ **C.** 802.1Q
- ○ **D.** VTP

13. You are in privileged mode on R1. Provide all configuration commands in order to configure this device as a router on a stick (ROAS) using the following information:

Physical Interface: GigabitEthernet 0/1

Subinterfaces: GigabitEthernet 0/1.10 (VLAN 10); GigabitEthernet 0/1.20 (VLAN 20)

VLANs: 10; 20

Protocol: 802.1Q

IP addressing: 10.1.10.1/24 (VLAN 10); 10.1.20.1/24 (VLAN 20)

---

14. What type of routing protocol is OSPF?

- ○ **A.** Distance vector
- ○ **B.** Link state
- ○ **C.** Hybrid
- ○ **D.** Path vector

15. What is the criterion for filtering that you can use with a standard ACL?

- ○ **A.** Destination IP address
- ○ **B.** Protocol Port Number
- ○ **C.** Source MAC address
- ○ **D.** Source IP address
- ○ **E.** Destination MAC address

16. What keyword enables the use of PAT in your NAT configuration?

- ○ **A.** Load
- ○ **B.** Ports
- ○ **C.** Overload
- ○ **D.** Pool

17. How many syslog levels are there with Cisco equipment?

- ○ **A.** 8
- ○ **B.** 6
- ○ **C.** 4
- ○ **D.** 16

18. What value do you change to have a router ignore its own startup-config on boot?

- ○ **A.** flash-boot
- ○ **B.** nvram.ini
- ○ **C.** configuration register
- ○ **D.** system-start

19. Examine the topology shown here. How many collision domains exist between the PC and Router 1?

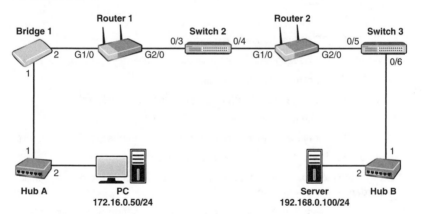

- ○ **A.** 0
- ○ **B.** 1
- ○ **C.** 2
- ○ **D.** 3

20. Which of the following provides a secure method to transfer files in your Cisco network?

- ○ **A.** TFTP
- ○ **B.** FTP
- ○ **C.** Telnet
- ○ **D.** SCP

21. Examine the topology shown in the figure. The PC has sent a Ping request to the Server. Which devices in the network operate only at the physical layer of the OSI reference model? (Choose 2)

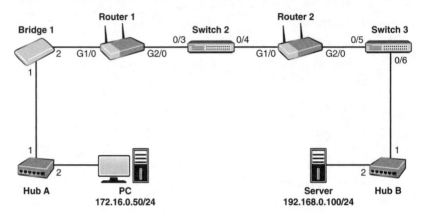

- ○ **A.** Ethernet cabling
- ○ **B.** Bridge 1
- ○ **C.** Router 2
- ○ **D.** Hub A
- ○ **E.** Switch 3
- ○ **F.** PC Network Interface Card

22. Which of the following are true on a typical Cisco access-layer switch? (Choose 2.)

- ○ **A.** It can have IP routing enabled
- ○ **B.** It can have an IP address configured for management
- ○ **C.** It can be used for NAT or PAT
- ○ **D.** A default gateway allows the switch to access remote networks
- ○ **E.** Ports default to no switchport mode

23. From the list, which of the following would be correct best practices for device hardening measures? (Choose two.)

- ○ **A.** Disable VTY login using the VTY line configuration command: **no login**
- ○ **B.** Disable Telnet on the VTY lines using the command: **transport input ssh**
- ○ **C.** Disable all banner messages
- ○ **D.** Disable the use of the plain text passwords in the configurations
- ○ **E.** Disable SSH on the VTY lines

24. Examine the switch configuration shown. What problem exists with this suggested configuration change?

```
SW1
configure terminal
interface fa0/10
switchport trunk encapsulation isl
switchport mode trunk
switchport port-security
switchport port-security max 2
no shutdown
```

- ○ **A.** Port security can only support a single secure MAC address.
- ○ **B.** Port security can be used on trunks (depending on the switch), but it is likely there will be many more than two learned MAC addresses on that port.
- ○ **C.** Port security can only be used with 802.1Q trunks.
- ○ **D.** A violation mode for port security must be selected.

25. Which of the following would be the preferred transport layer protocol for carrying Voice over IP (VoIP) when speed and throughput is a priority?

- ○ **A.** IP
- ○ **B.** TCP
- ○ **C.** UDP
- ○ **D.** HTTPS
- ○ **E.** ICMP

26. Examine the topology shown in the figure. If OSPF, EIGRP, and RIPv2 were all enabled on each interface on each router, which routing protocol would be used by R4 to determine the best route to 10.77.67.0/24?

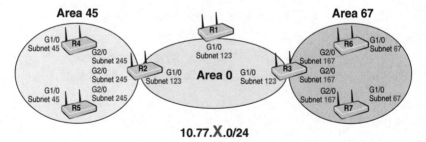

10.77.X.0/24

- ○ **A.** EIGRP because its metric considers bandwidth and delay
- ○ **B.** OSPF because its cost is derived from bandwidth and delay
- ○ **C.** OSPF because it is an advanced distance vector routing protocol
- ○ **D.** EIGRP because of administrative distance

27. You decided to reduce the size of your existing Layer 2 broadcast domains by creating new VLANs. A network device that forwards packets between those VLANs would be operating (at a minimum) at which OSI level?

 ○ **A.** A switch at Layer 1

 ○ **B.** A switch at Layer 2

 ○ **C.** A router at Layer 2

 ○ **D.** A router at Layer 3

28. Examine the topology shown in the figure. Provide the Router 2 configuration for RIP version 2 to enable RIP on G2/0. The G2/0 IP address is 192.168.0.1/24. Also, ensure that RIP will not perform automatic summarization.

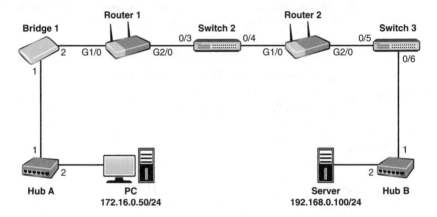

29. Which of the following statements regarding ICMP is correct?

 ○ **A.** ICMP functions at the Network layer of the OSI model.

 ○ **B.** ICMP relies on TCP for reliable packet delivery.

 ○ **C.** ICMP relies on UDP for efficient packet delivery.

 ○ **D.** ICMP functions at the Session layer of the OSI model.

30. What device can use a dual-band approach and 802.11 standards for connecting end users to the network?

 ○ **A.** Firewall

 ○ **B.** WLC

 ○ **C.** AP

 ○ **D.** Router

31. What type of physical topology is created when using a Layer 2 switch or a hub on the LAN?

 ○ **A.** Mesh

 ○ **B.** Hybrid

○ **C.** Partial mesh

○ **D.** Star

32. What is the last usable host address given the IP address and subnet mask of 172.16.10.101 with 255.255.224.0?

_____

33. What command produced the following output?

```
MK5 unit 0, NIM slot 1, NIM type code 7, NIM version 1
idb = 0x6150, driver structure at 0x34A878, regaddr = 0x8100300
IB at 0x6045500: mode=0x0108, local_addr=0, remote_addr=0
N1=1524, N2=1, scaler=100, T1=1000, T3=2000, TP=1
buffer size 1524
DTE V.35 serial cable attached
RX ring with 32 entries at 0x45560 : RLEN=5, Rxhead 0
00 pak=0x6044D78  ds=0x6044ED4 status=80 max_size=1524 pak_size=0
```

_____

34. What type of IP address is used to send traffic to one specific receiver from one specific source?

○ **A.** Multicast

○ **B.** Broadcast

○ **C.** Unicast

○ **D.** Anycast

35. Which of the following addresses is a private use only address?

○ **A.** 12.43.56.120

○ **B.** 177.12.34.19

○ **C.** 201.92.34.100

○ **D.** 10.123.23.104

36. What must be in place before you can route other devices IPv6 traffic through your Cisco router?

○ **A.** The command **dual-stack routing**

○ **B.** A loopback 0 interface with an IPv4 address assigned

○ **C.** IPv4 interfaces

○ **D.** The **ipv6 unicast-routing** global configuration command

37. What happens when a switch receives a broadcast frame?

○ **A.** The switch floods the frame out all ports

○ **B.** The switch floods the frame out all ports except for the receiving port

○ **C.** The switch floods the frame out of all ports for the appropriate VLAN except the receiving port

○ **D.** The switch buffers the frame until the MAC address is learned

38. What two address fields exist in a Layer 2 Ethernet frame? (Choose two.)

○ **A.** Destination IP address

○ **B.** Source MAC

○ **C.** Source IP

○ **D.** Destination MAC

39. What command would you use on a Cisco Layer 2 switch in order to verify errors regarding sending or receiving frames?

○ **A.** show controllers

○ **B.** show interface

○ **C.** show collisions

○ **D.** show version

40. Your Cisco switch is currently in VTP Client mode. You issue the **vlan 100** command in global configuration mode to create a new VLAN. What is the result?

○ **A.** The switch produces an error message.

○ **B.** The switch sends VLAN 100 configuration information to the VTP Server.

○ **C.** The switch reverts to Transparent mode.

○ **D.** The switch configures the VLAN, but on the local device only.

41. Which VLAN is not tagged by default on a Cisco Layer 2 switch trunk port?

○ **A.** 4094

○ **B.** 1

○ **C.** 20

○ **D.** 30

○ **E.** 0

42. What global configuration command allows you to disable CDP on an entire Cisco switch?

○ **A.** no cdp

○ **B.** no cdp enable

○ **C.** no cdp run

○ **D.** no cdp search

43. When you enable port security for a switch port, what is the default violation mode?

○ **A.** Restrict

○ **B.** Shutdown

○ **C.** Protect

○ **D.** Passive

44. What is the default administrative distance for internal EIGRP?

   ○ **A.** 20

   ○ **B.** 110

   ○ **C.** 120

   ○ **D.** 90

45. What layer of the Cisco hierarchical model would most likely feature intense security mechanisms?

   ○ **A.** access

   ○ **B.** distribution

   ○ **C.** core

   ○ **D.** workstation

46. Examine the configuration that follows. What is the next hop for 10.10.20.0/24?

`ip route 10.10.20.0 255.255.255.0 172.16.1.1`

   ○ **A.** 255.255.255.0

   ○ **B.** 10.10.20.1

   ○ **C.** 172.16.1.1

   ○ **D.** 0.0.0.0

47. What file transfer option uses UDP in its operation?

   ○ **A.** SCP

   ○ **B.** SFTP

   ○ **C.** TFTP

   ○ **D.** FTP

   ○ **E.** HTTP

48. What service provides name resolution for network requests?

   ○ **A.** ICMP

   ○ **B.** NAT

   ○ **C.** DNS

   ○ **D.** NTP

49. What tool produced the output shown?

```
Server:         8.8.8.8
Address:        8.8.8.8#53

Non-authoritative answer:
www.yahoo.com    canonical name = fd-fp3.wg1.b.yahoo.com.
Name:     fd-fp3.wg1.b.yahoo.com
Address: 98.139.183.24
```

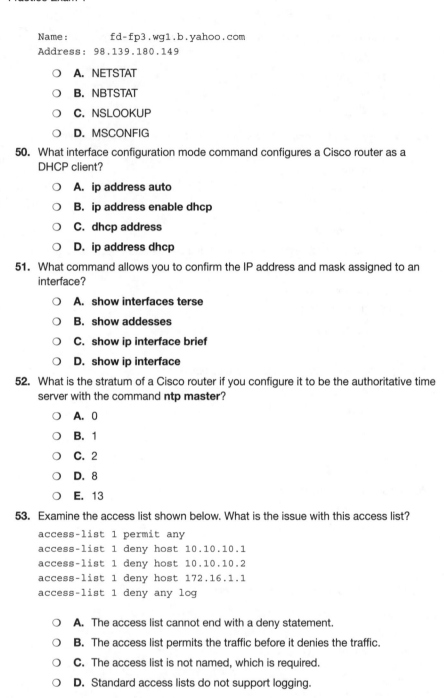

```
Name:       fd-fp3.wg1.b.yahoo.com
Address: 98.139.180.149
```

- ○ **A.** NETSTAT
- ○ **B.** NBTSTAT
- ○ **C.** NSLOOKUP
- ○ **D.** MSCONFIG

50. What interface configuration mode command configures a Cisco router as a DHCP client?

- ○ **A.** ip address auto
- ○ **B.** ip address enable dhcp
- ○ **C.** dhcp address
- ○ **D.** ip address dhcp

51. What command allows you to confirm the IP address and mask assigned to an interface?

- ○ **A.** show interfaces terse
- ○ **B.** show addesses
- ○ **C.** show ip interface brief
- ○ **D.** show ip interface

52. What is the stratum of a Cisco router if you configure it to be the authoritative time server with the command **ntp master**?

- ○ **A.** 0
- ○ **B.** 1
- ○ **C.** 2
- ○ **D.** 8
- ○ **E.** 13

53. Examine the access list shown below. What is the issue with this access list?

```
access-list 1 permit any
access-list 1 deny host 10.10.10.1
access-list 1 deny host 10.10.10.2
access-list 1 deny host 172.16.1.1
access-list 1 deny any log
```

- ○ **A.** The access list cannot end with a deny statement.
- ○ **B.** The access list permits the traffic before it denies the traffic.
- ○ **C.** The access list is not named, which is required.
- ○ **D.** Standard access lists do not support logging.

54. What do we use in dynamic NAT configuration in order to identify the traffic we intend to translate?

- ○ **A.** An access list
- ○ **B.** A pool
- ○ **C.** A NAT list
- ○ **D.** An interface reference

55. What is the most detailed level of debug on a router?

- ○ **A.** 6
- ○ **B.** 7
- ○ **C.** 8
- ○ **D.** 9

56. What configuration represents the configuration that will persist after a reboot of the device and is typically stored in NVRAM?

- ○ **A.** startup-config
- ○ **B.** back-config
- ○ **C.** store-config
- ○ **D.** running-config

57. What is the effect of the **no login** command in **line vty 0 4**?

- ○ **A.** This command has no effect.
- ○ **B.** Telnet is disabled.
- ○ **C.** Users can not access a VTY.
- ○ **D.** Users are not asked for a password.

58. Examine the configuration below. What statement is false?

```
no service password-encryption
!
enable secret rtYHS3TTs
!
username admin01 privilege 15 secret Cisco123
!
line vty 0 4
password ChEeEs&WiZ
login
transport input telnet
```

- ○ **A.** Telnet users will be required to provide a password for Telnet access.
- ○ **B.** Telnet users will be required to provide enable password of ChEeEs&WiZ for access to privileged mode.
- ○ **C.** The admin-level user account's password is not very secure.
- ○ **D.** New plain-text passwords will not be encrypted.

59. A new Layer 2 switch in its default configuration has just been powered up. In addition to a console connection there are two Windows hosts, and an IP Phone (using POE) connected to its Ethernet ports. Which of the following are true? (Choose two.)

○ **A.** If either Windows host has successfully completed an ARP resolution, the switch would have learned the MAC address of both Windows hosts.

○ **B.** The switch would see the two Windows hosts directly connected devices from CDP.

○ **C.** The switch won't know if the IP phone is a Cisco IP phone, or a third party IP phone until a call is initiated from the phone.

○ **D.** The switch can be configured with an IPv4 address on interface VLAN 1.

60. Refer to the network topology that follows. Your senior network administrator is concerned about network security. He has asked that you ensure the PC-10 device in VLAN 10 is the only device that is permitted to connect to Port 0/2 on the switch. How should you respond? (Choose two.)

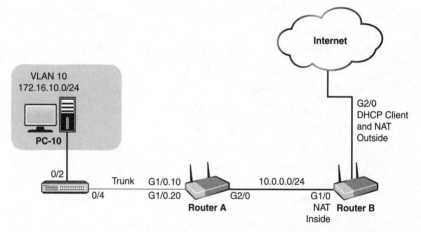

○ **A.** Configure RIP on all network devices and use MD5 authentication,

○ **B.** Configure the service password-encryption command on the switch,

○ **C.** Configure Port Security on interface 0/2 of the switch,

○ **D.** Configure Router A to route traffic sourced from any device other than PC-10 to Null0,

○ **E.** Configure a static MAC address as part of port security,

Answer Key to Practice Exam 1

Answers at a Glance to Practice Exam 1

1. B
2. 11
3. C
4. 1–15
5. D
6. B
7. C
8. B
9. A
10. 00:1b:77:12:34:56
11. C
12. C
13. ```
    configure
    terminal
    !
    interface
    gi0/1
    no shutdown
    !
    interface
    gi0/1.10
    encapsulation
    dot1q 10
    ip address
    10.1.10.1
    255.255.255.0
    !
    interface
    gi0/1.20
    encapsulation
    dot1q 20
    ip address
    10.1.20.1
    255.255.255.0
    ```
14. B
15. D
16. C
17. A
18. C
19. C
20. D
21. A, D
22. B, D
23. B, D
24. B
25. C
26. D
27. D
28. ```
    router rip
    version 2
    no
    auto-summary
    network
    192.168.0.0
    ```
29. A
30. C
31. D
32. 172.16.31.254
33. **show controllers**
34. C
35. D
36. D
37. C
38. B, D
39. B
40. A
41. B
42. C
43. B
44. D
45. B
46. C
47. C
48. C
49. C
50. D
51. D
52. D
53. B
54. A
55. B
56. A
57. D
58. B
59. A, D
60. C, E

Answers with Explanations

1. **Chapter 1 Network Fundamentals: Models and Designs—Answer B is correct.** There are two transport layer protocols listed here. Therefore, you should be able to narrow this question down to two options immediately—B. TCP and C. UDP. Of these two, TCP provides reliability features like sequencing of packets and synchronization. UDP does not.

2. **Chapter 4 LAN Switching Fundamentals: Switching Concepts—11 is correct.** Every port on a Layer 2 switch creates a collision domain by default. Here we have 9 workstations connected for 9 collision domains, and we have a collision domain for each of the 2 interswitch links. This makes a total of 11 collision domains. This Layer 2 switch concept is often called *microsegmentation*.

3. **Chapter 6 LAN Switching Fundamentals: Port Security—Answer C is correct.** Notice this is a default configuration of Port Security. Every value is set to default. This means the default number of MAC addresses is 1 and the default violation mode is Shutdown. This violation mode will log violations.

4. **Chapter 10 Infrastructure Services: DNS, DHCP, NTP—1–15 is correct.** The stratum is a numeric value from 1 to 15. It indicates how far away a device is from the reference clock source. 1 is considered the "best" value.

5. **Chapter 7 Routing Fundamentals: Routing Concepts—Answer D is correct.** The default administrative distance for iBGP is very bad at 200. Contrast this to External BGP (eBGP) as an excellent value of 20.

6. **Chapter 2 Network Fundamentals: IPv4—Answer B is correct.** 224.0.0.0 to 239.255.255.255 is the IPv4 multicast address range. This range permits the sending of a single packet to a group of machines that "subscribe" to the traffic. This is unlike a broadcast where a single packet is sent to all systems. In IPv6, broadcast traffic is eliminated in favor of multicast.

7. **Chapter 17 Infrastructure Maintenance: IOS Troubleshooting Tools—Answer C is correct.** A TTL is used with Traceroute. The default range for the TTL is 1 to 30.

8. **Chapter 15 Infrastructure Maintenance: Device Hardening—Answer B is correct.** The username command defaults to privilege level 1 for the user when a level is not specified.

9. **Chapter 3 Network Fundamentals: IPv6—Answer A is correct.** In IPv6 environments, it is common to have ISPs assigning blocks of addresses to an enterprise. This is due to the massive address space that is possible and a lack of need for private use only addressing.

10. **Chapter 4 LAN Switching Fundamentals: Switching Concepts— 00:1b:77:12:34:56 is correct.** The Layer 2 addressing information appears under the Ethernet II section. There is the Src for Source and Dst for Destination in the output of the packet capture shown.

11. **Chapter 14 Infrastructure Maintenance: Initial Device Configuration—Answer C is correct.** Hostnames on most Layer 2 switches running IOS 12.x must start with a letter, end with a letter or digit, and have as interior characters only letters, digits, and hyphens. Names must be 63 characters or fewer. C is the only option that conforms to the naming requirements.

12. **Chapter 5 LAN Switching Fundamentals: VLANs and Interswitch Connectivity—Answer C is correct.** An access port supports a single data VLAN. Multiple data VLANs are supported on trunk ports. 802.1Q is the current trunk port standard.

13. **Chapter 8 Routing Fundamentals: Inter-VLAN Routing—the following configuration is correct:**

```
configure terminal
!
interface gi0/1
no shutdown
!
interface gi0/1.10
encapsulation dot1q 10
ip address 10.1.10.1 255.255.255.0
!
interface gi0/1.20
encapsulation dot1q 20
ip address 10.1.20.1 255.255.255.0
```

    Notice this configuration features no IP address on the physical interface, and uses subinterfaces set for 802.1Q encapsulation and appropriate IP addresses for the different VLANs.

14. **Chapter 9 Routing Fundamentals: Static and Dynamic Routing—Answer B is correct.** OSPF is a link state routing protocol. RIP is an example of a distance vector protocol. EIGRP is a hybrid protocol. Finally, BGP is a path vector protocol.

15. **Chapter 11 Infrastructure Services: ACLs—Answer D is correct.** Standard ACLs can only filter based on a single criterion: source IP address.

16. **Chapter 12 Infrastructure Services: NAT—Answer C is correct.** The overload keyword implies the use of Port Address Translation.

17. **Chapter 13 Infrastructure Maintenance: Syslog and Device Management—Answer A is correct.** Syslog levels 0 through 7 are available on most Cisco devices.

18. **Chapter 16 Infrastructure Maintenance: Device Maintenance—Answer C is correct.** The Configuration Register settings can permit a router to ignore its own startup-config during boot.

19. **Chapter 4 LAN Switching Fundamentals: Switching Concepts—Answer C is correct.** There are two collision domains. The hub does not create collision domains off its ports. The bridge does. So there are two collision domains created by the bridge.

20. **Chapter 16 Infrastructure Maintenance: Device Maintenance—Answer D is correct.** The Secure Copy Protocol (SCP) relies upon SSH technology for its operation. It is the only protocol listed here with security and encryption capabilities for file transfer.

21. **Chapter 1 Network Fundamentals: Models and Designs—Answers A and D are correct.** The cabling and the hub are Layer 1 components. Bridges and Switches include Layer 2 components. The router includes a Layer 2 and Layer 3 component.

22. **Chapter 4 LAN Switching Fundamentals: Switching Concepts—Answers B and D are correct**. Layer 2 access switches will typically have IP addresses assigned for management purposes. A default gateway permits a managed switch to access remote networks, again for management purposes.

23. **Chapter 15 Infrastructure Maintenance: Device Hardening—Answers B and D are correct**. You should disable the use of Telnet by using the **transport input ssh** command. Also, use the **service password-encryption** command to hide plain text passwords. Depending on the AAA configuration (or lack thereof), the command **no login** removes the requirement for a login password on the VTY lines.

24. **Chapter 6 LAN Switching Fundamentals: Port Security—Answer B is correct**. Port security can be used on configured access or trunk ports, but not on a dynamic port. When used on a trunk, it is likely there will be many devices MAC addresses crossing the trunk, so the limit of two MAC addresses would likely be too restrictive.

25. **Chapter 1 Network Fundamentals: Models and Designs—Answer C is correct**. VoIP uses UDP for efficient transport.

26. **Chapter 7 Routing Fundamentals: Routing Concepts—Answer D is correct**. Here EIGRP is preferred due to its lower administrative distance.r

27. **Chapter 8 Routing Fundamentals: Inter-VLAN Routing—Answer D is correct**. A router at Layer 3 provides the Inter-VLAN communications. Note that this is often in the form of route processor inside a multilayer switch. This could also be implemented as a router on a stick (ROAS).

28. **Chapter 9 Routing Fundamentals: Static and Dynamic Routing—the following configuration is correct**:

```
router rip
version 2
no auto-summary
network 192.168.0.0
```

29. **Chapter 1 Network Fundamentals: Models and Designs—Answer A is correct.** ICMP operates at the Network layer of the OSI model. It is encapsulated directly in IP packets and does not rely on UDP or TCP for its operation. Note that ICMP possesses its own protocol number like OSPF or EIGRP, which also do not rely on TCP or UDP.

30. **Chapter 1 Network Fundamentals: Models and Designs—Answer C is correct.** A wireless access point (AP) is a device designed to connect users to the network. The device is typically dual band, allowing 2.4 GHz and 5 GHz bands for access by several different 802.11 standards, including 802.11n, 802.11ac and others.

31. **Chapter 1 Network Fundamentals: Models and Designs—Answer B is correct.** Both the hub and switch form a physical star topology.

32. **Chapter 2 Network Fundamentals—IPv4: 172.16.15.254 is correct.** There are 3 subnet bits. The increment is 32. The host range for this subnet is 172.16.0.1 to 172.16.31.254.

33. **Chapter 1 Network Fundamentals: Models and Designs—show controllers is correct.** This is output from **show controllers**. Note the type of serial cable connected is displayed regarding a serial interface.

34. **Chapter 2 Network Fundamentals: IPv4—Answer C is correct.** Unicast addresses are used for a specific host to send traffic to a specific host.

35. **Chapter 2 Network Fundamentals: IPv4—Answer D is correct.** Here are examples of private IPv4 address ranges 10.0.0.0–10.255.255.255; 172.16.0.0–172.31.255.255; 192.168.0.0–192.168.255.255.

36. **Chapter 2 Network Fundamentals: IPv4—Answer D is correct.** Cisco routers are able to support IPv6 on interfaces by default. They cannot, however, route other devices IPv6 traffic without the added global command.

37. **Chapter 5 LAN Switching Fundamentals: VLANs and Interswitch Connectivity—Answer C is correct.** The switch will send broadcast frames to all ports associated with that VLAN (including access and trunk ports), except the port the frame was received on.

38. **Chapter 4 LAN Switching Fundamentals: Switching Concepts—Answers B and D are correct.** The frame header includes destination and source MAC addresses (each six octets in length), the EtherType field and, optionally, an IEEE 802.1Q tag.

39. **Chapter 4 LAN Switching Fundamentals: Switching Concepts—Answer B is correct.** The show interface command is very valuable for troubleshooting issues like collision, and also for verifying the overall status of a switch or router interface.

40. **Chapter 5 LAN Switching Fundamentals: VLANs and Interswitch Connectivity—Answer A is correct.** VLANs cannot be created on VTP Client devices. If you attempt to do this, you receive an error message.

41. **Chapter 5 LAN Switching Fundamentals: VLANs and Interswitch Connectivity—Answer B is correct.** The native VLAN is the untagged VLAN. The default native VLAN is VLAN 1.

42. **Chapter 5 LAN Switching Fundamentals: VLANs and Interswitch Connectivity—Answer C is correct. no cdp run** is used to disable CDP globally on the device. To disable a CDP just on a single interface, use the **no cdp enable** command in interface configuration mode.

43. **Chapter 6 LAN Switching Fundamentals: Port Security—Answer B is correct.** When you configure port security, the default violation mode is shutdown.

44. **Chapter 9 Routing Fundamentals: Static and Dynamic Routing—Answer D is correct**. The default admin distance for internal EIGRP is 90.

45. **Chapter 1 Network Fundamentals: Models and Designs—Answer B is correct.** The distribution layer typically features the most intense security mechanisms, such as access control lists to control traffic. Note that the workstation layer and the access layer are the same. This rules out A and D as options.

46. **Chapter 9 Routing Fundamentals: Static and Dynamic Routing—Answer C is correct.** The static route is **ip route 10.10.20.0 255.255.255.0 172.16.1.1**. The

next-hop is the last IP address shown in this command. On a point-to-point link, the local exit interface can be used as part of the command instead of the next-hop address of the next router in the path.

47. **Chapter 16 Infrastructure Maintenance: Device Maintenance—Answer C is correct.** TFTP is the only protocol here that relies on UDP.

48. **Chapter 10 Infrastructure Services: DNS, DHCP, NTP—Answer C is correct.** DNS provides resolution of names to IP addresses.

49. **Chapter 10 Infrastructure Services: DNS, DHCP, NTP—Answer C is correct.** The NSLOOKUP tool is a common utility for DNS issues. The tool is excellent and displays information that you can use to diagnose Domain Name System (DNS) infrastructure problems and misconfigurations.

50. **Chapter 10 Infrastructure Services: DNS, DHCP, NTP—Answer D is correct.** It is simple to configure your Cisco device to acquire an address via DHCP. Under interface configuration mode, after bringing up the interface, use the **ip address dhcp** command.

51. **Chapter 14 Infrastructure Maintenance: Initial Device Configuration—Answer D is correct.** The show ip interface brief command provides a nice summary of the IP addresses assigned to your interfaces and their status. It does so in an easy-to-read, table-like format. This command is often typed as simply **sh ip int br**. This command does not provide mask information, however. For that, you can use **show ip interface**.

52. **Chapter 10 Infrastructure Services: DNS, DHCP, NTP—Answer D is correct.** A stratum 1 device is the most authoritative time server on the network. When you use the command **ntp master** and do not specify the stratum: the default stratum is 8.

53. **Chapter 11 Infrastructure Services: ACLs—Answer B is correct.** The order of access list statements is very important; they are processed from top to bottom. Here, the permit statement that begins the list permits all traffic before the deny statements are processed. On many IOS routers, the subsequent "deny" access control entries wouldn't even be allowed, and would generate a message indicating a conflict due to the **permit any** entry already being in place.

54. **Chapter 12 Infrastructure Services: NAT A is correct.** Dynamic NAT uses an ACL to identify the addresses to translate. The NAT commands also can include a pool to indicate the addresses that will be used for the translations.

55. **Chapter 17 Infrastructure Maintenance: IOS Troubleshooting Tools—Answer B is correct.** There are 8 syslog levels on a Cisco router. They are numbered 0 through 7. 7 provides the most detail.

56. **Chapter 16 Infrastructure Maintenance: Device Maintenance—Answer A is correct.** The running-configuration exists in RAM and cannot survive a reboot. The startup-configuration is stored in NVRAM and is loaded into RAM after a reboot.

57. **Chapter 14 Infrastructure Maintenance: Initial Device Configuration—Answer D is correct.** The **no login** command is very confusing. When it is issued, it indicates that the password should not be checked when connecting to the router on those VTY lines. Effectively it means that no login is required.

58. **Chapter 15 Infrastructure Maintenance: Device Hardening—Answer B is correct.** Here the Telnet password will be ChEeEs&WiZ, but to access privileged mode, rtYHS3TTs is required.

59. **Chapter 4 LAN Switching Fundamentals: Switching Concepts—Answers A and D are correct.** When the Windows hosts send at least 1 frame into the network, the switch would learn their respective MAC addresses. The switch can be configured with a management VLAN 1 IP address for the benefit of management of the switch. A default gateway is also required for the switch to communicate back to the management computer if that management computer is not on the same IP subnet as the switch.

60. **Chapter 6 LAN Switching Fundamentals: Port Security: Answers C and E are correct.** Here, a solution is port security with a static port security MAC address assignment.

Practice Exam 2

Are you ready to assess your preparedness for the actual ICND1 exam? Practice Exam 1 and this Practice Exam 2 are here for this purpose.

As you take this practice exam, please consider the following test-taking tips:

▶ **Read each question twice if necessary:** Be sure to read each question carefully so that you can fully understand the question. Sometimes this will necessitate reading the question twice.

▶ **Read the answers starting from the bottom:** When you read the answers from the bottom, you force yourself to carefully read each answer. If you read the answers from the top, you might find yourself quickly selecting an answer that looks right and skipping over the other answers. This is dangerous since there might be a better answer later in the options.

▶ **Time yourself:** The CCENT exam is a 90-minute exam. Time yourself during this practice exam to make sure that you stay within this time limit.

▶ **If you do not know the answer to a question, make a note of it:** Go back and review any trouble areas later. Be sure that you are mastering the topic area, not just looking up the answer to this one question. If you are unsure about one aspect of a topic, chances are you might be unsure about other areas related to that same topic. The Answer Key provides a chapter reference for you to make looking up trouble spots much easier for you.

▶ **Prepare mentally to take a test:** To properly assess yourself, take this practice exam as you would take the real exam. This means that you should find a quiet place without any distractions so that you can focus on each question. Provide scratch paper and a pen and pencil for yourself. No other tools (such as calculators) may be used in your actual exam or in your practice here.

▶ **If you cannot determine the correct answer(s), begin by eliminating incorrect answer(s):** If there are four options and you know that three are absolutely wrong, the fourth option has to be the correct one.

▶ **Consider taking this practice exam, as well as the next one, multiple times until you get perfect scores:** When you can consistently score high on these practice exams, the better you are likely to perform in the actual exam.

▶ **Pay close attention to the Answer Key:** You will note that many exam answers lie in store for you in our explanations to questions as well!

▶ **Enjoy the fill-in-the-blank style questions:** Although these question types are rare for the actual exam, we use them here to make this exam much tougher! These questions also provide me with the ability to test you in a simulation style manner—where you must provide correct configurations.

▶ **Use the CD-ROM materials:** There are even more practice exams waiting for you on the CD-ROM that accompanies this text. Be sure to use those materials as well.

▶ **Don't despair:** Do not be overly upset if on your first attempt at this practice exam, you do not score well. It only means that you need to continue studying. Be glad that you are able to spot your weak areas now and not after taking the actual exam. Go back through and review your problem areas now to ensure you are ready!

Congratulations in your pursuit of this valued IT certification!

1. Examine the NAT configuration shown in the exhibit. What is the problem with this NAT configuration?

```
interface gi0/0
 ip address 10.10.10.1 255.255.255.0
 ip nat inside
 !
interface gi0/1
 ip address 10.10.20.1 255.255.255.0
 ip nat inside
 !
interface serial 0/0
 ip address 172.16.10.64 255.255.255.0
 !
ip nat pool MYPOOL 172.16.10.1 172.16.10.1 prefix 24
ip nat inside source list 7 pool MYPOOL overload
access-list 7 permit 10.10.10.0 0.0.0.31
access-list 7 permit 10.10.20.0 0.0.0.31
```

_____

2. What syslog level in Cisco uses the name emergencies?

○ **A.** 1

○ **B.** 2

○ **C.** 0

○ **D.** 7

3. The user at the PC shown in the figure that follows is copying a file from the Server with a program that uses a connectionless transport protocol. Which protocols on the left match up to the layers on the right regarding the encapsulation done by the PC? (Not all protocols are used.)

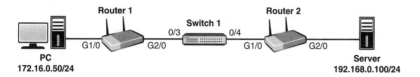

Protocols	Layers
UDP	Application
Serial	
TFTP	Transport
ICMP	
TCP	
Ethernet	Internet
IP	
FTP	Network Access

4. Where does the startup-configuration typically reside on a Cisco router?

- **A.** NVRAM
- **B.** Flash
- **C.** RAM
- **D.** USB

5. What is the effect of the **no login** command under the virtual terminal lines?

- **A.** It prevents log in to the device using the VTY lines.
- **B.** It redirects login to the console port.
- **C.** It triggers AAA only access to the VTY lines.
- **D.** It does not require login on the VTY lines.

6. Examine the configuration that follows. Why is the configuration producing an error when pasted into the CLI?

```
Current configuration : 2945 bytes
!
!
version 15.6
service timestamps debug datetime msec
service timestamps log datetime msec
```

```
no service password-encryption
!
hostname Router-A
!
boot-start-marker
boot-end-marker
!
no aaa new-model
!
mmi polling-interval 60
no mmi auto-configure
no mmi pvc
mmi snmp-timeout 180
!
!
!
ip cef
no ipv6 cef
!
multilink bundle-name authenticated
!
redundancy
!
!
!
interface GigabitEthernet0/0
 no ip address
 shutdown
 duplex auto
 speed auto
 media-type rj45
!
interface GigabitEthernet0/1
 ip address 172.16.1.64 255.255.255.224
 duplex auto
 speed auto
 media-type rj45
!
ip forward-protocol nd
!
!
no ip http server
no ip http secure-server
ip route 10.10.10.0 255.255.255.0 172.16.1.2
!
!
!
access-list 101 permit ip 10.10.0.0 0.0.255.255 any
access-list 101 deny   ip host 10.10.10.1 any
```

```
access-list 101 deny    ip any any log
!
control-plane
!
!
line con 0
line aux 0
line vty 0 4
 password cisco
 no login
 transport input telnet ssh
!
no scheduler allocate
!
end
```

- ○ **A.** Because there is no enable password set
- ○ **B.** Because the hostname is not legal
- ○ **C.** The transport input command lists both Telnet and SSH
- ○ **D.** Because of a bad IP address and mask combination

7. When is a login banner displayed on a Cisco router?

- ○ **A.** Before the Username: prompt
- ○ **B.** After entry to user mode
- ○ **C.** After entry to privileged mode
- ○ **D.** After entry via Virtual Terminal lines only

8. What hashing mechanism is used for the enable secret on your Cisco router?

- ○ **A.** MD5
- ○ **B.** Level 7 Cisco
- ○ **C.** DES
- ○ **D.** IPsec

9. Where is the full compressed IOS image typically stored on a Cisco router?

- ○ **A.** TPM
- ○ **B.** RAM
- ○ **C.** NVRAM
- ○ **D.** Flash

10. What is true regarding a network device that receives the packet as shown in the protocol analyzer output that follows? (Choose two.)

```
⊟ Ethernet II, Src: ca:00:1a:a4:00:1c (ca:00:1a:a4:00:1c), Dst: IntelCor_12:34:56 (00:1b:77:12:34:56)
  ⊞ Destination: IntelCor_12:34:56 (00:1b:77:12:34:56)
  ⊞ Source: ca:00:1a:a4:00:1c (ca:00:1a:a4:00:1c)
    Type: IP (0x0800)
⊞ Internet Protocol Version 4, Src: 198.133.219.25 (198.133.219.25), Dst: 10.0.0.2 (10.0.0.2)
⊞ Transmission Control Protocol, Src Port: http (80), Dst Port: d-cinema-rrp (1173), Seq: 0, Ack: 1, Len: 0
```

- ○ **A.** A bridge would forward the packet based on the layer 1 destination address.
- ○ **B.** A hub would forward the packet based on the Layer 2 destination address.
- ○ **C.** A switch would forward the frame based on the Layer 2 destination address.
- ○ **D.** A router would forward the packet based on the Layer 2 source address.
- ○ **E.** A router would forward the packet based on the Layer 3 source address.
- ○ **F.** A router would forward the packet based on the Layer 3 destination address.

11. What protocol does Ping use?

- ○ **A.** TCP
- ○ **B.** ICMP
- ○ **C.** UDP
- ○ **D.** ARP

12. Map the layers on the left to the protocols on the right. Not all layers are used, and some layers may be used more than once.

Layers	TCP/IP Protocols

Layers
Application
Presentation
Session
Transport
Network/Internet
Datalink
Physical

TCP/IP Protocols
CDP
TCP
PPP
SMTP
Serial
IP

13. What is the equivalent of the OSI presentation layer in the TCP/IP model?

- ○ **A.** Internet Layer
- ○ **B.** Network Access Layer
- ○ **C.** Transport Layer
- ○ **D.** Application Layer

14. What transport layer protocol provides sequencing and synchronization?

- ○ **A.** HTTP
- ○ **B.** TCP
- ○ **C.** ICMP
- ○ **D.** UDP

15. What device protects "internal" networks from "external" networks?

- ○ **A.** WLC
- ○ **B.** Firewall
- ○ **C.** AP
- ○ **D.** Layer 2 Switch

16. What layer of the classic Cisco network model is typically not collapsed in a simplified two-layer design?

- ○ **A.** Access
- ○ **B.** Internet
- ○ **C.** Core
- ○ **D.** Distribution

17. What topology provides the most overhead in a network design?

- ○ **A.** Bus
- ○ **B.** Full mesh
- ○ **C.** Star
- ○ **D.** Partial mesh

18. What is the standard maximum frame size in a typical Ethernet network?

- ○ **A.** 1500
- ○ **B.** 1600
- ○ **C.** 1900
- ○ **D.** 9000

19. In the network depicted, the user at PC1 has asked about which program to
use that will copy a file from the server to PC1 using a reliable Layer 4 transport
protocol. Which of the following would meet both requirements? (Choose two.)

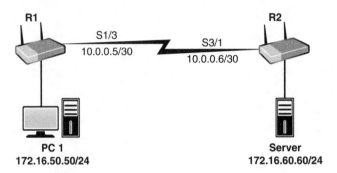

- ○ **A.** OSPF
- ○ **B.** TFTP
- ○ **C.** FTP
- ○ **D.** SCP
- ○ **E.** DNS

20. What is the typical size of the host portion of an IPv6 address?

- ○ **A.** 64 bits
- ○ **B.** 32 bits
- ○ **C.** 16 bits
- ○ **D.** 8 bits

21. What technology is used in order to allow a switch port to carry the traffic of
multiple Data VLANs from one device to another in a Cisco network?

- ○ **A.** VLAN hopping
- ○ **B.** Trunking
- ○ **C.** Port Security
- ○ **D.** VTP

22. What port security violation mode does not increment any security violation
conters?

- ○ **A.** Restrict
- ○ **B.** Protect
- ○ **C.** Shutdown
- ○ **D.** Disable

23. What port security approach is considered a mix of dynamic and static configuration?

   ○ **A.** Trunking

   ○ **B.** Violation null

   ○ **C.** Sticky learning

   ○ **D.** Blocked learning

24. Your junior administrator is examining a Cisco routing table and ask you what the meaning of the D he sees in routing table entries. What does this indicate?

   ○ **A.** OSPF

   ○ **B.** BGP

   ○ **C.** RIP

   ○ **D.** EIGRP

   ○ **E.** RIP version 2

25. At what layer of the OSI model do you find bits?

   ○ **A.** Physical

   ○ **B.** Transport

   ○ **C.** Network

   ○ **D.** Data Link

26. Examine the command shown here, what is the purpose of the last entry in this command (121)?

```
ip route 10.10.10.0 255.255.255.0 172.16.1.1 121
```

   ○ **A.** This is a sequence number.

   ○ **B.** This is the metric value for the route entry.

   ○ **C.** This is an administrative distance value to create a floating static route.

   ○ **D.** This is a weight value.

27. Which of the following is used by an IPv6 link local address?

   ○ **A.** f080::/10

   ○ **B.** fe80::/10

   ○ **C.** f880::/10

   ○ **D.** f008::/10

   ○ **E.** fe80::/8

28. What networking device provides instructions to APs in the modern network?

   ○ **A.** Router

   ○ **B.** Firewall

   ○ **C.** Switch

   ○ **D.** WLC

29. What is the name of the 802.1Q trunked VLAN that is not tagged and is intended for management traffic?

   ○ **A.** The Native VLAN

   ○ **B.** The Default VLAN

   ○ **C.** The System VLAN

   ○ **D.** The Prime VLAN

30. Your company has contracted with a service provider, who will be providing a T1 connection to connect your company to the Internet. You have 15 internal hosts, currently connected to a workgroup Ethernet switch. Which of the following physical elements would be required to use the service provider's connection?

   ○ **A.** A Layer 2 switch with a T1 interface

   ○ **B.** A Layer 2 switch with a serial interface and at least 1 available Ethernet port

   ○ **C.** A router with an Ethernet and serial interface

   ○ **D.** A router with two Ethernet interfaces and configured with NAT

31. In the network depicted, the Server is sending HTTP content back to the PC that requested it. Which of the following is true as the packets are forwarded over the network?

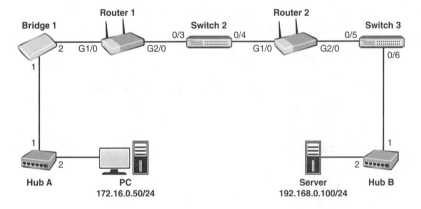

   ○ **A.** The bridges and switches use Ethernet addresses to make forwarding decisions.

   ○ **B.** The hubs, bridges, and switches use Ethernet addresses to make forwarding decisions.

○ **C.** The routers, bridges, and switches use Ethernet addresses to make forwarding decisions.

○ **D.** The hubs, routers, bridges, and switches use Ethernet addresses to make forwarding decisions.

32. Based on the network depicted, provide the complete syntax for a standard ACL for Router 2 G2/0 that permits traffic sourced from the PC but denies all other traffic. This ACL must use the number 10, and it must use the most efficient syntax possible.

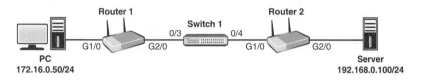

_____

33. Which of the following statements are true?

○ **A.** Hosts use ARP to learn the IP address associated with a URL such as www.yahoo.com.

○ **B.** ARP is used by a host to learn a default gateway's Layer 2 address.

○ **C.** SMTP and TFTP are both application layer services using TCP at the transport layer.

○ **D.** IPv4 clients in large networks can be assigned IP addresses dynamically using DNS.

34. Which port security configuration approach requires an administrator to save the running-configuration in order to be effective?

○ **A.** Dynamic learning

○ **B.** Static learning

○ **C.** Sticky learning

○ **D.** Age-based learning

35. Examine the topology and the configurations that follow. Why is R1's loopback interface unable to Ping the loopback interface of R3?

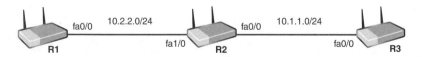

```
R1#
R1#show running-config
Building configuration...
Current configuration : 1270 bytes
!
!
```

```
upgrade fpd auto
version 15.0
service timestamps debug datetime msec
service timestamps log datetime msec
no service password-encryption
!
hostname R1
!
boot-start-marker
boot-end-marker
!
!
no aaa new-model
!
!
!
ip source-route
no ip icmp rate-limit unreachable
ip cef
!
!
!
no ip domain lookup
no ipv6 cef
!
multilink bundle-name authenticated
!
!
!
redundancy
!
!
ip tcp synwait-time 5
!
!
!
interface Loopback0
 ip address 1.1.1.1 255.255.255.255
 !
!
interface FastEthernet0/0
 ip address 10.2.2.1 255.255.255.0
 duplex half
 !
!
interface FastEthernet1/0
 no ip address
 shutdown
```

```
  duplex auto
  speed auto
  !
 !
 interface FastEthernet1/1
  no ip address
  shutdown
  duplex auto
  speed auto
  !
 !
 router rip
  version 2
  network 1.0.0.0
  network 10.0.0.0
  no auto-summary
 !
 ip forward-protocol nd
 no ip http server
 no ip http secure-server
 !
 !
 !
 no cdp log mismatch duplex
 !
 !
 !
 control-plane
  !
 !
 !
 mgcp fax t38 ecm
 mgcp behavior g729-variants static-pt
 !
 !
 !
 gatekeeper
  shutdown
 !
 !
 line con 0
  exec-timeout 0 0
  privilege level 15
  logging synchronous
  stopbits 1
 line aux 0
  exec-timeout 0 0
  privilege level 15
  logging synchronous
  stopbits 1
```

```
line vty 0 4
 login
!
end
R1#
R2#
R2#show running-config
Building configuration...
Current configuration : 1280 bytes
!
upgrade fpd auto
version 15.0
service timestamps debug datetime msec
service timestamps log datetime msec
no service password-encryption
!
hostname R2
!
boot-start-marker
boot-end-marker
!
!
no aaa new-model
!
!
!
ip source-route
no ip icmp rate-limit unreachable
ip cef
!
!
!
!
no ip domain lookup
no ipv6 cef
!
multilink bundle-name authenticated
!
!
!
redundancy
!
!
ip tcp synwait-time 5
!
!
!
```

```
interface Loopback0
 ip address 2.2.2.2 255.255.255.255
 !
!
interface FastEthernet0/0
 ip address 10.1.1.2 255.255.255.0
 duplex half
 !
!
interface FastEthernet1/0
 ip address 10.2.2.2 255.255.255.0
 duplex auto
 speed auto
 !
!
interface FastEthernet1/1
 no ip address
 shutdown
 duplex auto
 speed auto
 !
!
router rip
 version 2
 network 2.0.0.0
 network 10.0.0.0
 no auto-summary
!
ip forward-protocol nd
no ip http server
no ip http secure-server
 !
 !
 !
no cdp log mismatch duplex
 !
 !
 !
control-plane
 !
 !
 !
mgcp fax t38 ecm
mgcp behavior g729-variants static-pt
 !
 !
 !
```

```
gatekeeper
 shutdown
!
!
line con 0
 exec-timeout 0 0
 privilege level 15
 logging synchronous
 stopbits 1
line aux 0
 exec-timeout 0 0
 privilege level 15
 logging synchronous
 stopbits 1
line vty 0 4
 login
!
end
R2#
R3#show running-config
Building configuration...
Current configuration : 1270 bytes
!
!
upgrade fpd auto
version 15.0
service timestamps debug datetime msec
service timestamps log datetime msec
no service password-encryption
!
hostname R3
!
boot-start-marker
boot-end-marker
!
!
no aaa new-model
!
!
!
ip source-route
no ip icmp rate-limit unreachable
ip cef
!
!
!
!
no ip domain lookup
no ipv6 cef
!
```

```
multilink bundle-name authenticated
!
!
!
!
!
!
!
!
!
redundancy
!
!
ip tcp synwait-time 5
!
!
!
!
!
!
!
!
interface Loopback0
 ip address 3.3.3.3 255.255.255.255
 !
!
interface FastEthernet0/0
 ip address 10.1.1.3 255.255.255.0
 duplex half
 shutdown
 !
!
interface FastEthernet1/0
 no ip address
 shutdown
 duplex auto
 speed auto
 !
!
interface FastEthernet1/1
 no ip address
 shutdown
 duplex auto
 speed auto
 !
!
router rip
 version 2
 network 3.0.0.0
```

```
 network 10.0.0.0
 no auto-summary
 !
ip forward-protocol nd
no ip http server
no ip http secure-server
 !
 !
 !
no cdp log mismatch duplex
 !
 !
 !
 !
 !
 !
control-plane
  !
 !
 !
mgcp fax t38 ecm
mgcp behavior g729-variants static-pt
 !
 !
 !
gatekeeper
 shutdown
 !
 !
line con 0
 exec-timeout 0 0
 privilege level 15
 logging synchronous
 stopbits 1
line aux 0
 exec-timeout 0 0
 privilege level 15
 logging synchronous
 stopbits 1
line vty 0 4
 login
 !
end
R3#
```

36. Your junior admin notes that when he just performed a Ping, one of the packets failed. What is the most likely cause of the following results?

```
Router1# ping 10.255.0.126
Type escape sequence to abort.
Sending 5, 100-byte ICMP Echos to 10.255.0.126, timeout is 2
seconds:
.!!!!
Success rate is 80 percent (4/5), round-trip min/avg/max =
35/72/76 ms
```

- ○ **A.** Load balancing, with one of the next hops being unavailable
- ○ **B.** ARP resolution
- ○ **C.** Half Duplex operation
- ○ **D.** 10Mbps being used instead of FastEthernet or GigabitEthernet

37. Router A is assigning IP addresses to hosts in VLAN 10 as shown in the depicted network that follows. The user at PC-10 powers up their computer and checks www.cnn.com for news. What is the correct sequence of the first four protocols used by PC-10 when it first powers up?

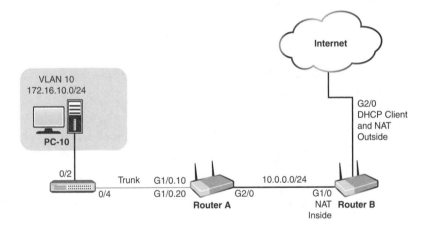

Protocol	Order
OSPF	1st
ARP	
HTTP	2nd
DNS	3rd
DHCP	
ICMP	4th

38. Given the following address and mask 172.16.10.1 255.255.248.0, what is the broadcast address for the subnet?

   ○ **A.** 172.16.15.255

   ○ **B.** 172.16.8.0

   ○ **C.** 172.16.16.255

   ○ **D.** 172.16.255.255

39. What is the multicast address used by RIP version 2 in its operation?

   ○ **A.** 224.0.0.9

   ○ **B.** 224.0.0.1

   ○ **C.** 172.16.1.1

   ○ **D.** 10.10.10.1

40. What is the RFC that was created in order to attempt to solve the IPv4 address shortage?

   ○ **A.** RFC 1002

   ○ **B.** RFC 2001

   ○ **C.** RFC 2002

   ○ **D.** RFC 1918

41. What is the method used by IPv6 to automatically generate a host portion of an IPv6 address?

   ○ **A.** SLAAC

   ○ **B.** DHCPv6

   ○ **C.** Modified EUI-64

   ○ **D.** ARPv6

42. What command does a client use to enable stateless auto configuration of IPv6 address information on an interface?

   ○ **A. ipv6 address autoconfig**

   ○ **B. ipv6 address dhcp**

   ○ **C. ipv6 address enable**

   ○ **D. ipv6 enable**

43. RIP version 2 is properly configured and working on both routers shown in the depicted network. The following was added to Router X: **ip route 10.255.0.128 255.255.255.224 10.255.0.75 89.** What will be the result?

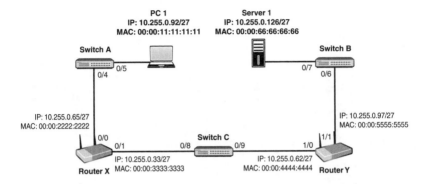

- ○ **A.** The static route will have an administrative distance that is better than RIP.
- ○ **B.** There will be a Layer 2 loop.
- ○ **C.** Router X will attempt to send packets destined to subnet 10.255.0.128/27 to PC 1.
- ○ **D.** This will cause a broadcast storm.

44. Examine the topology shown. PC1 is sending an HTTP packet to Server 1. What is true about this traffic as it is forwarded through Switch C? (Choose three.)

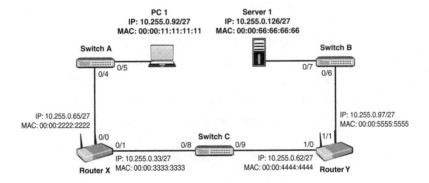

- ○ **A.** Source physical address will be 0000.3333.3333.
- ○ **B.** Source layer 2 address will be 00:00:11:11:11:11.
- ○ **C.** Source address will be 10.255.0.92.
- ○ **D.** Destination physical address will be 00:00:66:66:66:66.
- ○ **E.** Destination address will be 0000.4444.4444.

45. The Switch MAC address table is shown below the topology here. PC1's ARP cache is empty, and the user at PC 1 uses Ping to test the IP address reachability of Sever 1. Which of the following is true when the user presses enter?

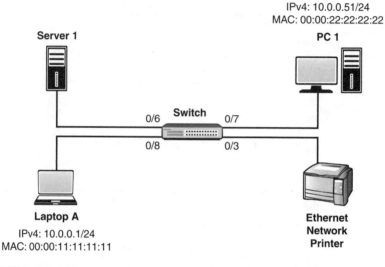

IPv4: 10.0.0.51/24
MAC: 00:00:22:22:22:22

PC 1

Server 1

0/6 **Switch** 0/7

0/8 0/3

Laptop A
IPv4: 10.0.0.1/24
MAC: 00:00:11:11:11:11

Ethernet
Network
Printer

MAC address	VLAN	Port
0000.1111.1111	1	0/8
0000.2222.2222	1	0/7
0000.6783.BEEF	1	0/6

- ○ **A.** The first frame will be sent out port 0/6 only.
- ○ **B.** The switch will add the printer's MAC address to the MAC address table.
- ○ **C.** The first frame from PC1 will be forwarded out all ports, except 0/7.
- ○ **D.** The reply to the PING request will cause the Server's MAC address to be added to the table.
- ○ **E.** The first frame will have a destination MAC address of Server 1.

46. A host runs the command **ipconfig** on their local system. The results are as follows:

```
Ethernet adapter:
    Connection-specific DNS Suffix  . :
    IPv4 Address. . . . . . . . . . . : 172.18.62.255
    Subnet Mask . . . . . . . . . . . : 255.255.248.0
    Default Gateway . . . . . . . . . : 172.18.63.254
```

Which of the following are true? (Choose two.)

○ **A.** The broadcast address for the host's subnet is 172.18.71.255.

○ **B.** The network the host is connected to is a Class B private address.

○ **C.** The subnet the host is connected to could support up to 2048 hosts.

○ **D.** The host with an IP of 172.18.64.5 would be on the same network as the host in the question.

○ **E.** The host address is on the 172.18.56.0/21 network.

47. Which of the following are valid host addresses when using a mask of 255.255.248.0? (Choose three.)

○ **A.** 34.45.56.0

○ **B.** 40.50.60.0

○ **C.** 50.60.70.255

○ **D.** 51.61.71.255

○ **E.** 60.70.80.0

○ **F.** 60.70.80.255

48. Refer to the depicted network. All the switches and R1 have had their startup configurations deleted, and then were rebooted before saving to NVRAM. These devices are now running in their default configuration. Which of the following are true? (Choose three.)

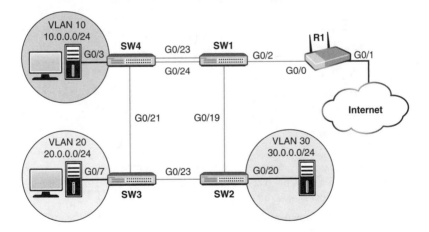

○ **A.** Clients shown in the diagram as being on VLANs 10, 20 and 30 will now all be on the same VLAN.

○ **B.** SW1 will see CDP neighbors on at least three interfaces.

○ **C.** The commands **show protocols, show ip interface, show interface** or **show ip interface brief** can be used to confirm that R1 G0/0 is up/up.

○ **D.** If the command: **ip address 10.0.0.1 /24** was added for G0/0 on R1, SW1 would learn that IP address within 60 seconds.

○ **E.** SW2 will see 2 CDP neighbors.

49. Provide the switch configuration to meet these requirements:

○ Create a user account BOB with a password of ToUgH1!23; this password should be stored using MD5.

○ Telnet should be disabled on the switch.

○ SSH should be enabled on the switch.

○ The local user accounts should be used to authenticate on the VTY lines.

○ Existing and future plain text passwords should be encrypted.

○ The password to get into privileged mode should be iTsMe@HeRe$, and it should be stored using MD5.

○ The management interface should use the default VLAN and have the IP address of 10.20.30.75/27.

○ The default gateway should be set to 10.20.30.94.

50. CSMA/CD technology is critical for what type of Ethernet network?

○ **A.** Full mesh

○ **B.** Partial mesh

○ **C.** Star

○ **D.** Half-duplex

51. Your VoIP users are complaining about their Cisco IP Phones not functioning properly. There have been changes to the local switch that connects these users. What is the most likely problem?

○ **A.** CDP was disabled.

○ **B.** Telnet was no longer permitted.

○ **C.** Service Password Encryption was used.

○ **D.** SSH is now mandatory.

52. How is CDP carried on the network?

- ○ **A.** Using 802.1Q messages
- ○ **B.** Using VTP messages
- ○ **C.** Using Layer 2
- ○ **D.** Using Layer 1

53. What is the default administrative distance of iBGP?

- ○ **A.** 20
- ○ **B.** 90
- ○ **C.** 120
- ○ **D.** 200

54. What two options exist for the next hop information in a static route? (Choose two.)

- ○ **A.** Specifying the next hop IP address
- ○ **B.** Specifying the next hop MAC address
- ○ **C.** Specifying the next hop CDP ID
- ○ **D.** Specifying the exit interface

55. What is the default lease duration for a Cisco DHCP server?

- ○ **A.** 1 hour
- ○ **B.** 1 day
- ○ **C.** 1 week
- ○ **D.** 1 month
- ○ **E.** 1 year

56. How do you configure a Cisco router to act as the reference time source on a network?

- ○ **A.** Using the **ntp server** command
- ○ **B.** Using the **ntp master** command
- ○ **C.** Using the **ntp source** command
- ○ **D.** Using the **ntp clock** command

57. What is the default privilege level for a local user account created with the **user-name** command?

- ○ **A.** 0
- ○ **B.** 1
- ○ **C.** 8
- ○ **D.** 15

58. What VTY line command causes the local username database to be checked for remote access?

- ○ **A. login**
- ○ **B. local**
- ○ **C. login local**
- ○ **D. aaa login local**

59. What command do you use in order to upgrade an IOS image on your local device with an image from a TFTP server?

- ○ **A. move**
- ○ **B. copy**
- ○ **C. tftp server**
- ○ **D. upgrade**

60. How many probes does Ping send by default?

- ○ **A.** 1
- ○ **B.** 2
- ○ **C.** 3
- ○ **D.** 5
- ○ **E.** 8

Answer Key to Practice Exam 2

Answers at a Glance to Practice Exam 2

1. This configuration fails to define the outside NAT interface.

2. C

3. Application: TFTP; Transport: UDP; Internet: IP; Network Access: Ethernet

4. A

5. D

6. D

7. A

8. A

9. D

10. C, F

11. B

12. CDP: Datalink; TCP: Transport; PPP: Datalink; SMTP: Application; Serial: Physical; IP: Network

13. D

14. B

15. B

16. A

17. B

18. A

19. C, D

20. A

21. B

22. B

23. C

24. D

25. A

26. C

27. B

28. D

29. A

30. C

31. A

32.
```
access-list 10
permit host
172.16.0.50

access-list 10
deny any
interface
gi2/0
ip access-
group 10 out
```

33. B

34. C

35. The Fa0/0 interface on R3 is administratively down.

36. B

37. 1st: DHCP; 2nd: ARP; 3rd: DNS; 4th: HTTP

38. A

39. A

40. D

41. C

42. A

43. A

44. A, C, E

45. C

46. B, E

47. B, C, F

48. A, B, E

49.
```
username
BOB secret
ToUgH1!23

!
line vty 0 15
transport
input ssh
login local
!
service
password-
encryption
!
enable secret
iTsMe@HeRe$
!
```

```
interface
vlan 1
ip address
10.20.30.75
255.255.255.
224!
ip default-
gateway 10.20.30.94
```

50. D

51. A

52. C

53. D

54. A, D

55. B

56. B

57. B

58. C

59. B

60. D

Answers with Explanations

1. **Chapter 12 Infrastructure Services: NAT — "This configuration fails to define the outside interface" is correct.** Notice here we are doing a form of dynamic NAT. Also, we are overloading a single routable address. This means we are doing Port Address Translation or PAT. This configuration is fine, except it does not specify the outside NAT interface (serial 0/0).

2. **Chapter 13 Infrastructure Maintenance: Syslog and Device Management — Answer C is correct.** There are 8 syslog levels on a Cisco router. They are numbered 0 through 7. 0 is the most severe condition and has the name emergencies. 7 is the least severe (and has the most detail) and is debug.

3. **Chapter 1 Network Fundamentals: Models and Designs — "Application: TFTP; Transport: UDP; Internet: IP; Network Access: Ethernet" is correct.** Here the connectionless application is TFTP. UDP is the connectionless transport protocol used by TFTP. IP is the Internet layer protocol, whereas Ethernet is used at the Network Access.

4. **Chapter 16 Infrastructure Maintenance: Device Maintenance — Answer A is correct.** The running-configuration exists in RAM and cannot survive a reboot. The startup-configuration is stored to survive a reboot; this location is typically NVRAM.

5. **Chapter 14 Infrastructure Maintenance: Initial Device Configuration — Answer D is correct.** The no login command can be very confusing. When it is issued, it indicates that the password should not be checked upon login, so it does not prevent login, but actually makes login possible without security.

6. **Chapter 14 Infrastructure Maintenance: Initial Device Configuration — Answer D is correct.** A valid IP address can't have all zeroes for the host portion, which is the problem with this attempted configuration. As a side note, on some Cisco devices, hostnames must begin with a letter, end with a letter or digit, and have as interior characters only letters, digits, and hyphens. Names must be 63 characters or fewer. In this example, the hostname was not the problem.

7. **Chapter 15 Infrastructure Maintenance: Device Hardening — Answer A is correct.** A configured login banner will appear before the Username: prompt.

8. **Chapter 15 Infrastructure Maintenance: Device Hardening — Answer A is correct.** MD5 is the hashing algorithm used for the enable secret.

9. **Chapter 16 Infrastructure Maintenance: Device Maintenance — Answer D is correct.** Flash memory is like the hard drive on a PC; it is typically where the operating system is stored.

10. **Chapter 7 Routing Fundamentals: Routing Concepts — Answers C and F are correct.** Switches forward based on the destination MAC (Layer 2) address, whereas routers forward based on the destination Layer 3 address (the IP address).

11. **Chapter 17 Infrastructure Maintenance: IOS Troubleshooting Tools — Answer B is correct.** Ping is a troubleshooting tool that relies upon ICMP.

12. **Chapter 1 Network Fundamentals: Models and Designs — CDP: Datalink; TCP: Transport; PPP: Datalink; SMTP: Application; Serial: Physical; IP: Network**. Be prepared to map technologies to the correct layer of the OSI model as done here.

13. **Chapter 1 Network Fundamentals: Models and Designs — Answer D is correct.** The presentation layer of the OSI model is rolled into the Application layer of the TCP/IP model.

14. **Chapter 9 Routing Fundamentals: Static and Dynamic Routing — Answer B is correct.** TCP at the Transport layer provides connection oriented, reliable features. This includes the sequencing and synchronization of packets.

15. **Chapter 1 Network Fundamentals: Models and Designs — Answer B is correct.** Firewalls are specialized devices that protect internal networks from external networks. Keep in mind, they can be software implementations or hardware appliances. These days, they can even be virtual.

16. **Chapter 1 Network Fundamentals: Models and Designs — Answer A is correct.** A collapsed core design is one where the distribution layer meshes into the core. You often see this in smaller networks, where the complexity of a three-layer design just really is not needed.

17. **Chapter 1 Network Fundamentals: Models and Designs — Answer B is correct.** The mesh topology is often implemented as full or partial. The full mesh provides the best redundancy, but it typically comes at the cost of complexity and the cost of many links.

18. **Chapter 4 LAN Switching Fundamentals: Switching Concepts — Answer A is correct**. The standard frame size and MTU is 1500 bytes in Ethernet networks.

19. **Chapter 16 Infrastructure Maintenance: Device Maintenance — Answers C and D are correct.** OSPF is a routing protocol and not a file transfer protocol used in the network. TFTP uses UDP and does not provide reliability. Finally, DNS is used for name resolution and not file transfer.

20. **Chapter 3 Network Fundamentals: IPv6 — Answer A is correct.** The host portion of an IPv6 address is typically 64 bits in length.

21. **Chapter 5 LAN Switching Fundamentals: VLANs and Interswitch Connectivity — Answer B is correct.** Trunking, specifically 802.1Q, permits the transport of multiple Data VLANs between devices.

22. **Chapter 6 LAN Switching Fundamentals: Port Security — Answer B is correct.** There are three possible violation modes; of them, protect is the only one that does not alert an administrator to a security violation.

23. **Chapter 6 LAN Switching Fundamentals: Port Security — Answer C is correct.** Port security sticky learning means the port will initially dynamically learn the MAC address and added to the running configuration. Then this MAC address can be saved (using the command **copy running-config startup-config**) in the startup configuration as a static MAC address assignment for port security when the switch reboots.

24. **Chapter 9 Routing Fundamentals: Static and Dynamic Routing — Answer D is correct**. EIGRP routes appear in the routing table with a D designation.

25. **Chapter 1 Network Fundamentals: Models and Designs—Answer A is correct**. Bits are the PDU at the physical layer.

26. **Chapter 9 Routing Fundamentals: Static and Dynamic Routing—Answer C is correct**. Administrative distance is added to the **ip route** command in order to create floating static routes.

27. **Chapter 3 Network Fundamentals: IPv6—Answer B is correct**. Link local IPv6 addresses use the fe80::/10 prefix.

28. **Chapter 1 Network Fundamentals: Models and Designs—Answer D is correct.** The Wireless LAN Controller is the device in the modern network that controls and manages Access Points.

29. **Chapter 5 LAN Switching Fundamentals: VLANs and Interswitch Connectivity—Answer A is correct**. The Native VLAN is a special VLAN on the trunk that does not use an 802.1Q tag by default.

30. **Chapter 1 Network Fundamentals: Models and Designs—Answer C is correct.** Here, a router completes the network design. This router should possess an Ethernet interface for connection to the switched network, and a serial interface for connection to the service provider network.

31. **Chapter 1 Network Fundamentals: Models and Designs—Answer A is correct.** Switches and bridges use Layer 2 Ethernet addresses to forward traffic.

32. **Chapter 11 Infrastructure Services—ACLs**: the correct syntax:
```
access-list 10 permit host 172.16.0.50
access-list 10 deny any
interface gi2/0
ip access-group 10 out
```

33. **Chapter 4 LAN Switching Fundamentals: Switching Concepts—Answer B is correct.** ARP provides the IP address (Layer 3) to MAC address (Layer 2) to resolution in an Ethernet network.

34. **Chapter 6 LAN Switching Fundamentals: Port Security—Answer C is correct.** Sticky learning requires the running configuration be saved. This places the dynamically learned entries into the startup configuration as static entries.

35. **Chapter 9 Routing Fundamentals: Static and Dynamic Routing—The Fa0/0 interface on R3 is administratively down**. Notice the shutdown command is in place under the interface configuration for Fa0/0.

36. **Chapter 4 LAN Switching Fundamentals: Switching Concepts—Answer B is correct.** Initial Ping packets might fail as a result of the initial ARP that must be performed.

37. **Chapter 10 Infrastructure Services: DNS, DHCP, NTP—1st: DHCP; 2nd: ARP; 3rd: DNS; 4th: HTTP.** This system broadcasts for its local DHCP server. It then performs ARP for its default gateway. Finally, this device uses DNS for domain name resolution and HTTP to access the website.

38. **Chapter 2 Network Fundamentals: IPv4—Answer A is correct.** Here the increment is on 8 as there are 5 bits of subnetting used. The host range of this subnet is 172.16.8.1 to 172.16.15.254.

39. **Chapter 2 Network Fundamentals: IPv4—Answer A is correct.** Notice that only two of these options are multicast addresses: A and B. A is the address used by RIP version 2.

40. **Chapter 2 Network Fundamentals: IPv4—Answer D is correct.** RFC 1918 defines private use IPv4 addresses.

41. **Chapter 3 Network Fundamentals: IPv6—Answer C is correct.** IPv6 uses modified EUI-64 technology in order to automatically generate a 64-bit host portion.

42. **Chapter 3 Network Fundamentals: IPv6—Answer A is correct.** The ipv6 address autoconfig command is used on the client.

43. **Chapter 9 Routing Fundamentals: Static and Dynamic Routing—Answer A is correct.** Here the AD of the static route (89) is less (better) than the AD of RIP, which is 120.

44. **Chapter 7 Routing Fundamentals: Routing Concepts—Answers A, C, and E are correct**. Without NAT, the source and destination IP addresses never change. The Layer 2 header information as the frame goes through Switch C will show a source MAC address of Router X and a destination MAC address of Router Y.

45. **Chapter 4 LAN Switching Fundamentals: Switching Concepts—Answer C is correct.** The first frame would be an ARP request, sent as a broadcast and it is sent out all ports for that VLAN except the switch port where the original frame entered the switch.

46. **Chapter 2 Network Fundamentals: IPv4—Answers B and E are correct**. This host is on the 172.18.56.0/21 network with a 172.18.56.1: 172.18.63.254 host range.

47. **Chapter 2 Network Fundamentals: IPv4—Answers B, C, and F are correct.** Host addresses can't have all 1s or all 0s for the host portion of their addresses. Below is the breakdown for the relevant networks, given this mask.

    NOTE: 255.255.248.0 or /21

	Subnet	Range	Broadcast
7	x.x.56.0	x.x.56.1– x.x.63.254	x.x.63.255
8	x.x.64.0	x.x.64.1– x.x.71.254	x.x.71.255
9	x.x.72.0	x.x.72.1– x.x.79.254	x.x.79.255
10	x.x.80.0	x.x.80.1– x.x.87.254	x.x.87.255
11	x.x.88.0	x.x.88.1– x.x.95.254	x.x.95.255
12	x.x.96.0	x.x.96.1– x.x.103.254	x.x.103.255
13	x.x.104.0	x.x.104.1– x.x.111.254	x.x.111.255

48. **Chapter 5 LAN Switching Fundamentals: VLANs and Interswitch Connectivity—Answers A, B, and E are correct.** The clients are now on the same VLAN, the default VLAN if 1. SW1 will see SW4, SW2, and R1 via CDP. SW2 will see SW1 and SW3 via CDP.

49. **Chapter 15 Infrastructure Maintenance: Device Hardening—Here is the solution configuration:**

```
username BOB secret ToUgH1!23
!
line vty 0 15
transport input ssh
login local
!
service password-encryption
!
enable secret iTsMe@HeRe$
!
interface vlan 1
ip address 10.20.30.75 255.255.255.224!
ip default-gateway 10.20.30.94
```

50. **Chapter 4 LAN Switching Fundamentals: Switching Concepts—Answer D is correct.** CSMA/CD allows devices to react properly when collisions occur on half-duplex network connections.

51. **Chapter 14 Infrastructure Maintenance: Initial Device Configuration—Answer A is correct.** Cisco IP Phones use CDP in order to communicate key information with the switch.

52. **Chapter 16 Infrastructure Maintenance: Device Maintenance—Answer C is correct.** CDP is transported directly over Layer 2. This ensures devices can see each other.

53. **Chapter 7 Routing Fundamentals: Routing Concepts—Answer D is correct.** iBGP is not considered compared to IGPs for distribution of prefixes inside an AS. As a result, it has a very high admin distance of 200.

54. **Chapter 9 Routing Fundamentals: Static and Dynamic Routing—Answers A and D are correct.** The next hop property can take an IP address of the next router or the local exit interface of the sending router.

55. **Chapter 10 Infrastructure Services: DNS, DHCP, NTP—Answer B is correct.** The default lease duration is one day.

56. **Chapter 10 Infrastructure Services: DNS, DHCP, NTP—Answer B is correct.** The **ntp master** command sets the local device as an authoritative time source.

57. **Chapter 14 Infrastructure Maintenance: Initial Device Configuration—Answer B is correct.** The default privilege level is very low: It is 1. This permits user mode access only.

58. **Chapter 14 Infrastructure Maintenance: Initial Device Configuration—Answer C is correct.** The **login local** command ensures the use of the local user accounts database on the device when connecting to the VTY lines.

59. **Chapter 16 Infrastructure Maintenance: Device Maintenance—Answer B is correct.** The **copy** command allows the transfer of files and images.

60. **Chapter 17 Infrastructure Maintenance: IOS Troubleshooting Tools—Answer D is correct.** The Ping utility sends 5 packets by default.

Glossary

A

802.1Q This technology inserts tags into frames in order to identify traffic belonging to specific VLANs over a trunk link.

ACE An access control entry is a permit or deny statement in an access control list.

ACL An access control list is a list of access control entries that are checked to match traffic on a Cisco device; these ACLs are often used to filter traffic when assigned to an interface.

administrative distance A value that ranges from 0 through 255, which determines the believability of a source's routing information; lower is more preferred.

advanced distance vector protocol A routing protocol that combines some of the characteristics of both distance vector and link-state routing protocols. Cisco Enhanced Interior Gateway Routing Protocol (EIGRP) is considered an advanced distance vector protocol.

anycast The ability to assign identical IP addresses to different nodes. The network then calculates and forwards traffic to the "closest" device to respond to client requests.

APs   Access points connect end users to the network using IEEE wireless technologies; these devices are often dual band.

application layer   The highest layer of the OSI model (Layer 7). It represents network services to support end-user applications such as email and FTP.

ARP (Address Resolution Protocol)   A protocol used to map a known logical address to a physical address. A device performs an ARP broadcast to identify the physical Layer 2 address of a destination device on an Ethernet network. This physical address is then stored in local cache memory for later use.

AS (autonomous system)   A group of networks under common administration that share a routing strategy.

attenuation   A term that refers to the reduction in strength of a signal. Attenuation occurs with any type of signal, whether digital or analog. Sometimes referred to as signal loss.

B

backup configuration   The version of the Cisco device configuration stored in the NVRAM of the system; this is more frequently called the startup configuration. Note that backup configuration could also refer to a copy of the configuration that exists on a remote TFTP or FTP server.

bandwidth   The available capacity of a network link over a physical medium.

BGP (Border Gateway Protocol)   An exterior routing protocol that exchanges route information between autonomous systems.

Bidirectional NAT   Network Address Translation (NAT) that features address translation from the inside network to the outside network as well as translation of traffic flowing from the outside network to the inside network.

boot field   The lowest four bits of a 16-bit configuration register. The value of the boot field determines the order in which a router searches for Cisco IOS software.

bridge   A device used to segment a LAN into multiple physical segments. A bridge uses a forwarding table to determine which frames need to be forwarded to specific segments. Bridges isolate local traffic to the originating physical segment but forward all nonlocal and broad-cast traffic.

broadcast   A data frame that is sent to every node on a local segment.

C

CAM   Content-addressable memory is the specialized memory used to store the CAM table—the dynamic table in a network switch that maps MAC addresses to ports. It is the essential mechanism that separates network switches from hubs; the

CAM table is often considered to be synonymous with the MAC address table.

CDP (Cisco Discovery Protocol) A Cisco proprietary protocol that operates at the data link layer. CDP enables network administrators to view summary protocol and address information about other directly connected Cisco devices.

channel A single communications path on a system. In some situations, channels can be multiplexed over a single connection.

checksum A field that contains calculations to ensure the integrity of data.

CIDR (classless interdomain routing) Implemented to resolve the rapid depletion of IP address space on the Internet and to minimize the number of routes on the Internet. CIDR provides a more efficient method of allocating IP address space by removing the concept of classes in IP addressing. CIDR enables routes to be summarized on powers of 2 boundaries; therefore, it reduces multiple routes into a single prefix.

classful addressing Categorizes IP addresses into ranges that are used to create a hierarchy in the IP addressing scheme. The most common classes are A, B, and C, which can be identified by looking at the first three bits of an IP address.

classless addressing Classless addressing does not categorize addresses into classes and is designed to deal with wasted address space.

client DNS configurations Domain Name Services configured on the client permit the device to resolve fully qualified domain names (www.yahoo.com) to IP addresses needed for network communication.

collapsed core network designs A simplified version of the three-layer network model from Cisco Systems; this version takes the distribution layer and collapses it into the core layer, resulting in the core and the access layer.

collisions The result of two frames colliding on a network. In modern Ethernet networks, this condition is avoided through the use of switches.

configuration register A 16-bit storage location that is set as a numeric value (usually displayed in hexadecimal form) used to specify certain actions on a router, such as where to look for the IOS image or whether to load the startup configuration from NVRAM.

congestion A situation that occurs during data transfer if one or more computers generate network traffic faster than it can be transmitted through the network.

console A direct access to the router for configuring and monitoring the router.

convergence The result when all routers within an internetwork agree on routes through the internetwork.

CPE (customer premise equipment) Terminating equipment such as telephones and modems, installed at the customer site and connected to the network.

CRC (cyclic redundancy check) An error-checking mechanism by which the receiving node calculates a value based on the data it receives and compares it with the value stored within the frame from the sending node.

CSMA/CA (carrier sense multiple access/collision avoidance) A physical specification used in wireless networks to provide contention-based frame transmission. A sending device first verifies that data can be sent without contention, before it sends the data frame.

CSMA/CD (carrier sense multiple access/collision detection) A physical specification used by Ethernet to provide contention-based frame transmission. CSMA/CD specifies that a sending device must share physical transmission media and listen to determine whether a collision occurs after transmitting. In simple terms, this means that an Ethernet card has a built-in capability to detect a potential packet collision on the internetwork.

D

data access ports Ports on a switch used to accept traffic from a single VLAN from workstations. Contrast this to a trunk port, which carries the traffic of many data VLANs.

DCE (data communications equipment) The device at the network end of a user-to-network connection that provides a physical connection to the network, forwards traffic, and provides a clocking signal used to synchronize data transmission over the network.

de-encapsulation The process by which a destination peer layer removes and reads the control information sent by the source peer layer in another network host.

default mask A binary or decimal representation of the number of bits used to identify an IP network. The class of the IP address defines the default mask. The mask can be presented in dotted-decimal notation or as the number of bits making up the mask.

default route A network route used for packets that don't have a better match in the routing table.

default VLAN In a Cisco switch with the default factory configuration, the default VLAN is VLAN 1. This VLAN permits all ports to participate in it by default.

delay The amount of time necessary to move a packet through the internetwork from source to destination.

demarc The point of demarcation is between the carrier's equipment and the customer premise equipment (CPE).

device access The ability to connect to a Cisco device for management using a wide variety of methods, including SSH, Telnet, and local login.

DHCP The Dynamic Host Configuration Protocol. This communication protocol permits a server to automatically assign the IP address information required by clients on the network. There are DHCP servers and DHCP clients that make up the process.

DHCP relay A device on the network that forwards DHCP requests from clients as unicast traffic to a DHCP server on a remote network segment.

distance vector protocol An interior routing protocol that relies on information from immediate neighbors only, instead of having a full picture of the network. Most distance vector protocols involve each router sending all or a large part of its routing table to its neighboring routers at regular intervals.

DNS (domain name system) A system used to translate fully qualified hostnames or computer names into IP addresses.

dotted-decimal notation A method of representing binary IP addresses in a decimal format. Dotted decimal notation represents the four octets of an IPv4 address in four decimal values separated by decimal points.

DTE (data terminal equipment) The device at the user end of the user-to-network connection that connects to a data network through a data communications equipment (DCE) device.

dynamic NAT Network Address Translation that uses a pool of addresses for translation and access lists to define the addresses that will be translated.

dynamic port security This variation of port security features MAC addresses that are dynamically learned and secured on the switch port.

dynamic route A network route that adjusts automatically to changes within the internetwork. These routes are learned dynamically via a routing protocol.

E

EGP (Exterior Gateway Protocol) A routing protocol that conveys information between autonomous systems; it is widely used within the Internet. Border Gateway Protocol (BGP) is an example of an exterior gateway protocol.

EIGRP (Enhanced Interior Gateway Routing Protocol) A Cisco-proprietary routing protocol that includes features of both distance vector and link-state routing characteristics. EIGRP is considered an advanced distance vector protocol.

encapsulation Generally speaking, encapsulation is the process of wrapping data in a particular protocol header. In the context of the OSI model, encapsulation is the process by which a source peer layer includes header and trailer control information with a protocol data unit (PDU) destined for its peer layer in another network host. The information encapsulated instructs the destination peer layer how to process the information. Encapsulation occurs as information is sent down the protocol stack.

err-disable recovery   This Cisco device feature permits error conditions to be recovered from automatically after a duration of time.

errors   There are many different error conditions that might occur in an Ethernet network. The **show interface** command is used to see these errors for an interface.

escalation   The process of taking a troubleshooting issue to other parties for their assistance.

Ethernet frame format   The common fields found in modern Ethernet frames. These fields include a source MAC address and destination MAC address, critical fields for Ethernet switches.

Ethernet switching   Ethernet switching permits full duplex communication that is collision free in modern LANs.

EXEC   The user interface for executing Cisco router commands.

Extended ACL   These access control lists permit the matching of traffic using many different criteria, including source IP address and destination IP address.

Extended options   Both Ping and Traceroute permit the use of extended IP options for using various parameters in network tests.

F

fault isolation   The process of determining exactly where a problem exists in the network.

FCS (frame check sequence)   Extra characters added to a frame for error control purposes. FCS is the result of a cyclic redundancy check (CRC).

file system management   The process of managing the various storage facilities within a Cisco device. These include components like RAM, NVRAM, Flash, and USB.

firewalls   These devices seek to protect networks or devices at specific points in the network.

flash   Router memory that stores the Cisco IOS image and associated microcode. Flash is erasable, reprogrammable ROM that retains its content when the router is powered down or restarted.

floating static route   These routes have an artificially high administrative distance value in order to make dynamic routes more preferred. These are used as backup routes as a result of this configuration.

flow control   A mechanism that throttles back data transmission to ensure that a sending system does not overwhelm the receiving system with data.

frame flooding   The process where a switch sends traffic out all ports except for the port where the traffic entered. This is done for broadcast frames and unknown unicast frames.

frame rewrite   Routers manipulate address information inside of packets they are sending. Specifically, they rewrite MAC address information.

frame switching   The processes used on an Ethernet switch in order to efficiently forward and filter traffic in the LAN.

frame tagging   A method of tagging a frame with a unique user-defined virtual local-area network (VLAN). The process of tagging frames allows VLANs to span multiple switches.

FTP (File Transfer Protocol)   A protocol used to copy a file from one host to another host, regardless of the physical hardware or operating system of each device. FTP identifies a client and server during the file-transfer process. In addition, it provides a guaranteed transfer by using the services of the Transmission Control Protocol (TCP).

full duplex   The physical transmission process on a network device by which one pair of wires transmits data while another pair of wires receives data. Full-duplex transmission is achieved by eliminating the possibility of collisions on an Ethernet segment, thereby eliminating the need for a device to sense collisions.

G

Gateway of Last Resort   The route to send traffic to when the exact destination of the traffic is not in the local routing table.

global configuration mode   A router mode that enables simple router configuration commands— such as router names, banners, and passwords—to be executed. Global configuration commands affect the whole router rather than a single interface or component.

Global unicast   The IPv6 address information that is used for Internet routing.

H

half duplex   The physical transmission process where only a single device in the broadcast domain can send data at a time. In a half-duplex Ethernet network, CSMA/CD is used.

header   Control information placed before the data during the encapsulation process.

hierarchical routing protocol   A routing environment that relies on several routers to compose a backbone. Most traffic from non-backbone routers traverses the backbone routers (or at least travels to the backbone) to reach another non-backbone router.

hop count The number of routers a packet passes through on its way to the destination network.

host route The most specific route possible in the routing table. This route features a 32-bit or 128-bit mask depending on the use of IPv4 versus IPv6.

hostname A logical name given to a Cisco device.

hybrid topology A network that features the use of multiple topologies. For example, the network might use a star topology that connects to a full mesh topology.

I

ICMP (Internet Control Message Protocol) A protocol that communicates error messages and controls messages between devices. Multiple types of ICMP messages are defined. ICMP enables devices to check the status of other devices and is used as part of the functions with ping and traceroute.

IEEE (Institute of Electrical and Electronics Engineers) An organization whose primary function is to define standards for network LANs.

implicit deny all This statement ends every ACL. It is an implied deny statement that ensures that packets not matching an explicit entry are denied.

initial configuration dialog The dialog used to configure a router the first time it is booted or when no configuration file exists. The initial configuration dialog is an optional tool used to simplify the configuration process.

initial device configuration This configuration is provided by an administrator or is provided by the Cisco factory default. It configures the basic parameters of the device.

inside global The term to describe your inside addresses after they have been translated with Network Address Translation (NAT). Inside global addresses are registered addresses that represent your inside hosts to your outside networks.

inside local The addresses on the inside of your network before they are translated with Network Address Translation (NAT).

interfaces Router components that provide the network connections in which data packets move in and out of the router. Depending on the model of router, interfaces exist either on the motherboard or on separate, modular interface cards. Interfaces could also be logical, such as loopback interfaces.

interior routing protocol A routing protocol that exchanges information within an autonomous system. Routing Information Protocol (RIP) and Open Shortest Path First (OSPF) are examples of interior routing protocols.

interswitch links Trunk links connect Cisco devices in order to move the traffic of multiple VLANs from device to device.

interVLAN routing This is the process of using a routing engine (RE) in order to move packets from one VLAN to another. Remember, VLANs usually have a one-to-one correlation with IP subnets in a Cisco network.

IOS Recovery This is the process of copying a valid IOS image to a Cisco device that has a troubled operating system. This is often done from a TFTP server that stores backup or upgraded IOS files.

IOS Tools There are many powerful troubleshooting and monitoring tools built right in to the IOS.

IP (Internet Protocol) One of the many protocols maintained in the TCP/IP suite of protocols. IP is the Layer 3 network-level mechanism used for Transmission Control Protocol (TCP) and User Datagram Protocol (UDP).

IP extended access list An access list that provides a way of filtering IP traffic based on the source and/ or destination IP address, TCP port, UDP port, ICMP-type and more.

IP standard access list An access list that provides a way of filtering IP traffic on a router interface based on only the source IP address or range.

IPv6 autoconfiguration The ability of an IPv6 device to receive its IPv6 address information automatically with little to no administrator intervention.

IPv6 Stateless Address Auto Configuration The IPv6 process for assigning full IPv6 address information to devices that require it.

K

keepalive frames Protocol data units (PDUs) transmitted at the data link layer used for multiple purposes, including verifying that an interface is up and available.

L

LAN protocols Sets of rules used for the transmission of data within a local-area network (LAN). A popular LAN protocol used today is Ethernet.

Layer 2 protocols Various protocols like CDP that operate at Layer 2 of the OSI model.

licensing The process of making your software powering your Cisco device legal.

link-local A special IPv6 address used to permit communications between devices sharing the same local link.

link-state advertisement A packet that contains the status of a router's links or network interfaces.

link-state protocol An interior routing protocol in which each router sends the state of its own network links across the network to every router within its autonomous system or area. This process enables routers to learn and maintain full knowledge of the network's exact topology and how it is interconnected. Link state protocols use a "shortest path first" algorithm. An example is OSPF.

LLC (Logical Link Control) sublayer A sublayer of the data link layer. The LLC sublayer provides some of functions supporting the data link layer.

LLDP Link Layer Discovery Protocol. This open standard Layer 2 technology permits devices to learn information about each other over the local link.

local authentication This refers to a Cisco device performing the security checks required to prove the identity of a user requesting access to the device, using its running configuration on the local router.

log events Information recorded about the health and operation of the device thanks to the local Syslog system.

logging The process on a Cisco router of using Syslog to report about the operation and health of the local device.

logical addressing Network layer IP addressing is most commonly referred to as logical addressing (versus the physical addressing of the data link layer). A logical address consists of two parts: the network and the node.

login banners These messages are presented to users just before the username prompt on the device. They are often used for security warnings.

loopbacks These virtual interfaces are used for many maintenance and monitoring techniques. They can also provide stable connections between devices that have multiple physical paths, in the event one of those paths goes down, since loopbacks should always be available as long as one physical interface remains functional.

M

MAC (Media Access Control) address A physical Layer 2 address used to define a device uniquely.

MAC address table The database on a Layer 2 switch that lists the MAC addresses known by the device and the ports these MAC addresses relate to.

MAC aging The process of removing stale MAC addresses from a Layer 2 switch.

MAC learning The process of recording the source MAC addresses for incoming frames on a Layer 2 switch.

MD5 verify This Cisco device feature permits the integrity verification of an IOS acquired from Cisco Systems.

mesh topologies These are topologies that feature full connections or partial connections between all network nodes.

metric The relative cost of sending packets to a destination network over a specific network route. Examples of metrics include hop count and cost.

Modified EUI 64 This method of assigning an IPv6 node with its host address portion is one of the many time saving features of IPv6.

multicasting A process of using one IP address to represent a group of IP hosts. Multicasting is used to send messages to a subset of IP addresses in a network or networks.

multi-area OSPF A feature of OSPF that divides the routed system into hierarchical areas, allowing greater control over routing update traffic. Router loads are generally reduced, as is the frequency of SPF recalculation. Multi-area OSPF systems can scale to large deployments.

multipath routing protocol A routing protocol that load balances over multiple optimal paths to a destination network. This is often used when the costs of the paths are equal.

multiplexing A method used by the transport layer in which application conversations are combined over a single channel by interleaving packets from different segments and transmitting them.

N

named ACL An access control list that uses a name as an identifier instead of a number.

NAT (Network Address Translation) The process of translating internal IP addresses to routable registered IP addresses on the outside of your network.

Native VLAN This is the single VLAN in the Cisco network that is not tagged with an 802.1Q VLAN identifier.

network mask The subnet mask used with an IP address.

next hop The IP address of the next device in a path to reach a network destination.

NIC (network interface card) An adapter or circuitry that provides network communication capabilities to and from a network host.

NTP Network Time Protocol provides IP network–based synchronization of device clocks, facilitating log and transaction analysis, and improving quality-of-service (QoS) responsiveness in Voice and Video over IP systems.

numbered ACL An access control list that uses a number in order to identify it instead of a name.

NVRAM (nonvolatile random-access memory) A memory area of the router that stores permanent information, such as the router's backup configuration file. The contents of NVRAM are retained when the router is powered down or restarted.

O

OSI (Open Systems Interconnection) model A layered networking framework developed by the International Organization for Standardization. The OSI model describes seven layers that correspond to specific networking functions.

OSPF (Open Shortest Path First) A hierarchical link-state routing protocol that was developed as a successor to the distance vector Routing Information Protocol (RIP).

P

packet switching A process by which a router moves a packet from one interface to another.

passive-interface A routing protocol command that places a router interface into "receive-only" mode; no routing updates are sent out, but those that are received are processed. This allows the passive interface's network to be advertised out other interfaces, without generating unnecessary routing protocol traffic on the passive interface network.

password recovery The process of resetting the password on a Cisco device in order to permit access to the device. This typically requires local access to the device.

PDU (protocol data unit) A unit of measure that refers to data that is transmitted between two peer layers within different network devices. Segments, packets, and frames are examples of PDUs.

peer-to-peer communication A form of communication that occurs between the same layers of two different network hosts.

ping A tool for testing IP connectivity between two devices. Ping is used to send multiple IP packets between a sending and a receiving device. The destination device responds with an Internet Control Message Protocol (ICMP) packet to notify the source device of its existence.

Port Address Translation This form of NAT allows many different inside devices to share a single address for translation.

Port security A system of MAC-based switch port security capabilities that can limit or deny access to certain hosts attempting to connect to a switch port.

prefix This refers to the network portion of a Layer 3 logical address.

presentation layer Layer 6 of the OSI model. The presentation layer is concerned with how data is represented to the application layer.

private IPv4 addressing These IPv4 addresses are for use in internal networks only. This technology allows for the duplication of addressing behind corporate network boundaries and helped ward off the IP address shortage. RFC 1918 lists most of the private IPv4 address space.

privileged mode An extensive administrative and management mode on a Cisco router. This router mode permits testing, debugging, and commands to modify the router's configuration.

protocol A formal description of a set of rules and conventions that defines how devices on a network must exchange information.

R

RAM (random-access memory) A memory area of a router that serves as a working storage area. RAM contains data such as route tables, various types of caches and buffers, in addition to input and output queues and the router's active configuration file. The contents of RAM are lost when the router is powered down or restarted.

RIP (Routing Information Protocol) A distance vector routing protocol that uses hop count as its metric.

ROM (read-only memory) ROM stores the bootstrap program and power-on diagnostic programs.

ROM Monitor mode A mode on a Cisco router that allows basic functions such as changing the configuration register value, or loading an IOS image to flash from a TFTP server.

route aggregation The process of combining multiple IP address networks into one superset of those networks. Route aggregation is implemented to reduce the number of route table entries required to forward IP packets accurately in an internetwork.

route table An area of a router's memory that stores the route forwarding information. Route tables contain information such as destination network, next hop, and associated metrics.

routed protocol A protocol that can be routed, such as IP.

router on a stick This refers to a router on a trunk link. This router is used to route between the VLANs on the trunk.

router modes Modes that enable the execution of specific router commands and functions. User and privileged are examples of router modes that allow you to perform certain tasks.

routing algorithms Well-defined rules that aid routers in the collection of route information and the determination of the optimal path.

routing protocols Routing protocols use algorithms to generate a list of paths to a particular destination and the cost associated with each path. Routers use routing protocols to communicate among each other the best route to use to reach a particular destination.

running configuration This is the configuration in RAM on a Cisco device. It is the configuration currently being used by the device.

S

Secure Copy Protocol SCP permits the secure transfer of files in the network. This technology relies upon SSH for the security mechanisms.

Secure Shell (SSH) A protocol that allows for secure communication between a client and a router. It is a secure alternative to Telnet.

service set identifier (SSID) A 32-byte unique identifier that is used to name a wireless network.

session layer   As Layer 5 of the OSI model, the session layer establishes, manages, and terminates sessions between applications on different network devices.

setup mode   The router mode triggered on startup if no configuration file resides in nonvolatile random-access memory (NVRAM).

sliding windows   A method by which TCP dynamically sets the window size during a connection, enabling the receiving device involved in the communication to slow down the sending data rate.

SMTP (Simple Mail Transfer Protocol)   A protocol used to pass mail messages between devices, SMTP uses Transmission Control Protocol (TCP).

SNMP   Simple Network Management Protocol is a standards-based protocol that allows remote monitoring and management of networked devices.

socket   The combination of the source and destination Transmission Control Protocol (TCP) port numbers and the source and destination Internet Protocol (IP) addresses defines a socket. Therefore, a socket can be used to define any User Datagram Protocol (UDP) or TCP connection uniquely.

source addressing   This refers to the management technique of specifying the source of traffic coming from a router. This often allows a more consistent or reliable management traffic approach.

source NAT   This refers to NAT of the source address in traffic packets.

SSH   The Secure Shell protocol is a secure alternative to Telnet.

standard ACL   This is an ACL that can filter using source IP address information.

star topology   The star topology is what you have with a switch connecting workstations today. Note: If drawn with the switch in the center of the network diagram, it literally resembles a star.

startup configuration file   The backup configuration file on a router, stored in NVRAM.

static NAT   This refers to NAT with a single source address being mapped to a specific translated address.

static route   A network route that is manually entered into the route table. Static routes function well in simple and predictable network environments.

sticky learning   This is the process of recording dynamically learned MAC addresses as static entries in the running configuration of a switch running port security.

stratum   This is a measure of the "distance" from an authoritative time source.

subinterface   One of possibly many virtual interfaces on a single physical interface.

subnetting   A process of splitting a classful range of IP addresses into multiple IP networks to allow more flexibility in IP addressing schemes.

Subnetting overcomes the limitation of address classes and allows network administrators the flexibility to assign multiple networks with one class of IP addresses.

subnet mask This is the network mask associated with an IP address. The purpose of this value is to distinguish between the network and host portions of the address.

SVI A switched virtual interface is a logical Layer 3 interface defined on a switch. These are also called VLAN interfaces because there is usually one defined for each VLAN, allowing inter-VLAN routing to be performed by a Layer 3 switch instead of by a router. Layer 2 switches can have only one SVI configured, which is used for switch management.

switch Provides increased port density and forwarding capabilities as compared to bridges. The increased port densities of switches enable LANs to be microsegmented, thereby increasing the amount of bandwidth delivered to each device.

syslog A network service that provides centralized log message archiving.

T

TCP (Transmission Control Protocol) One of the many protocols maintained in the TCP/IP suite of protocols. TCP provides a transport layer connection-oriented and reliable service to the applications that use it.

TCP/IP (Transmission Control Protocol/Internet Protocol) (TCP/IP) Model This represents the suite of protocols used in the IP protocol suite, including those at the application, transport, network, and data-link layers.

TCP three-way handshake A three-step process whereby a TCP session is established. In the first step, the sending device sends the initial sequence number with the SYN bit set in the TCP header. The receiver sends back a packet with the SYN and ACK bits set. In the third and final step, the sender sends a packet with the ACK bit set.

TCP windowing A method of increasing or reducing the number of acknowledgments required between data transmissions.

Telnet A standard protocol that provides a virtual terminal. Telnet enables a network administrator to connect to a router remotely.

Terminal Monitor This functionality permits a user with a remote session to a Cisco device, using Telnet or SSH to see logging messages produced by that local device.

TFTP (Trivial File Transfer Protocol) A protocol used to copy files from one device to another. TFTP is a stripped-down version of FTP.

Three-Tier Network Design This classic Cisco networking model defines the access, distribution, and core layers.

Timezones This is a clock setting possible on the Cisco device.

traceroute An IP service on a Cisco router that uses User Datagram Protocol (UDP) and the Internet Control Message Protocol (ICMP) to identify the number of hops between sending and receiving devices and the paths taken from the sending to the receiving device. Typically, traceroute is used to troubleshoot IP connectivity between two devices.

trailer Control information placed after the data during the encapsulation process. See encapsulation for more detail.

transport layer As Layer 4 of the OSI model, it is concerned with segmenting upper-layer applications, and in the case of TCP is concerned with establishing end-to-end connectivity through the network, sending segments from one host to another, and ensuring the reliable transport of data.

troubleshooting methodology This is an approach to troubleshooting using a defined sequence of steps.

trunk Supporting multiple virtual local-area networks (VLANs) on a single physical interface. The standardized protocol for trunks on Ethernet is 802.1Q.

U

UDP (User Datagram Protocol) One of the many protocols maintained in the TCP/IP suite of protocols, UDP is a Layer 4, best-effort delivery protocol and, therefore, maintains connectionless network services.

unicast This method of data transfer is from one specific system on the network to another specific system on the network.

unidirectional NAT This is a reference to Network Address Translation that occurs in one direction. For example, inside addresses being translated for outbound traffic, but no translation occurring for source addresses in the return path.

unique local addressing This is an IPv6 approach to private addressing similar to IPv4's RFC 1918 private address space.

User Datagram Protocol (UDP) This transport layer approach is the opposite of TCP. It provides no reliability in order to attempt to more efficiently send traffic due to less overhead.

user mode A display-only mode on a Cisco router. Only limited information about the router can be viewed within this router mode; no configuration changes are permitted. User mode is often referring to privilege level 1, which is the default for a new user account created on the local router.

V

V.35 A physical standard used serial connections.

VLAN (virtual local-area network) A technique of assigning devices to specific LANs based on the port to which they attach on a switch rather than the physical location. VLANs can extend the flexibility of LANs by allowing devices to be assigned to specific LANs on a port-by-port basis versus a device basis.

VLSM (variable-length subnet masking) VLSM provides more flexibility in assigning IP address space. (A common problem with routing protocols is the necessity of all devices in a given routing protocol domain to use the same subnet mask.) Routing protocols that support VLSM allow administrators to assign IP networks with different subnet masks. This increased flexibility saves IP address space because administrators can assign IP networks based on the number of hosts on each network.

voice port This refers to a switch-port that has been configured to carry Voice traffic in addition to data.

VTP (VLAN Trunking Protocol) A protocol for configuring and administering VLANS on Cisco network devices. With VTP, an administrator can make configuration changes centrally on a single Catalyst series switch and have those changes, such as the addition of VLANs, automatically communicated to all the other switches in the network.

Virtual Terminal Lines (VTY) These are virtual access ports on a Cisco device that allow connectivity using protocols like Telnet and SSH.

W

WANs (wide-area networks) WANs use data communications equipment (DCE) to connect multiple LANs. Examples of WAN protocols include Frame Relay, Point-to-Point Protocol (PPP), and High-Level Data Link Control (HDLC).

well-known ports A set of ports between 1 and 1,023 that are reserved for specific TCP/IP protocols and services.

Wildcard (Inverse) Mask This technique is used in Access Control Lists in order to mark bits as not being required to match. For example, a wildcard mask of 0.0.0.255 means the last octet of the associated IP address doesn't have to match.

Wireless LAN Controllers (WLCs) These devices are used to control and manage wireless Access Points in the network.

Index

Numbers

A

B

M

N

O

P

T